ROSES

ROSES

ROGER PHILLIPS & MARTYN RIX

Assisted by Alison Rix   Layout by Jill Bryan

Random House   New York

Acknowledgements

We are particularly grateful to Charles and Brigid Quest-Ritson for their help with the old and species roses, for giving us the benefit of their own observations, and for several of their photographs.

We should also like to thank the following for their help and encouragement: Ted Allen, David Austin, Oliver Baxter, Peter Beales, Beverley Behrens, John Bond, Christopher Brickell, Humphrey Brooke, Ursula Buchan, Bev Dobson, Fred Edmunds, Bob Flood, Jim Gardiner, Alan and Caroline Hardy, Philip Harkness, Polly Hunt, Daryl Johnson, June Justice, Roy Lancaster, Sid Love, Donald Maginnis, Bob Mitchell, Mikinori Ogisu, Andrew Paterson, Graham Thomas, Peter Yeo, Peter Stone.

Most of the roses photographed came from the following gardens and we are grateful to the staff of these gardens for their help: The Royal Horticultural Society Gardens, Wisley; The National Trust, Mottisfont; the Savill Gardens, Windsor; The Gardens of the Rose, St Albans; The Royal Botanic Gardens, Kew; The University Botanic Garden, Cambridge; R. Harkness & Co; David Austin Roses; Fred Edmunds Roses; Eccleston Square Gardens, London; Justice Mini Roses, Oregon; the International Rose Test Gardens, Portland, Oregon; The Hillier Arboretum, Ampfield.

We also had kind help and photographs from Sue Hauser, Roseries Hauser, Vaumarcus, and from Richard Huber A.G., Dottikon, Switzerland, and tireless assistance from Brent Elliott and the staff of Lindley Library.

Library of Congress Cataloging-in-Publication Data

Phillips, Roger, 1932–
    Roses/Roger Phillips & Martyn Rix; assisted by Alison Rix; layout by Jill Bryan.
    p. ca.
    Includes index.
    ISBN 0-394-75867-6 (pbk.) : $19.95
    1. Roses—Identification—Pictorial works.
2. Roses—Identification. I. Rix, Martyn. II. Title.
SB411.3.P48 1988
635.9'33372—dc19

Photoset by Rowland Phototypesetting Ltd,
Bury St Edmunds, Suffolk
Printed by Toppan Printing Co (Singapore) Pte Limited
First American Edition
Second Printing 1988

Contents

Wild *Rosa chinensis* var. *spontanea* in S.W. Sichuan, China

Introduction

In this book we have illustrated and given the history of more than 1400 of the roses most commonly grown in gardens, and shown the wild species from which they have been raised. Although there are hundreds of other rose books, these illustrations, taken in the studio, will give a clearer picture than ever before of many of the roses, showing details of buds, open flowers and leaves. In addition, many of the wild species are shown here growing in their native habitat; some of those from China are still almost unknown in the west.

How to use this book

The roses are arranged in their groups, starting with the species and simple hybrids, followed by old Shrub roses, modern Shrub roses, Hybrid Teas and Floribundas, ending with Miniatures, and finally Hips. Within each section, the roses are arranged, as far as possible, by date of introduction, the oldest first. The book may be used in three ways; firstly, to see what a particular rose looks like; secondly, to look through the book and choose a rose of a particular colour, shape or height to order from a nursery; thirdly, to identify an unknown rose by comparing it with the pictures.

The text

In every case the text accompanying the picture is on the same or facing page. The text in a book of this kind can only be very brief. We have given a short description of the distinguishing features of the species, as these often depend on the position of hairs, glands, prickles, etc., and an account of their habitats and distribution in the wild.

For the cultivars, we have mentioned first the group to which they belong (see pp. 8–10 for details of the different groups), then the raiser and the date, if known, of introduction, as that, rather than the date when the cross was made, is the one generally recorded. Then the height, scent and any other features are given. Scent is generally mentioned only if it is good, or particularly lacking, as nearly all roses have some scent. Finally the parentage is given, where that is recorded or guessed at. The early raisers did not carry out careful cross-pollinations, but relied on the seeds and on selecting from many thousands of seedlings, hence the parentage of roses raised before about 1900 is likely to be unknown or at least uncertain.

Measurements are given in metres and centimetres. 1 metre equals about 3 feet, and 2½ centimetres equals about 1 inch.

Where wild roses grow

Roses are found wild all round the northern hemisphere from the Arctic as far south as North Africa, the Yemen, South India, Thailand and New Mexico, but are unknown in the southern hemisphere. The greatest diversity of species, in roses as in so many other genera, is found in western China. Representatives of seven different sections occur in that area, and there are large numbers of species in two sections; the section *cinnamomeae*, of which the best-known member is *R. moyesii*, contains 26 species, and the section *synstylae* (e.g. *R. filipes*) contains 19 species.

In Central Asia there is also a large number of species; here the yellow *pimpinellifoliae* section is well represented, as are the sections *cinnamomae* (26 species) and the dog roses or *caninae* (22 species).

In Europe the dog roses are also important, with 30 species, but there are only 12 species in all the other sections of the genus. In France there are 32 species, which include such important forerunners of cultivated roses as *R. sempervirens*, *R. gallica* and *R. majalis*, as well as the popular foliage rose *R. glauca* (*rubrifolia*).

Burnet Rose on dunes in South Wales

In England 14 species are considered native, not including *R. rugosa*, which is often naturalized on seaside dunes. *R. arvensis* is the only member of the *synstylae*; *R. pimpinellifolia* itself is common, while the remaining species are divided into three groups, i.e. dog roses, downy roses and sweet briars.

In North America there are only 25 native species. Three belong to subgenus *Hesperhodos*, a desert-loving group found in Arizona, New Mexico and Baja California, of which the commonest in cultivation is *R. stellata* var. *myrifica* (p. 18). The *synstylae* group, so important in China, contains only *R. setigera*, the Prairie rose. The other species fall into two groups, the *cinnamomae*, such as *R. californica*, and the *carolinae* which includes the eastern species *R. carolina*, *R. virginiana* and *R. nitida*.

Habitats of wild roses

Wild roses usually grow in somewhat disturbed habitats, on the banks of streams, on cliffs, and on hillsides where the forest has been cleared or where the climate is too harsh for forest to develop. Only the climbing species such as *R. gigantea*, and the *synstylae* such as *R. filipes*, could hope to survive in forest, by climbing and flowering through the tops of the trees. Since man kept domestic animals, and needed to keep them out of the crops, wild roses have found hedges an ideal habitat, and their seeds have been planted along the hedgerows by roosting birds. Wild roses have often been deliberately planted, such as *R. banksiae* var. *banksiae* in many parts of Yunnan (see p. 30). In North America, both *R. laevigata*, the Cherokee rose, and *R. bracteata* were originally planted as quick-growing hedges to combat soil erosion, and have, in many states, become naturalized.

Hardiness of wild roses

Roses are found in almost all northern hemisphere climates, from the Arctic to the tropics. Most species are hardy down to about −15°C (+5°F), and tolerate hot summers. Several of the Chinese species however, are killed by −10°C (+12°F), and it is because these, such as *R. gigantea*, have played an important part in the development of the Hybrid Tea roses, that some Hybrid Teas are tender. Ramblers of the *sempervirens* type also suffer below −10°C (+12°F), as does *R. roxburghii*. Among the hardiest species are *R. rugosa*, which grows on dunes in northern Japan and Siberia, and *R. wichuraiana*, also from Japan, as well as *R. pimpinellifolia*. These have been used to breed ultra-cold-tolerant hybrids for the eastern USA and Canada.

The species from Central Asia are cold hardy, but sometimes do not get enough sun in western Europe to ripen their wood properly. They grow softly, do not flower well, and succumb to disease or early frosts. Extreme desert species, such as *R. persica*, will flower only if grown under cover, watered in spring and kept dry in summer.

Rose classification

The species of the genus (or family) *Rosa* are grouped for convenience into subgenera (subfamilies), sections and groups of species within the sections, as follows:

Rosa species in their groups.

HULTHEMIA *R. persica* (p. 19).
HESPERHODOS *R. stellata* var. *myrifica* (p. 18), *R. minutifolia* (Baja California).
PLATYRHODON *R. roxburghii* (p. 18), *R. hirtula* (p. 18).
ROSA
  1. Chinenses *R. chinensis* (p. 32) *R. gigantea* (p. 33).
  2. Banksianae *R. banksiae* (p. 30), *R. cymosa* (p. 31), *R. collettii* (Burma).
  3. Laevigatae *R. laevigata* (p. 32).
  4. Bracteatae *R. bracteata* (p. 32), *R. clinophylla* (India).
  5. Pimpinellifoliae *R. pimpinellifolia* (p.21), *R. ecae* (p. 16), *R. primula* (p. 14), *R. kokanica* (p. 14), *R. xanthina* (p. 20), *R. hemisphaerica* (p. 14), *R. foetida* (p. 14), *R. sericea* (p. 16).
  6. Synstylae *R. arvensis* (p. 34), *R. sempervirens* (p. 34), *R. phoenicea* (western Asia and Greece), *R. moschata* (p. 34), *R. brunonii* (p. 39), *R. longicuspis* (p. 39), *R. glomerata* (China), *R. rubus* (China), *R. helenae* (p. 37), *R. filipes* (p. 39), *R. soulieana* (p. 215), *R. henryi* (China), *R. mulliganii* (p. 39), *R. leschenaultiana* (S. India), *R. setigera* (p. 34), *R. multiflora* (p. 39), *R. wichuraiana* (p. 34), *R. luciae* (Japan), *R. sambucina* (p. 34), *R. abyssinica* (Ethiopia). *R. bottaiana* (Yemen).
  7. Cassiorhodon or Cinnamomeae *R. beggeriana* (p. 29), *R. pisiformis* (Turkey) *R. iliensis* (p. 29), *R. willmottiae* (p. 17), *R. nanothamnus* (p. 23), *R. acicularis* (p. 215), *R. majalis* (p. 27), *R. glauca* (p. 18), *R. pendulina* (p. 25), *R. setipoda* (p. 23), *R. corymbulosa* (p. 215), *R. caudata* (p. 23), *R. sertata* (China), *R. davidii* (p. 25), *R. farreri* (p. 23), *R. rugosa* (p. 100), *R. laxa* (p. 21), *R. bella* (p. 25), *P. prattii* (p. 18), *R. wardii* (p. 25), *R. sweginzowii* (p. 25), *R. moyesii* (p. 23), *R. macrophylla* (p. 25), *R. forrestiana* (p. 23), *R. multibracteata* (p. 25), *R. giraldii* (p. 19), *R. webbiana* (p. 23), *R. fedtschenkoana* (p. 23), *R. blanda* (N. America), *R. californica* (p. 27), *R. arkansana* (p. 20), *R. nutkana* (p. 27), *P. pisocarpa* (p. 27), *R. woodsii* (p. 27), *R. yainacensis* (p. 27), *R. gymnocarpa* (p. 27), *R. colvillei* (p. 27), *R. suffulta* (p. 27).
  8. Carolinae *R. virginiana* (p. 27), *R. carolina* (p. 27), *R. foliolosa* (p. 27), *R. nitida* (p. 21), *R. palustris* (p. 21).
  9. Rosa *gallica* (p. 48).
  10. Caninae Caninae *R. canina* (p. 28), Villosae *R. mollis* (p. 28), *R. orientalis* (p. 29), Rubiginosae *R. rubiginosa* (p. 18), *R. serafinii* (p. 18), *R. iberica* (p. 28), *R. glutinosa* (p. 215).

Rosa glauca (*R. rubrifolia*) and Golden Elder

History of rose cultivation

There is no doubt that the Romans grew roses in large quantities for decoration, but we cannot be certain which varieties they grew. In the Dark Ages the Arabs kept much of classical civilization alive, and Damask roses were probably reintroduced to Europe from the Middle East by the Crusaders. *Rosa gallica* 'Officinalis' was grown in the thirteenth century near Paris and Provins became the centre of a perfume industry. It can be seen, with other southern European garden plants such as pomegranates, vines and figs, in the Portinari altarpiece in Ghent Cathedral, which dates from *c.* 1430. A semi-double white rose, *Rosa × alba* 'Semi-plena' can also be seen in paintings of that period. *Rosa × centifolia* first appears in Dutch flower paintings of the early seventeenth century, and Moss roses, which are sports or mutations of either Damasks or Centifolias, are first recorded with certainty at Leyden Botanic Garden in 1720, though reported earlier, in 1696, at Carcassonne. During the 18th century there was only slow development in rose cultivation, but at the end of the century the coincidence of two factors led to amazing activity in rose breeding.

These factors were the introduction from China of the repeat-flowering China roses (in 1792, 1793) and the Tea roses (1810–24), and the fashion for roses initiated by Josephine, wife of Napoleon, at Malmaison from 1799 until her death in 1814. The great rose breeder of the early nineteenth century, J. P. Vibert, founded his nursery near Paris in 1815, and many of his roses are still in cultivation. Two early chance hybrids between China and European roses occurred outside Europe, and when sent back became the basis for new strains: the Bourbons, from the island of Réunion (Île de Bourbon), and the Noisettes from Charleston, South Carolina. In France the vogue for roses continued through the nineteenth century, spreading to the rest of the world in the twentieth. Hybrids of all sorts have been made, often at random, and have led to the following groups of cultivated roses.

Gallica (Also called Rose of Provins) Grown since ancient times, these are varieties of *Rosa gallica*, a short suckering rose, native of southern Europe from France eastwards to central Turkey. They are very hardy, once-flowering, with strongly scented flowers ranging from pink, through crimson, to purple. Height up to 1.5 m (American hardiness zone IV).

Damask There are two groups of Damasks, the Summer Damask, once-flowering, and the Autumn Damask which has a second flowering in the autumn. Both have been grown since ancient times. The Summer Damask is a hybrid between *R. gallica* and *R. phoenicea*, a native of the eastern Mediterranean which looks like *R. multiflora*, with hairy leaves. The Autumn Damask is a hybrid between *R. gallica* and *R. moschata* (p. 34). They are rather less hardy than the Gallicas (American hardiness zone V),

A courtyard in old Bokhara

Honorine de Brabant

often taller, up to 2.5 m, with usually richly scented, red, pink or white flowers in loose clusters.

Alba The third ancient group, hybrids between a rose of the *R. canina* section such as *R. mollis* (p. 28) and *R. gallica*, or possibly a Damask. Alba roses are always white or pale pink flowered, sweet scented, with bluish leaves. They make large bushes up to 2.5 m, with rather few thorns (American hardiness zone IV).

Moss Moss roses originate as mutations or sports on normal roses. The first is recorded in 1720. At present they are known to have appeared three times on Centifolia roses, and less often on Damask roses, in which the moss is stiffer and brownish. A single-flowered Centifolia Moss which appeared in the early nineteenth century enabled hundreds of Moss hybrids to be bred, in addition to the numerous sports that had appeared in the eighteenth century.

Centifolia (also called Cabbage Rose, Holland Rose, Rose des Peintres, or Provence Rose). The original Centifolia roses probably appeared around the end of the sixteenth century, from a cross between the Autumn Damask and an Alba. They make large, rather floppy bushes with very double flowers hanging on weak branches (American hardiness zone V). A single or semi-double sport arose in the early nineteenth century, before which the group was sterile and the early varieties grown were all sports from the original cross.

Portland Portland roses were named after Margaret Cavendish Bentinck, 2nd Duchess of Portland. The original, a hybrid between an Autumn Damask and *R. gallica* 'Officinalis', has been known since 1792. Portland roses were valued for their late flowering as well as their rich red colour, and were soon crossed with Chinas to produce the forerunners of the Hybrid Perpetuals.

China roses had been cultivated and new varieties produced on a large scale in China for many centuries before the first were brought to gardens in Europe in 1792.

The dwarf, perpetual-flowering Chinas were mutants of the climber *R. chinensis* (p. 32), some possibly hybridized with *R. × odorata* (below). This mutation has been observed in cultivation with 'Little White Pet' being a dwarf perpetual-flowering sport of 'Felicité et Perpetué'. The original introductions from China were

China roses at Mottisfont

'Slater's Crimson China' (p. 69) introduced in about 1792, and 'Parson's Pink China', now called 'Old Blush', in 1793. The original Chinas are dwarf, up to 2 m, but usually around 1 m, and rather tender (American hardiness zone VII) with red or pink single or loosely double flowers.

Tea The Tea rose, *Rosa* × *odorata*, is a hybrid between *R. gigantea* and *R. chinensis*, that occurred long ago in China, and many varieties were cultivated there (see p. 179). Two of these were introduced to Europe: the pale pink 'Hume's Blush' tea-scented China (1809) and 'Park's Yellow' tea-scented China (1824), but unfortunately neither is now in cultivation in Europe. Their progeny, however, have survived, and a whole class of Tea roses was bred from them, by crossing with Bourbons and Noisettes. These, when crossed with Hybrid Perpetuals, became Hybrid Teas.

Tea roses are generally either climbers or small, sparse bushes, with a continuous succession of large flowers of great beauty, in shades of pink, buff or light yellow. They have few thorns and are rather tender (American hardiness zone VII), growing best around the Mediterranean, in California and in Australia.

Bourbon Before the opening of the Suez Canal (1871) the Île de Bourbon, now Réunion, east of Madagascar, was an important stopping point for French ships sailing between the Far East and Europe. By 1817, *R. chinensis* had been grown there, as had the Autumn Damask from Europe, and they were apparently planted together as mixed hedges. A French botanist, M. Bréon, noticed an intermediate between the two types in such a hedge and moved it to his botanic garden whence seeds were sent to M. Jacques in Paris. He raised from them the original Bourbon rose, which was painted by Redouté in 1824. It had semi-double, bright pink flowers, good scent inherited from the Damask, and good autumn flowering. The Bourbon roses were bred by crossing this original Bourbon with Gallica and Damask hybrids (American hardiness zone V).

Noisette The forerunner of the Noisette rose was a hybrid between *R. moschata* and 'Parson's Pink China' made by Champneys in 1802 in South Carolina and named 'Champneys' Pink Cluster'. It was a climber with bunches of semi-double pink flowers but summer flowering only like *R. moschata*. Seeds of 'Champneys' Pink Cluster' were raised by Phillipe Noisette in Charleston, and from these he selected 'Old Blush' or *R. noisettiana* which was illustrated by Redouté in 1821. This, when crossed with 'Park's Yellow China', produced the climbing yellow Noisettes such as 'Desprez à fleur Jaune' (p. 77), yellow Tea roses, and finally, large-flowered climbers such as 'Maréchal Niel' (p. 79). Most are not very hardy (American hardiness zone VII).

Hybrid Perpetual Over a thousand varieties of Hybrid Perpetual were raised in the latter part of the nineteenth century, of which probably less than a hundred survive today. The ancestor of this class was the Portland × China hybrid, 'Rose du Roi', which appeared in 1816. When crossed with both Hybrid Chinas (Gallica × China crosses) and Bourbons, in about 1835, a new class of 'Hybrides remontants' or Hybrid Perpetuals was born. Some of the first were raised by Laffay, notably 'La Reine' (p. 72) and 'Gloire des Rosomanes' (p. 71), the latest such as 'Arilaga' (p. 74) in the early twentieth century.

The Hybrid Perpetuals are usually rather coarse growing, usually red, mauve, pink or white, often with huge flowers and strong shoots which need to be pegged down so that they produce flowers along their length. Their Portland ancestry makes these hardier than the Noisettes, but they still need protection in cold areas (American hardiness zone IV–V).

Hybrid Tea These, with the Floribundas, are the common roses of the twentieth century. They are sometimes also called large-flowered roses, an unfortunate choice as it invites confusion with the Grandifloras, another new class which is intermediate between Hybrid Teas and Floribundas. Hybrid Teas arose in the mid-

'Eye Paint'

e.g. *R. gigantea*, *R. chinensis* and *R. moschata* are important ancestors of modern roses. Furthermore, it has been noted that the gene for climbing is dominant over the dwarf (or bush) gene. Therefore it is not surprising to find many climbing Hybrid Teas and Floribundas; some of them arose as seedlings, others as sports of normal roses, such as 'Climbing Iceberg' or 'Climbing Grandmère Jenny'. Many of these climbing sports are summer flowering only, others have some later flowers. More recent large-flowered climbers, many raised by McGredy, are regularly repeat flowering.

Ramblers Ramblers throw up long non-flowering shoots from near the ground in summer; these shoots produce clusters of flowers along their length the following year and are then finished and in gardens pruned away; Climbers, on the other hand, produce shoots that have a productive life of more than two years and often become very thick and woody. There are three major groups of Ramblers, distinguished by their ancestry:

Sempervirens Ramblers This was the earliest group to be raised, hybrids between the European Mediterranean *R. sempervirens* and other unknown roses. The most famous group such as 'Adelaïde d'Orléans' was raised by M. Jacques around 1827 (p. 85). They are the least hardy (American hardiness zone V–VI).

Multiflora Ramblers These were crosses between the Chinese *R. multiflora* and various Hybrid Perpetuals or Hybrid Teas made around the end of the nineteenth century. Some included *R. wichuraiana* in their parentage through 'Crimson Rambler', an old Japanese hybrid. These are mostly quite hardy (American hardiness zone IV).

Wichuraiana Ramblers Two very different looking groups belong here; the large flowered, such as 'Albertine' (p. 81) were mostly raised by Barbier at Orléans around 1900–20, and have large flowers similar to loose Hybrid Teas. *R. luciae*, a close relative of *R. wichuraiana*, was said to be one parent of these, with Teas or Hybrid Teas as the other.

The small-flowered, such as 'Dorothy Perkins' (p. 89), are said to be a cross between *R. wichuraiana* and a Hybrid Perpetual. Most of these were raised in the USA by Jackson Perkins, or M. H. Walsh. Other Ramblers of generally similar appearance have been produced using different members of the *synstylae* section, such as 'Kew Rambler' with *R. soulieana*, and 'Baltimore Belle' using the Prairie Rose *R. setigera*. This last should be exceptionally hardy.

nineteenth century, as crosses between Teas and Hybrid Perpetuals, and succeeded in combining something of the elegance of the Teas and their perpetual flowering, with the robustness and freedom of flowering of the Hybrid Perpetuals. The first Hybrid Tea is generally said to have been 'La France', raised by Guillot in 1867, although at the time it was considered just another Hybrid Perpetual. It was a nearly sterile triploid, as were the early Bourbons, but eventually some fertile tetraploid Hybrid Teas appeared, such as 'Mme Caroline Testout' (p. 95) in 1890, or 'Lady Mary Fitzwilliam' raised by Bennet in 1882.

The next major advance was the introduction of yellow into Hybrid Teas. Between 1883 and 1888 Pernet-Ducher in Lyon made many thousand pollinations of Hybrid Teas and Hybrid Perpetuals with *R. foetida* 'Persiana', itself highly sterile. Finally, he succeeded in raising a cross with the Hybrid Perpetual 'Antoine Ducher' which, when crossed with a Hybrid Tea, produced 'Soleil d'Or', the first bright yellow Hybrid Tea. From this and further crosses, a race called Pernetiana roses were produced, yellow or orange flowered, very thorny, with little scent, and highly susceptible to blackspot.

A second important breeding programme was the introduction by Brownells of Rhode Island of *R. wichuraiana* genes into Hybrid Teas in an effort to produce hardier varieties, more resistant to blackspot, suitable for growing in the north-eastern USA. They used the hybrid 'Dr W. van Fleet' (parent of 'New Dawn') and two other *wichuraiana* hybrids to produce so-called sub-zero Hybrid Teas, which appeared around 1945, e.g. 'Lafter' (p. 131), and some of these were used by Kordes to breed varieties suitable for Germany. Hybrid Teas vary in their hardiness, but a guide to the hardiness of a particular variety in the colder parts of Europe and the eastern USA can be had by noting where it was raised. Thus German-raised roses by Kordes or Tantau are likely to be hardier than those raised in France, England or New Zealand.

Climbers Many roses are natural climbers, and several of those,

Mme Caroline Testout climbing on a pillar

Yellow Charles Austin

Hybrid Musks These roses were mostly raised by the Revd Joseph Pemberton, at Havering-atte-Bower in Essex, using the rose 'Trier', a hybrid between a hybrid tea and a seedling of 'Aglaia', which had the musk rose in its ancestry. Thus the name Hybrid Musk is rather far-fetched though generally accepted. Pemberton crossed 'Trier' with various Hybrid Teas, producing several very beautiful, though sterile, seedlings; tall, repeat-flowering, scented shrubs, with large clusters of small flowers. 'Penelope' (1923) and 'Felicia' (1928) are well-known examples. Both 'Trier' and 'Aglaia' had been raised in Germany by Lambert, and further development took place there, with 'Wilhelm' a fertile tetraploid raised by Kordes in 1930. Kordes, Tantau and Boerner have bred further roses along these lines (American hardiness zone IV–V).

Rugosas These roses are seedlings or crosses of *R. rugosa*, a very hardy species from northern Japan and Siberia (p. 100). They are all thorny, with leaves with impressed veins, and generally well-scented flowers. Several hybrids were raised in the early part of this century of which the Grootendorsts (p. 103) are the most familiar; they were *R. rugosa* crossed with a *multiflora* hybrid (American hardiness zone IV).

Polyantha The first dwarf Polyanthas were perpetual-flowering dwarfs of *R. multiflora* crossed with a dwarf China. These were hardy and floriferous, but small-flowered and without scent. In around 1910 the Danish breeder Poulsen began to cross dwarf Polyanthas with Hybrid Teas to try to introduce more hardiness into Hybrid Teas. These were called Poulsen roses, or Hybrid Polyanthas. Few of these survive today, having been overtaken by the Floribundas which were derived from them.

Floribunda Poulsen's original Hybrid Polyanthas were back-crossed to Hybrid Teas and other rose species such as *R. wichuraiana*, *R. rubiginosa*, *R. rugosa* and *R. pimpinellifolia* were brought into the group. One aim here has been to produce roses which produce a mass of colour over a long season, so-called 'bedding' roses. Another has been to introduce flowers with veined or 'hand-painted' petals, and McGredy have successfully produced some of these using 'Frühlingsmorgen' (p. 105).

Grandiflora This group was established in the USA to accommodate large-flowered, tall Floribundas such as 'Queen Elizabeth' (p. 171) and other intermediates between Floribundas and Hybrid Teas.

English Roses David Austin had the foresight to see that the old Gallica, Damask and Centifolia roses, with their subtle colours, scent and many-petalled flowers, would become increasingly popular, and the good fortune that one of his early crosses was the wonderful 'Constance Spry' (p. 83). The parentage of this was 'Belle Isis' (a Gallica 1845) and 'Dainty Maid' (a Floribunda 1940). He has continued to breed along these lines, using other old roses such as 'Comte de Chambord' as well as more modern Hybrid Teas and Floribundas to produce continuous-flowering roses with the shapes of Gallicas but a wider colour range, including yellow, buff and salmon pink, and greater disease resistance and tolerance of wet (American hardiness zone V).

Boursault These large shrubs or semi-climbing roses raised in the early nineteenth century, were said to be derived from *R. pendulina* × *R. chinensis*, but their chromosome number suggests that either *R. majalis* or *R. blanda* were used, not *R. pendulina* proper. *R. blanda* has also been used to breed thornless roses in the USA.

Sweet Briars The most familiar of these hybrids of *R. rubiginosa* were made by Lord Penzance, using the semi-double form 'Janet's Pride', crossed with various China hybrids and *R. foetida*; these kept the scented foliage of the Sweet Briar which has been lost in later crosses.

Kordesii A hybrid between *R. rugosa* and *R. wichuraiana* named 'Max Graf' (1919) was a sterile diploid, but Kordes succeeded in raising three seedlings from it in 1940 and 1950–1 which were fertile tetraploids, the beginning of a new race of Kordesii hybrids, such as 'Parkdirektor Riggers' (see p. 115).

Pimpinellifolias The early Scotch or Burnet roses raised in about 1900 were selections of *R. pimpinellifolia*, some possibly crossed with *R. pendulina* to introduce red colour. Kordes, however, crossed varieties of the Burnet rose with Hybrid Teas, and produced a beautiful range of single-flowered shrubs such as 'Frühlingsmorgen' (1940) and 'Frühlingsgold' (1950).

Macrantha Using *R.* × *macrantha* 'Daisy Hill', possibly a hybrid between *R. canina* and *R.* × *alba*, Kordes produced several hybrids, one of which, 'Raubritter', is exceptionally beautiful; unfortunately it is triploid and sterile, so no further generations have been raised. A similar breeders' dead end has been 'Cerise

Ground cover roses at Wisley

Bouquet', a hybrid between *R. multibracteata* and a Hybrid Tea, 'Crimson Glory'.

Miniatures Modern miniatures were raised from the dwarf China rose, Roulettii (p. 203), long grown on cottage windowsills in Switzerland, and rediscovered by Henri Correvon in 1922. Mini-roses are particularly popular at present in America, for growing in small yards or indoors under lights; some of the larger varieties are known as Patio roses. New colours and shapes have been introduced by crossing with Floribundas, and singles by using *R. wichuraiana*. Other dwarf Chinas, such as 'Pompon de Paris', were very popular as pot plants in the nineteenth century.

Rose fields at R. Harkness & Co, Hitchin, Herts

How to grow roses

Buying roses Roses are best ordered in late summer from a nursery, so that they arrive either in autumn or early spring, bare rooted. This is better than buying roses growing in containers in summer. In winter the plants are dormant and they settle in better than when disturbed while in active growth.

The number of plants needed to fill a certain area depends on the type of rose, but the smaller Floribundas can be planted 30 cm apart, larger or more vigorous roses 50 cm, and shrub roses, either so that their branches will not interfere with one another, or close enough to make one huge bush.

Preparing the soil Most roses grow best in a roughly neutral soil, though they can tolerate both acid and chalky soils. Their other requirements are good drainage and, if possible, full sun. Break up the sub-soil below the planting hole, but keep the fertile top 20 cm or so separate and add to it peat, leaf mould, or old compost and bone meal, with some sharp sand if the soil is heavy, and some lime if the soil is acid. Plant only when the soil is dry and crumbly – not easy on clay soils in a wet season.

Planting the roses When the roses arrive bare rooted from the nursery, plant them as soon as conditions allow. If they cannot be planted immediately keep them cold but away from frost, open the top of the packing, but make sure that the roots do not dry out. Before planting, thoroughly soak the roots in a bucket of water, and cut them back to 20–25 cm; remove any which are broken or damaged in any way. Leave the top growth at about 45 cm if planting in autumn or winter, but prune the bush if planting in spring. The ideal planting hole is circular, wider than the root spread and about 30 cm deep, with a low cone in the middle round which the roots can be spread out before the hole is filled, to hold the plant firmly and give the roots a good start.

Extra rose fertilizer can be added round the roots if planting in spring, otherwise any fertilizing is best left till growth begins. Any firming of the soil must be done before watering, and dry and sandy soils pressed down more than wet or clay soils.

Manuring Any farmyard manure is best used only on the surface of the soil, so it reaches the roots gradually. Burnt soil and ash from a bonfire are excellent for roses, as they contain potash which is the most beneficial nutrient for healthy growth and good flowers. A good alternative to manure is a top dressing of coarse peat with a granular rose fertiliser such as Toprose added. It is a good idea to fertilize after the first flowering to ensure a good second crop.

Planting from containers Roses can be planted from containers at any time of year, provided that the soil is not too wet. Try to obtain bushes that have been potted in soil compost, rather than peat. In summer make sure that the plant in the container is well watered. Then place it in its hole, with as little disturbance as possible, and, after the container has been removed, put back the soil and again water well. If the rose has been grown in a peat compost it is advisable to dig it up in autumn and replant it, so that it does not sit overwinter in a heap of sodden peat.

Pruning Rose pruning is a simple operation, requiring only a knowledge of where on the bush the year's flowers can be expected to come. As a preliminary to the main pruning, all dead wood and any spindly shoots should be removed. Most modern roses, such as Hybrid Teas and Floribundas, flower best on the ends of new shoots that come from near the base of the plant. These roses can be pruned down to about half their unpruned height, leaving good outward-facing buds on last year's wood to grow up and flower. In

Shortening roots

Pruning a new H. T.

all except the mildest climates, the main pruning is best done in early spring. The harder the pruning, the fewer but larger flowers may be expected. Weaker plants need harder pruning than strong vigorous ones. After flowering, the dead heads should be cut off, leaving the full-sized leaves to encourage the new flowering shoots. Climbing Hybrid Teas should have their long vigorous shoots tied in and thinner side shoots should be shortened to a good bud.

Most shrub roses flower on short shoots coming off branches which have been formed the previous summer. At the spring pruning, shoots which have flowered the previous year are removed altogether and only these seven-month-old shoots are retained. Do not shorten these shoots but, if they are ramblers, train them and tie them in. If they are Hybrid Perpetuals, or very strong Damasks, bend them over carefully and peg them down. They will then flower along their length, not at the top only. If a second crop of flowers is expected, these roses also can be dead-headed and lightly pruned and fertilized to encourage the second crop of flowers. [Hybrid Musks profit from this light pruning after the first flowering.] Rose species and simple hybrids, and this includes the Gallicas, Albas and Centifolias, need little pruning. It is sufficient to remove any dead, very old or feeble wood, and also do a little gentle shaping here and there. These roses will flower year after year without any pruning, and more are spoilt by having their embryonic flowers cut off by overzealous pruners than by neglect. Very old branches should be removed completely, to encourage and give room for strong new shoots to come up from the base.

Control of pests and diseases

Most pests and diseases can now be controlled by using one 'cocktail' of sprays, such as 'Multirose', which is both contact and systemic insecticide and fungicide, and includes a foliar feed. How often do you read 'Spray at the first sign of disease' and how often is that good advice ignored! The pictures and descriptions below will help to identify some of the commoner pests and diseases.

Greenfly or blackfly, technically called aphids, are the commonest pests, and attack young shoots, particularly in dry weather, causing distortion of shoots and stunting. They breed phenomenally quickly, the females producing young almost daily, without the need of males (envy of the feminist!). They can soon completely cover a young shoot, or the juicy stalk of a small bud, with a heaving mass of tiny bodies. They can be gently rubbed or brushed off, but modern pirimicarb-based sprays are more effective.

Caterpillars of various flies and moths also like young shoots; some curl the leaves into a neat tube, others eat out the heart of developing buds. If the roses look healthy, but develop fewer flowers than expected, small caterpillars may be the culprits. They can be picked off but will be prevented from doing damage by an early spraying, as the leaves begin to expand.

Red spider mite is particularly resistant to sprays but, both in the greenhouse and in warm, sheltered places outside, the predator, *Phytoseiulus persimilis*, gives excellent control. Leaves damaged by red spider show minute yellow dots, later patches and finally the whole leaf looks yellow, with a fine web underneath; the minute brown spider-like mites can be seen with a lens, moving slowly, or sucking the leaf juices.

Japanese beetles These small brown beetles are the same shape as cockchafers, but only half their size. They can be very destructive, especially in North America, arriving in the garden in swarms and eating flowers and leaves. Regular spraying is the only means of control.

Mildew appears as a fine powdery deposit on the surface of leaves and shoots. It is usually worst in spells of dry weather, or when the plant is dry at the roots. It is not very damaging to the plant, but

Mildew on *Charles de Mills*   Rust on *R.* × *alba*

Black spot on *R. kokanica*   Black spot on 'Zéphirine Drouhin'

nevertheless unsightly, and can be controlled by sprays. Some roses are resistant to it, some especially susceptible, e.g. 'Dorothy Perkins', a rambler which suffers particularly when growing on a wall.

Black spot This is seldom serious on modern roses, but some species, especially the yellow-flowered ones such as *Rosa foetida* can be defoliated completely in wet summers. Spraying before the disease has taken hold, and clearing up all dead leaves in autumn, can control it, and it may be worthwhile spraying very susceptible varieties before an attack develops.

Rust This disease can be serious in some climates but can now be controlled by sprays, or kept at bay by high potash fertilizers.

Frost damage In cold winters roses may be damaged or even completely killed by frost. The different groups vary greatly in their hardiness and the zone numbers are put after each group. If there is any doubt about the hardiness of a rose it can be protected, after the first frost of autumn, with a mound of fine soil protected by coarse manure or peat, held down by conifer branches, so that the buds in the lower part of the plant are held at around freezing for as long as possible, and prevented from alternate freezing, thawing, and so drying in cold sunny weather.

The photographs

When shooting roses in the garden or the field, it is essential to work from a tripod so that you can take advantage of the opportunity to use a slow shutter speed and thus a smaller aperture, giving greater depth of field. In practice the best speed is normally 1/15 sec, although if there is a strong wind you may have to go up to 1/30 or in extremes 1/60.

The studio shots are taken on a Bronica 120, with a normal lens, with two Bowens quad units as light source. The field shots are taken with a Nikon FM. The film in both cases is Ektachrome 64, that used for the field shots pushed one stop in development.

R. kokanica

R. kokanica near Tashkent, central Asia

R. hemisphaerica in central Turkey

Rosa kokanica (Regel) Regel ex Juz.
(*R. xanthina* var *kokanica* (Regel) Boul.)
A suckering shrub up to 2 m, with reddish
pubescent young twigs. Leaflets 5–7, aromatic,
glandular beneath and on the margins. Flowers
around 5 cm across; petals soon curling back.
Sepals not leafy at their apex. Hips brownish.
Found on rocky slopes and stony places in
Afghanistan and in central Asia, in the Pamir
Alai and Tien Shan at 900–2800 m. Frequent in
the foothills near Tashkent, where the
photograph here was taken. Flowers from May
to July according to altitude. This species was
introduced into cultivation by Jelena de Belder.
It grows well, but is often defoliated by
blackspot and does not flower after a cool
summer, even in a hot dry position in full sun.

Rosa hemisphaerica J. Herrmann (*R. rapinii*
Boiss. & Bal.)   A much-branched bush up to
1.5 m, with many strong, curved prickles.
Leaflets 5–7 (–9), not strongly aromatic, grey
green above, glaucescent and finely pubescent
beneath, glandular on the rachis. Stipules often
toothed. Flowers 4–5 cm across, petals rather
pale yellow. Hips orange red. Native of Turkey,
Iran, the Kopet Dağ, and Soviet Armenia,
growing on dry slopes and roadsides from 800 to
1800 m; often cultivated within that range. Rare
in cultivation in England, requiring more heat
and drought in summer to flower well.
Photographed in Turkey, near Malatya.

Rosa hemisphaerica 'Flore Pleno' (*R.
sulphurea* Ait.)   This rose has been cultivated in
Europe since the early 17th century. It is similar
to *R. foetida* 'Persiana' but less satisfactory in
gardens as the flowers 'ball' in wet weather,
rotting before they have opened properly. They
also have a tendency to hang down. It needs a
hot, dry situation in full sun to have a chance of
success.

Rosa foetida J. Herrmann (*R. lutea* Miller)
Austrian Brier, Austrian Yellow   A shrub up to
3 m, with glabrous young twigs and few
straight, or slightly curved, slender prickles.
Leaflets 7–9, aromatic, sparsely glandular
beneath and on the margins, dull green on both
sides. Flowers around 6 cm across; petals often
suffused with red. Sepals becoming leafy at the
apex. Hips dark brick red. Native of south-west
Asia from Turkey to Pakistan and north to
Georgia and the Tien Shan, in hedges, scrub
and rocky slopes up to 2850 m, flowering from
April to June. Naturalized in southern and
eastern Europe. A good garden plant, cultivated
in England since before 1600, thriving in poor
soil and full sun. This species is cultivated
throughout its range and may have originated as
a hybrid between *R. kokanica* and
R. hemisphaerica.

Rosa foetida 'Bicolor' (*R. punicea* Miller)
Austrian Copper.   This cultivar of *R. foetida*
has been known since the 12th century, and
probably originated in Turkey, or Central Asia.
The petals are red inside, yellow in the reverse
but branches may revert to the plain yellow
form. It grows well in dry sunny gardens and is
frequently grown in warm climates such as
California. Graham Thomas mentions a double
form of this, which has apparently been lost.

Rosa foetida 'Persiana' Persian Double
Yellow.   This double form of *R. foetida*
probably also originated in western Asia. It was
introduced to England, probably in 1837, by Sir
Henry Willock. It differs from *R. hemisphaerica*
in its less drooping flowers and in its leaves.

Rosa primula Boulenger (*R. ecae* subsp.
primula (Boul.) Roberts)   The history of this
rose is covered in detail in Bean ed. 8 (1976). It
was raised from seed collected by F. N. Meyer
in 1910 near Samarkand in central Asia, but has
not been recognized in recent local Russian
Floras. It makes a bush up to 2 m high, with
very aromatic foliage and exceptionally long
leaves which may have 15 leaflets on strong
shoots, 9–13 on flowering side branches. It
differs from *R. ecae* (p. 16) and *R. kokanica*
(above) also in its pale yellow flowers.

Golden Chersonese   This hybrid between
'Canary Bird' and *R. ecae* (female) was raised by
E. F. Allen in 1963. It makes a shrub up to 2 m
high, flowering once, in late May. It combines
the aromatic foliage and deep yellow flowers of
R. ecae with the larger petals of R. 'Canary
Bird'.

R. foetida 'Bicolor'

R. foetida 'Persiana'

R. hemisphaerica 'Flore Pleno'

R. foetida

R. primula

Golden Chersonese

R. × reversa

R. sericea f. lutea

R. sericea subsp. omeiensis

Cantabrigiensis

R. ecae

Canary Bird

Helen Knight

R. xanthina f. hugonis

R. willmottiae
'Hadden's variety'

R. willmottiae

Albert Edwards

June 15th, from Valley Gardens, Windsor

R. ecae near Ferghana, central Asia

Rosa × reversa Waldst. & Kit.   This hybrid between *R. pimpinellifolia* and *R. pendulina* is known in the wild and combines the characters of the parents. It makes a bush up to 1.5 m high, with white or pink flowers, and usually dark purple pendulous fruits.

Rosa sericea f. lutea (*R. omeiensis* 'Lutea')   The yellow-flowered form of *R. sericea* does not appear to have been reported in the wild, except by Kingdon Ward in northern Burma. The plant shown here, *R. sericea* subsp. *omeiensis* 'Lutea', is probably the result of hybridization between *R. sericea* and *R. xanthina*, as it has 5 petals and a cup-shaped flower like *R. xanthina* f. *hugonis*.

Rosa sericea subsp. omeiensis f. pteracantha Franchet   The width of the large red thorns is very variable in the wild, plants with numerous broad thorns and those with hardly any growing side by side in western China; large-thorned plants are reported also from Manipur.

Rosa sericea subsp. omeiensis (Rolfe) Roberts.   A shrub up to 3 m, with arching branches and strong new shoots springing up from the base. It is these shoots that carry the best large red thorns which are such a striking feature of f. *pteracantha*. Leaflets 11–19, oblanceolate to elliptic. Flowers white, usually with 4 petals. Hips, with a fleshy stalk, yellow, red, purplish or red with an orange or yellow stalk, ripening within two months of flowering. *R. sericea* Lindley is native of the Himalayas from Nepal to central China, growing on dry hillsides, by streams and on roadsides from 1300 to 3600 m.

Subsp. *sericea* has thin, not fleshy, fruit stalks, often 5 petals, and 7–11 leaflets, while subsp. *omeiensis* has fleshy fruit stalks and more than 11 leaflets, and 4 petals. Subsp. *sericea* is found mainly in the west, subsp. *omeiensis* in Sichuan and Hubei. In Yunnan, however, where the plant is common around Dali and Lijiang, it has fewer leaflets (7–11), but fleshy fruit stalks. In the wild, flowering is from March to July, depending on habitat and altitude.

Rosa ecae Aitch. (*R. xanthina* var. *ecae* (Aitch.) Boul.)   A much-branched, suckering shrub growing to 1.5 m in the wild and 2.5 m in cultivation, with straight, flattened thorns. Branches often crooked, very thorny. Leaflets 7–9, up to 5 mm long, obovate or oblanceolate to broadly elliptic, glandular. Stipules very narrow with diverging auricles. Petals often not overlapping; flowers 20–30 mm across. Hips 5–7 mm long, red brown, sepals patent. Native of central Asia, from Afghanistan and Pakistan north to the Tien Shan, Pamir Alai and northern China (Shaanxi), growing on rocky hillsides in the mountains from 500 to 3000 m, flowering from April to June according to altitude. Photographed here in central Asia near Ferghana, flowering in May. Introduced into cultivation by Surgeon-Major Aitchison in 1880 while on the commission to delimit the borders of Afghanistan. It requires as dry and sunny a site as possible.

Cantabrigiensis   This hybrid occurred by chance in Cambridge Botanic Gardens in about 1931. It makes a robust upright bush up to 2 m high, with bristly young shoots, and somewhat cupped, scented flowers. Hips orange red. Said to be a hybrid between *R. xanthina* f. *hugonis* and *R. sericea*.

R. sericea near Baoxing, Sichuan

R. sericea subsp. *omeiensis* f. *pteracantha*

R. sericea near Lijiang, Yunnan

Canary Bird   A particularly well-coloured clone of *Rosa xanthina* (p. 20) of unknown origin, possibly a hybrid between f. *spontanea* and f. *hugonis*. It makes a bush up to 2 m high and across and requires full sun and exposure in well-drained soil.

Helen Knight   This seedling of *R. ecae* originated from a plant growing on the wall of the Director's house at Wisley. The other parent is said to be *R. pimpinellifolia* 'Grandiflora' which was growing nearby. It was raised by F. P. Knight, then Director, in 1966 and named after his wife. It makes a bush up to 3 m on a wall, with red-brown twigs and rich yellow flowers, larger than those of *R. ecae*.

Rosa xanthina* f. *hugonis (Hemsl.) Roberts (*R. hugonis* Hemsley)   This form of *R.*

xanthina is found in central China, as far south as the Min river in western Sichuan, growing in rather dry valleys. There it makes a bush up to 2.5 m, flowering in early May, and varying in colour from pale to bright yellow. The prickles vary greatly in type and number, consisting of bristles and/or flattened crimson thorns like *R. sericea*. Thorns of this type are found in the clone 'Hidcote Gold', sometimes considered a hybrid with *R. sericea*, but said to have been raised from wild seed. It is likely that f. *hugonis* consists of wild populations intermediate between *R. xanthina* and *R. sericea*. The clone illustrated here is characterized by its pale yellow cup-shaped flowers, and is thorny and bristly only on the young shoots.

Albert Edwards   This hybrid between *R. xanthina* f. *hugonis* and *R. pimpinellifolia* var.

altaica, makes a very free-flowering shrub up to 3 m high and across, with slightly scented flowers.

Rosa willmottiae Hemsley   A bush up to 3 m high and across, with very delicate shoots and usually 9 rounded leaflets. Flowers small, 2.5–3.75 cm across. Fruits with the sepals and top of the flesh falling off (p. 214) when ripe. Native of western China, in dry valleys in western Sichuan, from 2300 to 3150 m; introduced by Wilson in 1904. In gardens this species grows and flowers well both in the open and in woodland clearings. Two forms are shown here; a garden form and 'Hadden's Variety'. A third variety, 'Wisley', is in cultivation and is shown on p. 214. It has narrower leaflets, deeper pink flowers and the top of the fruit remains attached even when ripe.

R. rubiginosa

R. glauca

R. prattii

R. hirtula

R. roxburghii f. normalis

R. serafinii

R. stellata var. mirifica

R. giraldii

Edward Hyams

June 25th, from The Gardens of the Rose

R. × hardii

Rosa rubiginosa L. (*R. eglanteria* L.) Sweet Briar or Eglantine   A spreading bush up to 3 m, with stout curved and hooked prickles, bristles and stiff glandular hairs, especially on the flowering branches. Leaflets 5–7, rounded, double toothed, glandular beneath, giving the whole plant an aromatic scent in damp weather. Petals usually deep pink. Hips smooth or glandular, bright red. Native of Europe except Spain and Portugal and the far north, and western Asia growing among scrub, in hedges, by streams and on the edges of woods. In the British Isles *R. rubiginosa* is commonest on chalk in south-eastern England, but is present in scattered localities over the rest of the country. In gardens Sweet Briar is planted for its scented foliage and is useful for hedging.

Rosa glauca Pourret (*R. rubrifolia* Vill.)   A tall shrub up to 4 m with support but usually with arching branches and few thorns, easily recognized by its very grey or sometimes purplish leaves, and small deep pink flowers. Hips brownish red. Native of the mountains of Central Europe, from the Pyrenees and Alps eastwards to Poland, Romania and Albania, but not common. Introduced into cultivation in England before 1830, this rose has recently become excessively popular for its foliage, both in a garden setting and for use in flower arrangements. Beautiful specimen bushes grow on the terrace at Crathes Castle in Aberdeen.

Rosa prattii Hemsley   A bush from 1 to 2.5 m tall, with straight pale brown thorns and leaves with 10–15 small lanceolate to obovate leaflets. Flowers often 3 or more in an umbellate cyme, pale to deep pink. Fruit bottle shaped. Native of western Sichuan, especially around Kangting (Tachien-lu) at 2300–3000 m, where it flowers in June and July.

Rosa hirtula (Regel) Nakai (*R. roxburghii* var. *hirtula* (Regel) Rehd. & Wils.)   This rose, very close to *R. roxburghii*, differs primarily in its paler flowers and its leaflets, which are hairy beneath. It is native of central Honshu.

Rosa roxburghii f. normalis Rehd. & Wils. (*R. microphylla* Roxb. ex Lindl.)   A large shrub, finally reaching 5 m or more with peeling bark when old. Prickles few, in pairs. Leaflets 9–19. Flowers scented, 5–7.5 cm across. Sepals leafy. Hips prickly, falling when green, with persistent sepals. Native of western China where it is common both in western Sichuan near Mt Emei and in Yunnan around Dali, from 300 to 2000 m, growing on stream banks, in hedges and by paths between rice fields. It has also been found in Hubei. In cultivation in the British Isles *R. roxburghii* requires a warm position to flower freely, and is cut down only by exceptionally severe winters. It was introduced from China in 1908, probably by Wilson.

Rosa serafinii Viv.   A dwarf relative of *R. rubiginosa* up to 50 cm, with hooked or curved prickles. Leaflets 5–7, 8–12 mm long, glandular beneath, aromatic. Hips smooth, red. Native of Corsica, Italy, Sicily, Sardinia and Bulgaria where it grows on dry rocky mountains.

Rosa stellata var. mirifica (Greene) Cockerell   A low bush with young stems glandular and stellate pubescent, or glandular only in var. *mirifica*, and numerous long, nearly straight prickles. Leaflets 3, wedge shaped, toothed towards the apex, usually less than 1 cm long. Flowers solitary, without bracts. Native of western Texas, southern New Mexico, and northern Arizona, around the Grand Canyon in the upper Sonoran zone, growing in dry rocky places at about 2000 m, flowering from June to September. A very beautiful dwarf large-flowered species, requiring dry, hot, well-drained position, or a sunny frame.

Edward Hyams Collected by Edward Hyams near Shahrud in Iran in 1972, from among *Rosa persica*, this interesting hybrid was preserved and distributed by E. F. Allen. It has 5–7 leaflets, and the conspicuous red blotch of *R. persica* which distinguishes it from *R × kopetdaghensis*, a hybrid between *R. hemisphaerica* and *R. persica* known from several places in east and central Iran and in Russian Kopet Dağ. It has grown and flowered well both at the RNRS gardens in a frame and in Mr Allen's own garden, and has proved to be diploid. Its parentage is a matter of speculation.

Rosa giraldii Crépin A bush up to 2.5 m tall, with few straight, often paired prickles. Leaflets 7–9, oval or elliptic, sometimes hairy on both sides; flowers solitary or in clusters of 3–5; pedicels very short, often hidden by large bracts. Fruit globular or ovoid, red. Native of western China from Shaanxi southwards to Sichuan and western Hubei.

Rosa roxburghii Trattinnick The original *R. roxburghii* shown here was the double form, introduced from the Botanic Garden at Calcutta in about 1824, where William Roxburgh was superintendent. It was said to have been brought from Canton. It had earlier (1820) been described as *R. microphylla* by Lindley from a Chinese painting.

Rosa × coryana Hurst This hybrid between *R. roxburghii* and, probably, *R. macrophylla* was raised by Dr C. C. Hurst at Cambridge Botanic Gardens in 1926, and named after Reginald Cory who made a large bequest to the garden. It makes a dense bush up to 2 m high, with smooth stems and very bristly pedicels and ovaries. Flowers produced in June and July, with little scent.

Rosa persica Michx. ex Juss. (*R. berberifolia* Pall., *Hulthemia persica* (Michx.) Bornm.) A dwarf suckering and decumbent shrub up to 50 cm high, with numerous straight and curved prickles. Leaves simple, to 15 mm long, variable in shape, green or greyish, glabrous or pubescent, toothed. Flowers solitary; petals up to 15 mm long, yellow with a red blotch at the base. Anthers purple. Hips globose, bristly, blackish. Native of steppes and desert regions of Iran, Afghanistan and central Asia north to western Siberia, flowering from April to June. *Rosa persica* is common in Iran, often growing as a weed in cornfields, and being used for fuel after the wheat has been harvested. In cultivation, plants of Iranian origin have proved very difficult to flower, even in a frame, but plants from seed from Tashkent grew and flowered well in a frame at Wisley. Photographed here north of Tashkent, flowering on grassy hills in May.

Rosa × hardii Cels This chance hybrid of *R. persica* was raised by M. Hardy in about 1836, the pollen parent being supposed to be *R. clinophylla* which was growing nearby. It is still in cultivation but rare, being difficult to keep for long, and susceptible to mildew. It is best grown in a raised bed against a wall or in a large pot kept indoors in winter and put out in full sun in summer.

R. roxburghii f. normalis, by a paddyfield near Dali, Yunnan

R. persica near Tashkent, central Asia

R. × coryana

R. roxburghii

R. pimpinellifolia 'Nana'

R. nutkana var. hispida

R. arkansana

Mrs Colville

R. xanthina f. spontanea

R. pimpinellifolia 'Double White'

R. pimpinellifolia

R. pimpinellifolia 'Grandiflora'

June 16th, from University Botanic Garden, Cambridge

Rosa pimpinellifolia 'Nana'   This dwarf (up to 50 cm high) double-flowered form of the Scotch rose is possibly that shown in Andrews' *Roses* in 1805.

Rosa nutkana var. *hispida* Fernald (*R. spaldingii* Crépin)   A shrub up to 2 m high, with distinct pairs of slender prickles at the leaf bases. Leaflets 5–7, usually singly serrate without glandular teeth, glabrous or pubescent. Flowers usually solitary; sepals lanceolate, attenuate. Hips globose, purplish. Native of western North America from British Columbia south to Utah, mostly east of the Cascades, growing in woods or scrub in the mountains, flowering from May to July. Described from Clearwater, Oregon.

Rosa arkansana Porter   A low shrub with stems up to 0.5 m high, densely bristly and with straight prickles nearly to the summit. Leaflets

3–9, ovate or elliptic, obtuse or acute, without glands, glabrous, somewhat shining above. Flowers in a few to many-flowered corymbs; hips 1–1.5 cm in diameter, with persistent sepals. Native of the Mid-West from Wisconsin and Minnesota to Colorado and Kansas, growing on dry slopes and prairies, flowering from May to August. Very close to *R. acicularis* but differing in its glabrous, not glandular leaflets, and to *R. suffulta*, which, however, has leaflets softly pilose beneath.

Mrs Colville   This is like a deep pink *R. pimpinellifolia* in habit and appearance but is considered to be a probable hybrid with *R. pendulina* as is suggested by its somewhat elongated hips, not rounded as in *R. pimpinellifolia*. It is a selection of *R.* × *reversa* (see p. 16) but is only 1 m high. Its origin is not recorded.

Rosa xanthina f. spontanea Rehder   *Rosa xanthina* Lindl was a double-flowered plant, cultivated in China before 1800, and introduced to the Arnold Arboretum by Meyer in 1907. It can now be seen planted along the road from Beijing airport to the city. The single form of the species f. *spontanea*, is widespread in northern China and Korea, as far west as dry parts of Sichuan (f. *hugonis*). 'Canary Bird' (p. 17) is a particularly good form. *R. xanthina* requires dry, well-drained soil and full sun to grow well in England, where it can make a bush up to 3 m high and across with arching branches.

Rosa pimpinellifolia 'Double White'   This larger double white Scotch rose makes a suckering mass of stems up to 2 m high. It is vigorous, disease free and produces large numbers of scented flowers in early summer with the minimum of attention.

R. palustris

***Rosa pimpinellifolia* L.** (*R. spinosissima* L. pro parte) Scotch or Burnet Rose   A suckering thicket of low stems up to 1 m high, with both prickles and bristles, often extending as far as the inflorescence. Leaflets 5–11, glabrous, simply serrate; sepals undivided. Flowers usually creamy, occasionally white or pink, up to 5 cm across. Hips round, blackish. It is found wild on dunes and dry heathy or chalky pastures, from Iceland and Norway to France and eastwards to Turkey, south-western Russia and Central Asia. In the British Isles it can be found wild around the whole coastline and more rarely inland.

***Rosa pimpinellifolia* 'Grandiflora'**   This clone makes a large bush up to 2 m high and across, with suckers. It is distinct from wild *R. pimpinellifolia* in its larger size and larger paler flowers. The stems are prickly but not bristly. 'Grandiflora' was said to have been introduced from Siberia sometime before 1820. It is sometimes known as var. *altaica* (Willd.) Thory which name was originally given to a very bristly but not prickly plant. This rose was one of the parents of the popular shrub roses 'Frühlingsmorgen', 'Frühlingsgold' and an ancestor of 'Maigold'.

***Rosa nitida* Willd.**   A suckering shrub up to 1 m high, with slender canes covered with dark purple bristles and few straight prickles. Leaflets 7–9, shining and dark green above, narrowly elliptic or oblong, on flowering shoots 1–4 cm × 4–12 mm. Flowers solitary or few in a corymb, 4–6 cm across, scented like Lily-of-the-Valley in the evening; hips subglobose, dark red. Native of North America, from Newfoundland and Quebec south to Nova Scotia and southern New England, growing in bogs, wet thickets and the edges of ponds on acid soil, flowering from June to September according to altitude. Valuable in the garden for its striking shining leaves and deep red or purple autumn colour (p. 214).

***Rosa palustris* Marsh**   A suckering shrub up to 2.5 m high, with stout, often hooked, prickles at the base and at the leaf bases. Leaflets 5–9, dull green, oblong or elliptic, minutely pubescent beneath, 2–6 cm long. Flowers in corymbs or solitary, 4–5.5 cm broad. Hips with glandular bristles or smooth, red. Native of North America from Florida and Arkansas north to Quebec, Wisconsin and Minnesota, growing in swamps, marshes and the margins of lakes, flowering from June to August according to altitude. An attractive, late-flowering species.

***Rosa laxa* Retz.**   A shrub up to 2 m with arching stem, and green bark. Prickles large, few, downcurved and flattened, mixed with bristles. Leaflets 5–9, ovate to elliptic or oblong, glabrous or slightly downy beneath, 1.5–4.5 cm × 8–25 mm, obtuse. Flowers solitary or in groups of 3–6, 4–5 cm in diameter, pale pink or white. Hips globose or elliptic, usually smooth, with persistent erect sepals. Native of north-west China and Siberia to the Tien Shan and Pamir-Alai where it grows in steppes, open forests or by rivers and lakes, flowering from June to August.

R. pimpinellifolia 'Double White'

R. nitida

R. laxa

R. fedtschenkoana

Hillieri

Highdownensis

R. setipoda

Fargesii

R. webbiana

R. caudata

Geranium

R. moyesii

June 25th, from The Gardens of the Rose

R. nanothamnus

Highdownensis A seedling of *R. moyesii*, raised by Sir Frederick Stern at Highdown, Sussex, in 1928. A large shrub with shoots up to 3 m high, arching in their second year. Flowers in clusters with little scent. Hips freely produced (p. 216).

Rosa fedtschenkoana Regel A suckering shrub up to 2 m high, with greyish leaves and white flowers over a long season from June to September. Hips bristly, orange red (p. 214). Native of Central Asia, in the Ala-tau, Tien Shan and Pamir-Alai, extending in north-west China. The cultivated form, shown here, was introduced at the end of the 19th century. In its long season of flowering and short (around 2.5 cm long) fruit it differs from *R. fedtschenkoana* as described by Regel, which is very close to *R. webbiana*, and so is possibly a hybrid with *R. beggeriana*.

Hillieri A shrub up to 3 m, with spreading branches, not bushy. Flowers the darkest of this group. Hips large, not prolific. A seedling of *R. moyesii* raised at Hillier Nurseries around 1924; the pollen parent was possibly *R. willmottiae*, but it has not left much trace in its offspring.

Rosa setipoda Hemsley & Wilson A bush up to 3 m high; branches with bristles as well as prickles. Leaflets 7–9, acute or obtuse. Flowers up to 20 or more in a cluster, white in the centre. Pedicels and receptacle purple, glandular bristly. Hips large, coral red. Native of western China, in the north-west of Hubei and adjacent Sichuan, in mountain scrub from 2000 to 2600 m. Introduced by Wilson to Veitch's nursery in 1901.

Rosa webbiana Royle A shrub from 1–2 m high, with straight, slender, yellowish prickles. Leaflets 5–9, obovate or almost round, obtuse. Flowers borne singly, usually pink, sometimes with a white centre or all white. Pedicels smooth or glandular, often purplish or reddish, as are the young shoots. Hips bottle shaped or globular, red. Native of the western Himalayas from the Pamir in Soviet central Asia to Kashmir, Tibet and Afghanistan and north to Kashgar, usually found in rather dry valleys. The closely related species *R. bella* and *R. sertata* are found in western and northern China.

Fargesii (*R. moyesii* var. *fargesii* Rolfe) This is a bright pink form of *R. moyesii* of uncertain origin whose history is given in Bean, ed. 8 (1976), in some detail. It is significant mainly in that it has been found to be tetraploid, not hexaploid as are most *R. moyesii*, and so might be used in hybridizing with other tetraploid roses. The purple shoots and pedicels contrast well with the pink flowers.

Rosa caudata Baker A bush from 1–4 m high in the wild, close to *R. setipoda* but with a compact inflorescence so that the flowers are held among the leaves. Inflorescence many flowered, with bristly pedicels. Leaflets glabrous beneath. Tetraploid. Native of western Hubei, near Fang Xian, from 1800 to 2000 m, growing in scrub. Introduced by Wilson in 1908.

Geranium This is the commonest clone of *R. moyesii* in cultivation. It makes an open bush with few rather stiff stems up to 2.5 m high. The foliage is rather delicate light green, as are the stems. The fruits are large and, if anything, more striking than the flowers. 'Geranium' originated at Wisley as a seedling of *R. moyesii* in 1938. Most *moyesii* seedlings are pink flowered, and one such, selected for its fruits, is 'Sealing Wax' (p. 216).

Rosa moyesii Hemsley & Wilson A large, robust shrub up to 6 m high, often with many stems shooting up from the base. Leaflets 7–13, glabrous except on the midrib beneath, up to 3.75 cm long, elliptic, usually simply toothed. Flowers solitary or in groups of up to 4, red or pink, with glandular bristly or smooth pedicels and receptacle. Hips large (p. 217), usually with green sepals. Native of western China, in western Sichuan and Yunnan, in mountain scrub, from 2000 to 6300 m, flowering in June and July. In Sichuan it is common around Tachien-lu (Kangting) and in Yunnan known both from the Dali range and from Lijiang where it grows on limestone. In the wild both red and deep pink-flowered plants are found in the same area and most seedlings turn out pink. Illustrated here is a multi-stemmed form (T. 888) collected by Wilson.

R. farreri

Rosa nanothamnus Boulenger (*R. webbiana* var. *microphylla* Crép.) A dwarf, very prickly shrub up to 50 cm high, with long straight spines. Leaflets usually 5(–9), ovate or obovate, 3–15 mm long, glabrous or pubescent. Flowers solitary up to 3.75 cm in diameter. Hips globose or ovoid, 10–12 mm long, sepals persistent. Native of central Asia, from the Tien Shan and Pamir-Alai to Afghanistan and Kashmir, on dry rocky hillsides. Requires full sun and exposure to flower well. This is a dwarf, small-leaved form of *R. webbiana*.

Rosa farreri Rolfe 'Persetosa' Farrer's Threepenny-bit Rose A twiggy bush up to 2 m high and wide. Leaflets 7–9, around 1.5 cm long, ovate; flowers 1–3 together, deep pink in bud, opening paler. Hips around 1 cm long, with conspicuous sepals, pedicels glandular (p. 214). Native of north-western China, especially the province of Gansu, whence 'Persetosa' originated, selected by E. A. Bowles from Farrer 774. This rose is sometimes considered to be a form of *R. elegantula* Rolfe.

R. forrestiana

Rosa forrestiana Boulenger A spreading, upright shrub up to 2 m high, with straight- or upward-pointing paired prickles. Leaflets 5–7, to 1.25 cm long, oval or round, glabrous or glandular to hairy on the veins beneath. Flowers pale to bright pink, solitary or up to 5 in a group, with very short pedicels hidden by large leafy bracts. Sepals shorter than the petals. Styles exserted. Hips rounded, with persistent sepals, glandular bristly (p. 214). Native of China, in north-west Yunnan, collected by Forrest and introduced in 1918. Free flowering in cultivation and with rounded hips characteristically surrounded by a ruff of broad bracts.

'Eddie's Jewel' A *R. moyesii* hybrid raised by Eddie in 1962. It makes a large bush up to 3 m, with one main flowering and some later flowers up to 12.5 cm across. Hips ovoid. Parentage: 'Donald Prior' × *R. moyesii* hybrid.

Eddie's Jewel

R. pendulina

R. davidii

R. davidii var. elongata

R. sweginzowii

R. bella

R. acicularis var. nipponensis

R. macrophylla 'Rubricaulis'

R. macrophylla

R. wardii

June 25th, from The Gardens of the Rose

R. macrophylla in Kashmir

R. multibracteata

Rosa davidii Crépin   A large shrub up to 5 m; shoots glabrous with strong straight or slightly curved prickles. Leaflets 7–11, 1.5–5 cm long, pubescent beneath, usually ovate, obtuse or acute, simply toothed. Flowers pink, 4–12 or more in a loose corymb. Sepals up to 2 cm long, flattened towards the apex. Pedicels 2.5–3.75 long, slender, glandular. Hips scarlet, bottle shaped, around 2 cm long. Native of western Sichuan, around Wa-shan, and Baoxing (Moupine) where it was originally collected by Père David, flowering in July at 1600–3000 m, in mountain scrub. First introduced to cultivation by Wilson in 1903. *R. banksiopsis* Baker, from western Hubei, eastern Sichuan and possibly Gansu, differs mainly in its glabrous pedicels, and lack of prickles.

Rosa pendulina L. (*R. alpina* L.)   A suckering shrub up to 2 m high but often less, usually without prickles. Leaflets 7–11, usually pubescent and sometimes glandular beneath. Flowers solitary, 35–55 cm across, deep pink. Fruit pendant, bottle shaped, often glandular, red. Native of open woods and alpine scrub and meadows in the mountains of central and southern Europe, from the Pyrenees to the Caucasus (var. *oxyodon*). This is the European representative of the *Rosa moyesii* group, photographed here in Switzerland near Sierre. The rose illustrated opposite, was labelled *R. hawrana* at the Gardens of Kmet, but appears closest to *R. pendulina*.

Rosa davidii var. **elongata** Rehder & Wilson   Differs from var. *davidii* in its larger leaves up to 7 cm long, which may be glabrous beneath, by its fewer-flowered corymbs (3–7) and more elongated fruit. It was collected by Wilson both at Baoxing and at Wa-shan and probably only represents part of the natural variation of *R. davidii*.

Rosa sweginzowii Koehne   A large spreading shrub up to 4 m high, with reddish shoots and large flat prickles as well as bristles. Leaflets 7–11, oval, hairy on the veins beneath. Flowers pink, up to 4 or more in an umbel. Pedicels short, barely longer than the bracts, glandular bristly as are the hips. Native of western China from Sichuan north to Gansu, and Shanxi growing in scrub from 2600 to 3300 m, flowering in June and July. Close to *R. moyesii* but often with larger leaves and more rounded glandular fruit in denser bunches.

Rosa acicularis var. **nipponensis** (Crép.) Koehne   A shrub, usually less than 1 m high in the wild. Stems purplish; leaflets 7–9, oblong, obtuse to rounded, 1–3 cm long, with minute teeth. Flowers solitary or in small groups of up to 3, bright pink. Pedicel with long, glandular hairs. Fruit obovoid. Native of high mountains in central and southern Japan, in Honshu (on Mt. Fuji) and on Shikoku, flowering in June and July. *R. acicularis* Lindley itself is a taller leafy bush with fewer leaflets, found from Sweden and Finland eastwards across Siberia into northern Japan and Kamchatka, with another variety in North America.

Rosa bella Rehder & Wilson   A spreading bush up to 3 m high, with purplish bristly branches. Leaflets usually 7–9, shortly stalked, elliptic to ovate acute 1–2 cm long, 0.6–1.2 cm across, simply serrate, with curved teeth, smooth, glaucescent beneath, sometimes glandular on the ribs. Flowers bright pink, 4–5 cm in diameter, solitary or in a group of 2–3; pedicels up to 1 cm long, with stalked glands. Hips elliptic ovate, to 2 cm long, glandular setose. Native of north-western China, collected in seed by Purdom in the mountains of north-west Shanxi, and described from plants growing in the Arnold Arboretum in 1915. Close to both *R. moyesii* and. *R. sweginzowii* but has undivided sepals, a slender bud and slender prickles. Similar also to *R. webbiana* which has rounded, not acute, leaflets.

Rosa macrophylla 'Rubricaulis'   This is a striking clone of *R. macrophylla* with purplish red stems and rather crinkled leaves with rounded leaflets glaucous underneath. It has similarities with *R. davidii* var. *elongata* and was raised from Forrest 15309, collected in north-west Yunnan; a similar form 'Glaucescens' (F. 14958) was collected on the Mekong–Salween divide.

Rosa macrophylla Lindley   A large shrub up to 5 m high, often with dark red or purple stems and few prickles. Leaflets 7–11, around 5 cm long, pubescent and glandular beneath, rough above with impressed veins, simply or doubly toothed, ovate elliptic, often acute. Flowers deep pink, up to 5 in a corymb; pedicels glandular. Sepals to 3.5 cm long, entire, expanded at the tip. Hips very large, roundish, or bottle shaped, to 7.5 cm long, glandular. Native of the Himalayas, from Pakistan eastwards to Bhutan and western China, from 2100 to 3800 m, growing in scrub and open forests. This is the largest fruited of roses, and various exceptionally fine forms are in cultivation. 'Master Hugh', which was raised by

R. pendulina in Switzerland

Maurice Mason from seed collected by Stainton, Sykes and Williams at Kali Gandkhi in Nepal (SSW 7288) has very round hips (p. 216). Schilling 2079, also from Nepal, has the largest hips of all the forms in cultivation.

Rosa wardii Mulligan   A shrub up to 2 m high, with rather few slender prickles. Leaflets 5–9, up to 2 cm long, glabrous above, downy and glandular on the veins beneath. Flowers white or pale pink, up to 3 in a group. Sepals acuminate or caudate. Described from plants collected by Kingdon Ward in south-east Tibet (KW 6101). The original plants had white flowers and were described as a variety var. *culta*. The plant shown here differs in its pink flowers, and white, not purple disc. It is close to *R. sweginzowii* but for the lack of bristles.

Rosa multibracteata Hemsley & Wilson   A bushy shrub up to 3 m high, with delicate branches and slender straight spines in pairs. Leaflets 5–9, less than 1.5 cm long, obovate to round, glabrous above, downy beneath on the midrib. Flowers usually several in a paniculate cyme, around 3.75 cm across, bright pink. Styles exserted. Pedicels short, to 2 cm long, downy, glandular, with conspicuous bracts at the base. Hips bottle shaped, with long caudate sepals (p. 214). Native of western China, in western Sichuan, most common in the Min river valley, at 1600–3000 m, flowering from May to August. An attractive plant with a long flowering season and parent of the hybrid 'Cerise Bouquet' (p. 106).

R. pisocarpa

R. woodsii var. fendler

R. nutkana var. muriculata

R. gymnocarpa

R. woodsii var. ultramontana

R. majalis

Octet

R. yainacensis

R. covillei

R. suffulta

Rose d'Amour

June 25th, from The Gardens of the Rose

Rosa nutkana Presl Nootka Rose   A bush with stout stems up to 2 m high, with stout straight flattened prickles at the leaf bases or none. Leaflets 5–7, elliptical to broadly oval, 1.5–5 cm long. Flowers mostly solitary, 4–6 cm wide. Pedicels glabrous to glandular bristly; receptacle usually glabrous, petals obcordate. Hips globose, 15–18 mm in diameter, purplish. Shown here is var. *muriculata* (Greene) G. N. Jones, which differs in having glandular stipules and sepals glandular hispid not glabrous on the back. Native of western North America from northern California to Alaska, east to the Rockies, flowering from May to July.

Rosa pisocarpa Gray Cluster Rose   A bush with slender stems 2–2.5 m high. Prickles straight, few or none. Leaflets 5–7, oval to elliptic oblong, pale and pubescent beneath, 1–4 cm long. Flowers 1–5 in a corymb. Pedicels and receptacle glabrous. Sepals 13–15 mm, caudate-attenuate. Hips globose, 7–10 mm in diameter. Native of western North America from northern California to British Columbia, growing in open woods below 1600 m, flowering from June to August.

Rose d'Amour (*R. virginiana* 'Plena', *R.* × *rapa*)   A double form or hybrid of *R. virginiana*, known since the 18th century. It makes a large bush up to 2 m or higher if grown as a climber. Graham Thomas has distinguished this from the 'D'Orsay Rose' which is similar in flower, but has pairs of thorns at the base of the leaf, and narrower leaflets and stipules, without red staining on the leaf bases.

Rosa woodsii Lindl. **var. fendleri** (Crép.) Rydb.   A shrub up to 2 m, with straight, slender prickles; stipules and petioles glandular. Leaflets 5–7. Flowers usually around 3 together, sometimes solitary. Petals up to 2.5 cm long, pink. Hips globose, glabrous. Native of North America from Missouri to Minnesota and Ontario, flowering from June to August. var. *ultramontana* (Wats.) Jepson is a suckering thicket-forming shrub, with sparse prickles; leaflets oval 1–4 cm long; petals 1.5–2 cm long. Native of western North America from California east of the Sierra Nevada to British Columbia, Montana and Nevada, growing in damp valleys from 1200 to 3200 m.

Rosa gymnocarpa Nutt. Wood Rose   A low bush usually around 1 m high, with slender straight prickles. Leaflets 5–7, oval to roundish, 1–4 cm long, doubly serrate, glabrous. Stipules narrow, glandular ciliate, dentate. Flowers very small, usually solitary, petals 8–12 mm long. Hips globose, glabrous, 5–10 mm long. Sepals dropping at maturity. Native of western North America, from central California north to British Columbia and Montana, usually below 1800 m, flowering from May to July. A small-flowered species, close to *R. willmottiae* from China.

Rosa yainacensis Greene   A low shrub with slender straight prickles at the leaf base. Leaflets 5–7 oval, 1–2 cm long, dark green and glabrous above, pale and pubescent beneath. Flowers usually solitary. Pedicels and receptacle glabrous. Sepals attenuate, entire, sometimes with leafy tips. Native of southern Oregon, east of the Cascades.

Octet   This rose originated as a cross between two North American species, *R. rudiuscula* Greene from Montana and *R. subglauca* Rydb. from Alberta, made at the University of Michigan, and is an allopolyploid and fertile.

The history of this rose is described by E. F. Allen in *The Rose Annual* 1979 p. 136–8. It makes a suckering shrub up to 2.5 m, and is vigorous, hardy and disease free.

Rosa majalis J. Herrmann (*R. cinnamomea* L. (1759))   A suckering bush forming thickets of stems up to 2 m high. Bark reddish brown. Prickles slender, in pairs at the nodes. Leaflets 5–7, 1.5–4.5 cm long, elliptical to obovate, pubescent bluish-green, paler beneath. Flowers solitary. Bracts large, equalling or longer than the glabrous pedicels. Petals 18–30 mm, purplish pink. Sepals undivided. Hips glabrous, globose. Native of northern and central Europe from Germany and France south to Yugoslavia and eastwards across Siberia, often growing in damp places, flowering from May to July. This rose has been cultivated since the 16th century, and is naturalized in parts of Belgium and Holland; both double and single forms may be found as garden escapes.

Rosa covillei Greene   A low shrub up to 1 m high, with bristles and weak prickles. Stipules narrow, glandular-ciliate. Leaflets usually 7, oval or obovate, 15–20 mm long, glabrous above, paler and pubescent beneath. Sepals ovate, short acuminate, about 1 cm long. Hips glabrous, round ovoid. Native of Klamath Co., Oregon, in pine forests.

Rosa suffulta Greene (*R. arkansana* var. *suffulta*)   Stems up to 0.5 m; internodes usually densely bristly and thorny; stipules pubescent. Leaflets 9–11, pubescent beneath. Flowers corymbose, produced on sideshoots and on the end of the current year's growth. Native of the Mid-West from Indiana to Texas on dry, rocky slopes, flowering from May to August.

Rosa foliolosa Nutt.   A low shrub up to 0.5 m, with few prickles; leaflets usually 9, apex and base acute, upper surface glabrous and shining, up to 3 cm long. Flowers usually solitary; petals obcordate. Hips subglobose, smooth or glandular; sepals spreading, deciduous. Native of the prairies of Texas, Oklahoma and Arkansas, flowering in May and June.

Rosa virginiana Miller   A bush up to 2 m high, with pairs of stout decurved thorns at the leaf bases, and few other similar internodal thorns. Stipules usually glandular dentate. Leaflets 7–9, usually acute, glabrous or pubescent on the veins below. Flowers solitary or few together; pedicels and hips with glandular bristles. Sepals attenuate with leafy tips. Native of eastern North America from Newfoundland to Pennsylvania to Ontario and Arkansas.

Rosa carolina L.   A bush rarely more than 1 m high with numerous internodal thorns, those at the leaf base scarcely different from the rest. Leaflets usually 5, oblong to oval or nearly round; flowers usually solitary, often produced on the current year's stems. Pedicels and hips with glandular bristles. Sepals rarely with leafy tips. Native of upland wood, dunes and prairies from Nova Scotia and New York to Minnesota south to Maryland and Texas, flowering from May to July.

Rosa californica Cham. & Schlecht. 'Plena'   A form of the Californian rose, which makes a large bush up to 3 m high and across. Leaflets 5–7; flowers normally pink, in corymbs with leafy bracts, *c.* 4 cm across. The wild form is native of California and Oregon, growing in scrub and on roadsides, flowering from June to October.

R. californica 'Plena'

R. carolina

R. foliolosa

R. virginiana

R. canina in a hedge in Northamptonshire

R. gallica

Rosa canina L. Dog Rose   A bush up to 5 m, with strong curved prickles. Leaflets 5–7, ovate, obovate or elliptical, glabrous and without glands. Pedicels glabrous. Flowers solitary or in groups of 2–5. Petals pink to white, 15–30 mm long. Sepals deflexed, falling as the flowers fade, the outer pinnate. Hips 10–20 mm, glabrous. Native of most of Europe and western Asia except the far north, naturalized in North America. Common in hedgerows, on the edges of woods, by streams and in scrub on all types of soil. Often used as a stock for budding Hybrid Tea roses.

Rosa gallica L.   A suckering low shrub up to 0.8 m high, forming large patches. Stems with prickles and glandular bristles. Leaflets 3–7, 2–6 × 1.8–3 cm, rather stiff, ovate to narrowly elliptical, rounded at apex, double toothed, bluish green and glabrous above, paler pubescent and glandular beneath. Flowers solitary or 2–4 in a group, well scented, 6–9.5 cm across, deep pink. Pedicels with glandular bristles. Outer sepals pinnatifid, deflexed and falling after flowering. Fruit globose to ovoid, densely glandular bristly. Native of southern and central Europe, from France where it is locally frequent, and Belgium, eastwards to Turkey and the Caucasus. Naturalized in Spain and Portugal. This is the forerunner of most of the garden roses, and in its unimproved form makes a most attractive low shrub. It can be recognized by its low stature, large flowers and stiff leathery leaves.

Rosa mollis Smith   A shrub up to 2.5 m high, with arching branches and slender straight soft prickles. Young stems pruinose. Leaflets 5–7, 1.2–3.5 cm long, greyish green, pubescent on both surfaces. Petals around 2 cm long, often deep pink. Sepals pinnate. Pedicels and sepals with glandular bristles. Hips 1–1.5 cm, globose, often glandular, with persistent sepals (p. 215). Native of Europe and western Asia, from Scotland and Finland, south to Portugal and Albania and Turkey, but commonest in the north, in hedges, by rivers and in scrub. The specimen shown here was from Aberdeenshire. R. mollis differs from other similar species in the sepals which remain erect in fruit (p. 215), the small leaflets, pruinose young stems, and glandular bristly but not pubescent pedicels.

Rosa iberica Stev. (*R. rubiginosa* var. *iberica* (Stev.) Boiss.)   A bushy shrub up to 2 m high with curved and hooked prickles. Leaflets 5–7, sticky and aromatic, ovate to elliptic or obovate, 1.5–3.5 cm long, glandular on both surfaces. Flowers 1–6 together; sepals narrowly ovate, up to 2 cm with attenuate apex. Petals up to 2.5 cm, white or pale pink. Hips globose to ovoid, usually smooth or sparsely hispid. Native of north and eastern Turkey, the Caucasus, northern Iraq and Iran to Kopet Dağ, in scrub and woods and mountains from 1200 to 2500 m,

R. mollis

R. iberica

Wolley-Dod

R. beggeriana

R. orientalis

R. iliensis

flowering from May to July. A small species for a dry, sunny site, noted for its aromatic foliage.

Rosa orientalis Dupont ex Ser. (*R. heckeliana* subsp. *orientalis* (Dupont) Meikle)   A low bush up to 0.6 m. Young shoots densely pubescent. Prickles straight or slightly curved. Leaflets 5–7, up to 7 cm long, elliptic to suborbicular, greyish green and pubescent. Flowers solitary or 2–3 together. Sepals to 2.5 cm long, attenuate at apex. Petals up to 1.5 cm long, pink. Hips with glandular bristles and persistent sepals. Native of Yugoslavia, Greece and Albania eastwards to Iran and Iraq, from 1350 to 3400 m, in rocky places and on screes, usually on limestone, flowering in June and July. Shown here, EMR 3090 from near Erzurum, Turkey, photographed in cultivation.

Wolley-Dod (*R. villosa* 'Duplex')   A clone or hybrid of *R. villosa*, grown by the Col. A. H. Wolley-Dod at Edge Hall, Cheshire, author of *A Revision of the British Roses* (1931). Flowers semi-double. Hips smaller than those of typical *R. villosa*.

R. villosa L. is native of central and Southern Europe excluding Britain; close to *R. mollis* but distinct in its larger leaflets (3–5 cm) and fruit, 1–2 cm long, globose to pyriform, hence the synonym *R. pomifera*.

Rosa beggeriana Schrenk   An open shrub 1–2 m high, often with reddish young shoots. Prickles pale, curved, usually in pairs below the leaves. Leaflets usually 7, narrowly ovate to obovate; bracts ovate-lanceolate. Flowers in many-flowered corymbs or panicles, white, 2–3 cm or rarely 4 cm in diameter; sepals narrowly lanceolate, erect after flowering, but falling with the top of the hip, before ripening. Ripe hips red or purple, globose 5–10 mm in diameter. Native of Central Asia from Iran and Afghanistan, to the Tien Shan, Pamir Alai, and Chinese Turkestan (and apparently naturalized in Turkey) growing in rocky places and scrub in the mountains from 1200 to 3000 m, flowering from May to July. Shown here a collection from central Asia, near Ferghana, which was striking in its shrimp-pink young growth and persistent pea-like hips.

Rosa iliensis Chrshan   This species was described in 1950 from Ili, in Chinese Turkestan, but occurs also in Soviet Central Asia. Recent Soviet floras do not consider it worthy of separation from *R. beggeriana*, particularly var. *silverhjelmii* Crépin, in spite of its large black hips, with persistent, not caducous, sepals and disk. It has also been found to be diploid, whereas in previous counts *R. beggeriana* has been reported to be tetraploid.

R. *banksiae* var. *banksiae* planted as a hedge near Lijiang, Yunnan

R. *banksiae* var. *banksiae* in Yunnan

R. *banksiae* 'Lutea'

R. *banksiae* 'Lutescens'

Rosa banksiae R. Br. in Ait., var. **normalis** Regel   A rampant evergreen climber up to 15 m or more, with few prickles and no bristles. Leaflets 3–7, up to 6.5 cm long, acute, oblong lanceolate, hairy on the midrib below. Stipules thread like soon disappearing. Flowers in umbels, around 3 cm across, white (or yellow in cultivation), scented of violets. Sepals ovate, undivided, deciduous. Pedicels glabrous or hairy. Hips small, around 0.5 cm across, dull red. Native of central and western China from Hubei and Gansu to Yunnan, usually at low altitude but recorded up to 1800 m. It grows in valleys, by streams and rocky places, flowering from April to June. Photographed here at about 800 m on the dry side of a ravine above Dali in north-west Yunnan in May 1985. It differs from cultivated R. *banksiae* 'Lutea' in its more numerous thorns, longer narrower leaflets, usually 7 in number, and conspicuously notched petals. Single white R. *banksiae* was first introduced to Europe by Robert Drummond in 1796, and planted at Megginch Castle on Tayside, where it seldom flowered and remained unrecognized until cuttings were taken to Nice in 1905, where they flowered and were identified.

Rosa banksiae var. **banksiae** ('Alba Plena')   The first form of R. *banksiae* to be described was the double white which was introduced by William Kerr to Kew from

R. *banksiae* var. *normalis* near Dali, Yunnan

Canton in 1807 and was named after the wife of Sir Joseph Banks, then director of Kew. This form is rare in cultivation in Europe, having been superseded by the yellow-flowered forms. Another form is found in some parts of Yunnan, especially in the Lijiang valley where the photographs were taken. It is used to make hedges, notably in the village of Ulu Ky where Forrest recruited his collectors. With its 7 leaflets and backward curving thorns, it appears to be a double form of the single found at Dali.

***Rosa banksiae* 'Lutescens'** This single-flowered form of the yellow *R. banksiae* is of unknown origin and its date of introduction is not recorded. I have seen both the double and single forms apparently growing on the same plant in an old garden on the Riviera, and it may be that the single yellow appeared as a reverse sport on the commoner double.

***Rosa banksiae* 'Lutea'** The double-yellow *R. banksiae* was introduced in 1824 from China by John Parks but had been known earlier in the Botanic Garden at Calcutta to which it had been brought some years earlier. It is said to be the hardiest form, and grows well in Cambridge Botanic Gardens on the wall of the Director's office. On the whole, though, it requires a warmer, sunnier climate than is usual in England. It usually has 5 leaflets and few, if any, thorns, so may possibly be an ancient hybrid with a yellow Tea rose.

***Rosa cymosa* Tratt.** (*R. microcarpa* Lindl.) A scrambling or trailing rose with stems up to 5 m long. Leaflets 5–7, narrowly ovate, acute, glabrous or hairy. Stipules linear. Flowers numerous in a flat corymb, around 1.5 cm across. Sepals sometimes pinnate with spiny lobes. Styles exserted, but not united into a column. Hips small, dull red. Native of the warmer parts of China, from the coast to western Sichuan, up to around 1300 m, flowering from April to June. It grows in hedges and on the rocky banks of streams. Photographed here in late May near Baoxing (Moupine). *R. cymosa* is rare in cultivation, but has recently been introduced from China. It may be expected to be rather tender and need the protection of a cold greenhouse except in the south-west of the British Isles.

R. *cymosa*

R. *cymosa* in a ravine near Baoxing, Sichuan

R. chinensis var. spontanea in S. W. Sichuan

R. chinensis var. spontanea showing the flowers reddening as they age

R. bracteata

Cooper's Burma Rose

Rosa chinensis Jacq. **var.** **spontanea** (Rehder & Wilson) Yu & Ku   An evergreen climber or large bush up to 5 m, but usually around 2.5 m, with few thorns. Leaflets 3–5, shortly stalked, glabrous, dark green above, paler below, lanceolate, acuminate. Flowers solitary, or 2–3 together, opening pink, soon reddening, 5–6 cm across. Pedicels and receptacle glabrous or with glandular bristles. Sepals 1.5–3 cm, lanceolate, entire, reflexed after the flower opens. Hips orange. Native of western China, in north-west Sichuan at around 1000 m, where it was collected in fruit by Wilson, and western Hubei near Ichang where it was seen by Henry. The plants shown here were discovered and photographed by Mikinori Ogisu at 1700 m in Leibo, south-west Sichuan, in May 1983. They grow mostly on dry west-facing slopes from 1560 to 1950 m. This is the wild type of the cultivated *R. chinensis* which has had such a profound effect in gardens as ancestor of the Hybrid Tea and Floribunda roses.

Rosa bracteata Wendl.   An evergreen climber up to 6 m, with hooked prickles in pairs and bristles. Leaflets 5–11, obovate, obtuse, shining dark green above, glabrous or downy on the midrib beneath, up to 5 cm long. Flowers to 10 cm across, solitary on a short pedicel hidden by large downy laciniate bracts. Hips globose, orange red. Native of south-eastern China and Taiwan, it was introduced into cultivation in 1793 by Lord Macartney. It is rather tender, requiring a warm wall even in the warmest parts of England where it flowers continuously from June until early autumn.

Anemone (Anemonoides)   A hybrid Climber, up to 4 m, between *R. laevigata* and a Tea rose, raised by Schmidt in 1895. Evergreen, leaves glossy. Flowers 10 cm across. Good scent.

Ramona   A sport of 'Anemone' originating in California in 1913. Flowers deeper pink, paler outside. Good scent. Once flowering, but with odd later flowers. Both these roses need a warm sheltered wall to do well but are said to be hardier than *R. laevigata* itself.

Cooper's Burma Rose ('Cooperi')   This rose is sometimes considered a cultivar of *R. laevigata*, or else of *R. gigantea* or of *R. × odorata*. It was raised at Glasnevin from seeds sent to Ireland by Roland Cooper, collected in Burma, possibly in Maymyo Botanic Garden. It differs from typical *R. laevigata* by having red, not green, stems, softer leaves often with 5 leaflets, and looser flowers which become spotted with pink as they fade. It is tender in cold parts of England (damaged by less than −10°C on a wall) but freer flowering than *R. laevigata*.

Rosa laevigata Michaux Cherokee Rose   A robust evergreen climber up to 10 m or more, with hooked prickles and bristles on the smaller branches. Leaflets 3, glabrous, lanceolate to ovate, acute, leathery in texture. Stipules deciduous. Flowers up to 10 cm across, white. Pedicels and receptacle bristly. Hips bristly, orange red. Native of southern China, and

R. gigantea in Yunnan

Ramona

Anemone

Taiwan, as far west as western Hubei but widely naturalized elsewhere, notably in the warmer parts of North America; it was first described from Georgia. In the wild it grows in rocky places and by streams at up to 1000 m, flowering in April. In cultivation in England the species is too tender to thrive, being cut to the ground by hard frosts, and flowering poorly. In the south of France it grows well, flowering in April.

Rosa gigantea Collett ex Crépin A gigantic evergreen climber up to 30 m or more, with strong hooked prickles. Leaflets usually 7, oblong or ovate, acuminate, up to 8 cm long, glabrous. Flowers solitary, or in groups of 2–3; buds slender, yellow, opening cream or white,

more rarely pink, 10–14 cm across. Hips red or yellowish. Native of the eastern Himalayan foothills, from Manipur to Yunnan, growing on the edges of forest, by streams and scrambling over shrubs from 1300 to 2600 m, flowering from March to May. First introduced from the Shan Hills in Burma in 1888 and later by Kingdon Ward from Manipur, who reported the flowers white with orange stamens and the flowering period lasting six weeks. Forrest reported forms with yellow or pink flowers on bushes not more than 2 m tall, in north-western Yunnan, in the Dali and Lijiang valleys (f. *erubescens* Rehder & Wilson). Photographed in Yunnan by Roy Lancaster.

R. laevigata

R. moschata

R. setigera

R. sempervirens near Algeciras in Southern Spain

Rosa moschata Miller   A robust climber up to
10 m. Branches glabrous with very few prickles.
Leaflets 7, up to 5 cm long, broadly elliptic or
broadly ovate, or rarely obovate, acute or
acuminate at apex, smooth and shining above,
below glabrous or pubescent on the nerves,
simply toothed, without thorns on the rachis.
Flowers 4–6 cm across, corymbose or cymose,
very sweetly scented (of musk!). Pedicels
pubescent and glandular. Sepals entire or with
very narrow lateral lobes. Hips ovoid or
subglobose, usually pubescent and glandular.
Flowers from June to September, a month later
than *R. brunonii*. This rose is not known with
any certainty in the wild, but has long been
cultivated for use as a purgative. It is known
from southern Europe, Turkey, Iran,
Afghanistan and North Africa as a cultivated or
naturalized plant, and probably also from
Ethiopia (*R. abyssinica* R. Br.). The plant
shown here, flowering at Mottisfont in early
September, was found by Graham Thomas
growing in E. A. Bowles' old garden at
Myddelton House.

Rosa sempervirens L.   A rambler or climber
up to 4 m, with dark leathery evergreen leaves,
and few or no prickles. Leaflets 5–7, ovate
lanceolate, glossy above and beneath, glabrous,
2–5 cm long. Flowers in a panicle, usually few,
3–5 cm across, with some scent. Pedicels
glandular hispid. Styles usually pubescent. Hips
subglobose or ovoid, around 1 cm long, orange
red. Native of southern Europe from Spain
eastwards to Greece, Turkey and North Africa,
growing in scrub and thickets, flowering from
May to July. Photographed in southern Spain.

Rare in cultivation, but the parent of a group of
hybrids such as 'Félicité et Perpétue (p. 91).

Rosa setigera Michaux Prairie Rose   A shrub
with climbing or arching stems up to 5 m high.
Leaflets 3, rarely 5, ovate to oblong ovate, acute
to acuminate, serrate, pubescent on the midrib
beneath, 3–9 cm long. Flowers about 5 cm
across, pink fading to white, without scent, in
few-flowered corymbs. Styles exserted, united,
glabrous. Pedicels and hips with glandular
bristles. Hips red, 8 mm across. Native of
North America, from Ontario to Nebraska,
Texas and Florida. This is the only American
member of the synstylae, with united styles. It
flowers from June to August. In gardens it is
striking as a late flowering large-flowered
climber.

Rosa wichuraiana Crépin   A creeping rose,
sending out long, floppy branches to 3 m or
more, smooth green and with curved prickles.
Leaflets 5–9, shining green, broadly ovate to
almost round, up to 2.5 cm long, glabrous
except for the midrib beneath. Stipules ciliate.
Flowers 2.5–4 cm across, in loose corymbs,
opening in succession; pedicels glabrous. Hips
globose, orange red. Native of Japan, Korea and
China, mainly on the coast, where it grows on
dunes and rocks, the long shoots creeping down
the beach, flowering from June to July. In
cultivation this species flowers as late as August,
and is useful, though not showy, for growing on
a steep bank.

Rosa multiflora var. **cathayensis** Rehder &
Wilson   This variety of *R. multiflora* differs

from the Japanese in its larger corymbs of larger
flowers, which are usually pink tinged. It is
found in many parts of China, from Gansu and
Hubei to Sichuan and Yunnan, flowering from
April to June, usually by rivers and streams,
from 300 to 1600 m. Photographed here in
Yunnan, near Dali, in May.

Rosa arvensis Huds.   A trailing shrub with
low, arching branches, often scrambling over
hedges, up to 2 m. Prickles hooked. Leaflets
5–7, 1–3.5 cm long, ovate or ovate elliptic,
glabrous or pubescent on the ribs beneath.
Flowers 1–6 together, 3–5 cm across, well
scented. Pedicels with stalked glands. Sepals
less than 1 cm, ovate, acuminate, not leafy at the
apex. Styles glabrous, united. Fruit small, red,
usually globose. Native of western and southern
Europe, from Iceland to northern Spain,
eastwards to Germany and Greece, flowering
from May to July. This is the only member of
the synstylae native to the British Isles, where it
is commonest in the south, especially on chalk
and limestone, but very rare in Scotland.

Rosa sambucina Koidz.   A climbing shrub,
close to *R. luciae* and *R. wichuraiana*, but
differing in having entire stipules and 5–7
leaflets with the terminal larger than the others,
and all 5–10 cm long, varying in shape from
lanceolate to ovate and acute to acuminate,
glabrous beneath. Flowers 4–5 cm across,
white, in corymbs of 5–20. Pedicels and hips
glandular pilose. Native of Japan, in central
Honshu, Shikoku and Kyushu, growing on
cliffs, rocks and open places in the forest,
flowering in May and June.

R. multiflora var. cathayensis near Dali in Yunnan

R. arvensis, wild in Somerset

R. wichuraiana

R. sambucina in Honshu, Japan

R. brunonii

Polyantha Grandiflora

Treasure Trove

Ballerina

Phyllis Bide

R. helenae

R. multiflora var. nana

Paul's Himalayan Musk

R. filipes 'Kiftsgate'

July 10th, from Wisley

R. filipes 'Kiftsgate' at Limekilns, Suffolk

Betty Sherriff

Wickwar

Rosa brunonii Lindley Himalayan Musk Rose   A very rampant, usually deciduous, climber up to 10 m or more. Leaflets 5–9, usually 7, acute, bluish green, pubescent and glandular beneath, usually pubescent above; leaf stalks and rachis with hooked prickles. Flowers 2.5–4 cm across, well scented, in a conical paniculate corymb. Hips subglobose, around 1 cm long. Native of the Himalayas from Kashmir and Afghanistan to south-west China, growing in scrub, from 1200 to 2400 m, flowering from April to June. A beautiful species with its bluish-green leaves and scented flowers opening cream, fading to white. Very rampant when happy. The clone 'La Mortola' has densely pubescent greyish leaves and is reputed to be rather tender.

Polyantha Grandiflora ('Gentiliana')   A hybrid introduced by Bernaix in 1886. A beautiful rose of unknown parentage with growth up to 6 m and scent of oranges. Pedicels bristly.

Ballerina   A Hybrid Musk raised by Pemberton and introduced by Bentall in 1937. Compact growth up to 3.1 m. Perpetual flowering, well into autumn. Parentage: *R. multiflora* seedling.

Treasure Trove   A robust climber up to 6 m or more. A chance seedling found by John Treasure in his garden at Burford House, Herefordshire. Flowers in large corymbs, with very good scent. Parentage: Probably 'Kiftsgate' × a garden rose.

Phyllis Bide   A rambler up to 4 m, raised by Bide and Sons of Farnham in 1923. Flowering into autumn; good scent. Parentage: 'Perle d'Or' × 'Gloire de Dijon'.

Rosa helenae Rehder & Wilson   A robust climber up to 6 m or more, with hooked prickles. Leaflets 7–9, dark green above, greyish beneath, pubescent on the midrib and veins. Flowers 3–4 cm across, well scented, in small corymbs, 6–15 cm across. Pedicels glandular. Petals glabrous. Fruit ovoid 1–1.5 cm long, orange red or scarlet. Native of Shaanxi, western Hubei near Yichang and Sichuan, in hedges and by streams, up to 1500 m, flowering in June. Introduced by Wilson in 1900. Rather similar plants were found by Forrest in Yunnan. Distinguished by its large fruit.

Rosa multiflora var. **nana**   A dwarf form of *R. multiflora*, making a low bush up to 0.8 m high, perpetual flowering, either pale pink or white. Graham Thomas records that this rose can flower in two months from seed. It is possibly a dwarf, recurrent-flowering mutant of *R. multiflora*, in the same way that the perpetual China roses are dwarf mutants of the wild climber.

Paul's Himalayan Musk   A rampant climber up to 10 m or more, whose origin has been lost but is probably the *R. himalaica alba magna* of Paul of Cheshunt. The sprays of flowers hang down and are sweetly scented. Parentage: *R. brunonii* seedling.

***Rosa filipes* 'Kiftsgate'**   This clone of *R. filipes* (p. 39) is now the most famous of the Himalayan climbers. It was planted at Kiftsgate Court, close to the better known garden at Hidcote in Gloucestershire, it possibly reached England from the Roseraie de l'Haÿ. A plant of 'Kiftsgate' grows to a vast size, covering trees, buildings or anything in its path. The corymbs of small flowers may be 45 cm across, and are produced rather late in the rose season.

Wickwar   This beautiful rose makes a large spreading bush about 2 m high and more across, with greyish leaves similar to *R. brunonii* and creamy flowers with a very good scent. It is a seedling of *R. brunonii*, possibly with *R. soulieana* as the other parent, which originated in the garden of Keith Steadman at Wickwar, Gloucester.

Betty Sherriff   A graceful climber reaching 6 m with glossy leaves, red shoots and scented flowers flushed with pale pink. It was collected by Mrs Sherriff on a dry hillside on the Bhutan/Tibet border, but the exact locality is unknown. In vegetative characters it is closest to *R. longicuspis*, but its loose corymbs of small flowers are suggestive of *R. filipes*.

R. filipes

Wedding Day

R. mulliganii

Seagull

Rambling Rector

R. multiflora

July 16th, from The Gardens of the Rose

R. brunonii near Baoxing, Sichuan

Rosa filipes Rehder & Wilson   A rampant climber up to 6 m or more, with hooked prickles and purple young shoots. Leaflets 5–7, ovate oblong or lanceolate, acuminate, glabrous above, usually glabrous and glaucescent beneath, 4–7.5 cm long, with a few prickles on the midrib and petiole. Flowers 2–2.5 cm across, well scented, in a large loose corymb, up to 25 cm wide. Pedicels slender, 2–3 cm long, with short-stalked glands. Styles pilose. Hips globose, 8–12 mm across. Native of western China, in north-western Sichuan where it grows in thickets from 1300 to 2300 m, flowering in June and July. Found also in Gansu from which it was sent by Farrer to E. A. Bowles. For 'Kiftsgate' see p. 37.

Wedding Day   A rampant climber up to 8 m or more with flowers opening pale buff and petals with a mucronate apex. A seedling which occurred at Highdown, Worthing, Sussex and was introduced in 1950 by Sir Frederick Stern. It is very well scented and free flowering but the flowers are spoiled by rain, becoming spotted with dull red. Probably a hybrid of *R. sinowilsonii*.

Rosa mulliganii Boulenger   A rampant climber up to 6 m or more, with hooked prickles. Leaflets 5–7 glabrous above, dark shining green, the longest up to 6 cm long, glabrous above, pubescent on the nerves beneath. Flowers 4.5–5.5 cm across in a large loose corymb; pedicels, 2.5–3.5 cm long, thinly pubescent and with numerous stalked glands. Sepals attenuate, 1.2–1.8 cm long. Hips 11–13 mm long. Close to *R. rubus* but with more leaflets, 5 or 7, not 3–5, longer pedicels and larger flowers, or *R. brunonii* but with glabrous shining leaves. This rose appears frequently in cultivation but is not recognized in Chinese floras. It was described from plants growing at

Wisley, probably collected by Forrest in Yunnan.

Seagull   A climber up to 4 m long raised by Pritchard in 1907. Well scented. Once-flowering. Semi-double flowers in very large corymbs. Parentage: not recorded.

Rosa multiflora Thunb.   A bush with arching stems up to 5 m long, flowering in the second year, with numerous curved prickles. Leaflets 7–9, up to 5 cm long, glabrous, or downy beneath, obovate or elliptic. Stipules deeply laciniate. Flowers about 2.5 cm across, in a rather tight corymb. Sepals short. Hips ovoid to round, red. Native of Japan, Korea, China (var. *cathayensis*) and Taiwan, growing in sandy and rocky places by streams, flowering from April to June. Naturalized in America, particularly in the east. A very thorny rose, thriving in poor soil, making a fine show both in flower and fruit.

Rambling Rector   A hybrid of unknown origin, known since 1912, making a dense bush or climbing into a tree. Leaflets downy beneath; pedicels densely glandular. Anthers soon blackening. Parentage: probably *R. multiflora* × *R. moschata*.

Rosa brunonii Lindl. (Chinese form)   The Chinese form of *R. brunonii*, found in western Sichuan, differs from the western Himalayan in its glabrous shoots and nearly glabrous leaves. In these it is similar to *R. rubus*, but that is said to have only 5 leaflets, not 7 as is usual in *R. brunonii*. The photograph here was taken at about 1300 m in the valley of Baoxing (Moupine) near Ya'an in late May. This rose was making huge thickets of arching stems on the sides of the valley after the forest had been cleared.

R. longicuspis near Dali, Yunnan

Rosa longicuspis A. Bertoloni (*R. lucens Rolfe, R. yunnanensis* (Crép.) Boul.)   A robust climber up to 6 m or more, with stiff shining almost evergreen leaves and red-purple young shoots. Leaflets 3–7, narrowly ovate to lanceolate or elliptic more or less reticulate, leathery, green beneath, glabrous, 5–10 cm long. Flowers about 5 cm across, sweetly scented, from narrowly ovoid buds, in a panicle of up to 15; petals silky on the back. Pedicels and hips often glandular and hairy; hips ovoid, 1.5–2 cm long. Native of the eastern Himalayas from Assam to Yunnan and Sichuan where it is found on Mt Emei, growing in hedges, thickets and among rocks, from 1000 to 2000 m, flowering from May to July. Photographed here in May on dry slopes in western Yunnan above the city of Dali. *R. longicuspis* var. *sinowilsonii* (Hemsl.) Yu & Ku, differs in its larger leaves, no – or only slightly – hairy pedicels, and broader buds. Described from Mt Emei.

Great Maiden's Blush

R. gallica 'Versicolor'

Martin Frobisher

Alba Maxima

Comte de Chambord

Belle de Crécy

Tuscany Superb

Königin von Dänemark

Charles de Mills

July 10th, from Wisley

Königin von Dänemark

R. × alba 'Semiplena'

Maiden's Blush

Jeanne d'Arc

Great Maiden's Blush (La Royale, La Séduisante, Cuisse de Nymphe, La Virginale, Incarnata, *Rosa alba regalis* of Redouté)   An Alba rose, known since the 15th century. It makes a large shrub up to 2.5 m high with arching branches and glaucous leaves. Flowers sweetly scented. Free flowering from mid-June to early July, but not repeating.

***Rosa gallica* Versicolor** (Rosa Mundi, *R. gallica* 'Variegata')   This variegated sport of *R. gallica* 'Officinalis' has been known since the 16th century and often reverts to its non-variegated parent (see p. 48). It makes a low shrub up to 2 m high, needing some support if the stems are not to flop when weighed down by flowers. Alternatively, the stems can be pruned in spring to keep the bushes to about 1 m high.

Martin Frobisher   Although it looks like an old rose and is named after the Elizabethan seafarer, this rose was raised by Svedja at the Canadian Dept of Agriculture in 1968, reputedly from seed of Schneezwerg, a hybrid of *R. rugosa*. It makes a rounded bush about 1.5 m high, with one or two flowers continually open after the initial burst. Scented like *R. rugosa* but in leaves and general appearance much more like a large form of *R. pimpinellifolia*.

Alba Maxima (Great Double White, Jacobite Rose)   A large shrub up to 2 m, often found in old gardens. It has been known to revert to 'Alba Semiplena' which indicates that it was originally a sport of that variety. The leaves are coarse, greyish green. Young stems spring up from the base and arch over when in flower.

Comte de Chambord   This beautiful rose was raised by Moreau-Robert in 1860 from a Portland, probably crossed with a China rose. It has upright growth up to 1.5 m, with thin-petalled, purplish-pink, sweet-scented flowers, produced after the first flowering, in flushes into autumn. We noted this flowering well at Mottisfont Abbey Garden in early September.

Belle de Crécy   A Gallica of lax growth up to 1.3 m. The well-scented flowers open bright pink and soon fade in the sun to pale violet. Known since 1848, and possibly named after the Château de Crécy, near Dreux, the first of many houses embellished by Mme de Pompadour.

Tuscany Superb   A Gallica known since 1848, up to 1.5 m high. Similar to the original 'Tuscany' but with large, more double flowers, of only faint scent.

Königin von Dänemark (Queen of Denmark, Belle Courtisanne)   An Alba, probably crossed with a Damask, raised by James Booth, of Flottbeck Nurseries, near Hamburg (then in Denmark) 1826. Makes a lax bush up to 2 m high, with branches often weighed to the ground by the flowers, and particularly bluish-green leaves.

Charles de Mills (Bizarre Triomphant)   A Gallica forming an erect bush up to 1.5 m high, producing particularly fine, very flat flowers with good scent. Most beautiful in shades of crimson, fading to reddish purple. It is surprising that the raiser of this striking rose is not recorded.

***Rosa* × *alba* Semiplena**   One of the oldest varieties of *R.* × *alba* and said to be grown still in quantity in Bulgaria, around Kazanluk, north of Plovdiv, for attar. It makes a large bush, up to 2 m high, with arching branches well covered with scented flowers. This is one of the toughest roses and is tolerant of anything except shade.

Maiden's Blush   An Alba rose, a smaller version of 'Great Maiden's Blush', with slightly smaller flowers on a bush up to 3.3 m high. Known since the late 18th century.

Jeanne d'Arc   An Alba raised by Vibert in 1818. A smaller version of 'Alba Maxima' with flowers about 6 cm across on a bush up to 1.5 m high. Growth very twiggy. Although, in my garden, regularly defoliated by rust, it flowers well.

Henri Foucquier

Duchesse de Montebello

Georges Vibert

Surpasse Tout

Georges Vibert

Cramoisi Picoté

Pompon Blanc
Parfait

Celeste

July 3rd, from Mottisfont

Belle Amour

du Roi

Rose de Resht

Jacques Cartier

Mme le Gras de St Germain

Félicité Parmentier

July 1st, from Mottisfont

Duchesse de Montebello

Rose de Resht

Félicité Parmentier

Henri Foucquier A Gallica of unknown date. A lax bush with almost thornless stems. Henri Foucquier (1838–1901) was a writer and politician.

Duchesse de Montebello A Gallica–Damask hybrid, raised by Laffay, of spreading, vigorous, lax growth, up to 1.6 m high. Light green leaves and well-scented flowers. Known since 1829.

Georges Vibert A Gallica raised by Robert in 1853. Upright growth up to 1.5 m with rather small leaves. The flowers fade with age. Here the upper flower is fresh, the lower two faded.

Surpasse Tout (Cerisette La Jolie) A Gallica known since 1832. Growth strong and bushy, up to 1.3 m. Flowers first cupped, then reflexed.

Cramoisi Picoté A Gallica raised by Vibert in 1834. Thin, erect growth, up to 1.5 m, with small leaves. Flowers in clusters of three, upright; petals curling back to form perhaps the most reflexed of all rose blooms, not unlike a pompom dahlia. Little scent.

Pompom Blanc Parfait An Alba raised in 1876. Slender erect growth up to 1.6 m and small leaves and flowers. This has a longer flowering season than most Albas, with occasional flowers late in the season. Unlike other Albas, the flowers are in a tight cluster, like marshmallows, pink fading to white. Possibly an Alba crossed with a Multiflora hybrid.

Celeste (Celestial) An Alba which originated

in Holland around the end of the 18th century. It makes a large rounded bush up to 2 m high, with grey-green leaves typical of R. × alba, and exceptionally beautiful, sweetly scented flowers. Illustrated by Redouté under the name R. damascena 'Aurore'.

Belle Amour An Alba of unknown origin, possibly, as suggested by Graham Stuart Thomas, crossed with a Damask (or a China?), distinct in its thorns, and in its scent which contains a strong hint of aniseed.

Rose de Resht An Autumn Damask introduced by Miss Nancy Lindsay. A leafy bush, eventually up to 2 m high, producing flowers at six week intervals through the summer and autumn. Flowers with a sweet rich scent. Brought back from Iran: 'N.L. 849. Happened on it in an old Persian garden in ancient Resht, tribute of the tea caravans plodding Persia-wards from China over the Central Asian steppes; it is a sturdy, yard high bush of glazed lizard-green, perpetually emblazoned with full camellia flowers of pigeon's blood ruby, irised with royal-purple, haloed with dragon sepals like the painted blooms on oriental faience.' Cruel sceptics have suggested she found it in a garden in France.

du Roi A Portland–China hybrid raised in France in 1815 by Lelieur. It makes a low bush around 1 m high, with well-scented flowers throughout the summer. This rose and its sport, 'Rose du Roi à Fleur Pourpré' (1819), are said to be important as the forerunners of the Hybrid Perpetuals.

Jacques Cartier A Portland–China hybrid

raised by Moreau-Robert in 1868. Sweet-scented flowers with a button eye appear from summer to autumn on a bush up to 1.3 m high. We have noted this flowering well at the beginning of September and it should flower again at the end of October in a good season.

Mme le Gras de St Germain An Alba or Alba–Damask hybrid known since 1848, the first edition of William Paul's *The Rose Garden*. Upright growth up to 2 m, or 5 m with support. Flowers with yellowish centres and good scent.

Félicité Parmentier An Alba raised in 1834 which makes a bushy shrub up to 1.3 m. Like 'Belle Amour' this has some Damask characters. The flowers reflex after opening to form almost a sphere of white.

43

Sissinghurst Castle

Tuscany

Marcel Bourgouin

Agathe Royale

Petite Orléannaise

Aimable Rouge

Du Maître d'Ecole

Nestor

July 3rd, from Mottisfont

Sissinghurst Castle (Rose des Maures) An old Gallica found by Vita Sackville-West growing at Sissinghurst Castle in the ruins of the garden. It makes a mass of stems up to 1 m high.

Tuscany (Old Velvet) A suckering shrub up to 3.5 m high. It is one of the most ancient of the Gallicas, similar but smaller flowered than 'Tuscany Superb' and darker than 'Sissinghurst Castle'.

Marcel Bourgouin (Le Jacobin) A Gallica raised by Corboeuf in 1889. Magenta or, in good seasons, rich purplish flowers, the petals pale on the back. Growth short, up to 1 m.

Agathe Royale A Gallica hybrid, probably with *R. majalis* as the other parent (*R. × francofurtana*) known since 1820. Growth to 1.6 m, arching. Leaves soft. Flowers well scented. Very similar to its sister 'Empress Josephine' but more robust with narrower stipules.

Aimable Rouge (La Triomphe) A Gallica of unknown origin, probably dating from the 18th century, widely grown in Holland and France in the 1820s. Illustrated by Redouté, from Malmaison.

Petite Orléannaise A Centifolia with small flowers on a strong bush up to 1.5 m high. Of unknown origin, probably around 1900.

D'Aguesseau A Gallica raised by Vibert in 1823. Up to 1.7 m high. Flowers well scented, intense crimson on first opening, becoming deep pink. Strong growing.

Du Maître d'École A Gallica rose bought by Constance Spry from Pajotin-Chedane's nursery at La Maître École but apparently not raised by them. Flowers very well scented, red in bud, opening pink, fading to greyish mauve in the sun. Low sturdy growth to 1 m. Nearly thornless.

Nestor A Gallica, probably dating from around 1840. Growth more or less thornless, up to 1.3 m high. Flowers variable in colour, pale in bud opening usually bluish pink with deeper centres fading to grey.

Robert le Diable A late-flowering rose, in which the influence of both *R. gallica* and *R. chinensis* can be seen, known since 1850 in France. The sweetly-scented flowers contain purple and grey mixed with cerise and scarlet and become pale greyish mauve in hot weather. Growth up to 1.3 m, lax and sprawling. Susceptible to blackspot and damage by rain.

Conditorum An ancient Gallica cultivar preserved in the University Botanic Garden at Oxford, with well-scented flowers shaded purple in hot weather. Height up to 1.3 m. The thick petals keep their colour and scent when dry.

Violacea (La Belle Sultane, Cumberland, Maheka) An old Gallica known since the 18th century. Tall, up to 2 m. Almost without spines. Leaves rather drooping. Calyx winged, showing possible Centifolia influence. The well-scented flowers become violet as they mature.

Belle Isis A Gallica raised by Parmentier in 1845. Growth usually short, rather floppy, less than 1 m high. Stems thorny. Graham Thomas suggests that this may be a hybrid with a Centifolia rose.

Robert le Diable

Conditorum

Violacea

Belle Isis

D'Aguesseau

July 1st, from Mottisfont

Robert le Diable

Assemblage des Beautées

Président de Seze

Cardinal de Richelieu

L'Impératrice
Joséphine

Hippolyte

Agathe

La Plus Belle des Ponctuées

Anaïs Segales

July 1st, from Mottisfont

President de Seze

Cardinal de Richelieu

L'Impératrice Joséphine

Jenny Duval

Assemblage des Beautées (Rouge Éblouissante) A Gallica known since 1823, making a low bush up to 1 or 1.3 m. The vivid crimson flowers become purplish as they fade.

Président de Sèze (Mme Hébert) A Gallica raised by Hebert in 1836. It makes a loose bush up to 1.3 m high with remarkable flowers, pale lilac pink around the edge, crimson in the centre. This is one of the most striking and beautiful of all the Gallicas.

Cardinal de Richelieu A triploid Gallica–China hybrid raised by Laffay in 1840. It makes a good bush up to 1.6 m high, slightly less across, with few thorns. Flowers reflexing into a deep purple sphere, often with a green eye. Generous feeding and careful pruning are recommended for this variety.

L'Impératrice Joséphine (*Empress Josephine*) (Rosier de Francfort, Pius IX) A Gallica hybrid, probably with *R. majalis* as the other parent, known since 1820. It makes a low, bushy shrub, about 1.6 m high, with very few thorns, and can be recognized by its wide stipules.

Agathe This Gallica has been known since before 1815 and shows some characteristics of Damask roses with which it may be a hybrid. It is compact, up to 1.3 m in height, with thorny shoots and well scented flowers.

Hippolyte (Souvenir de Kean) A Gallica probably dating from the early 19th century. It makes a good bush up to 1.3 m high, with clusters of flowers hanging down on arching stems.

La Plus Belle des Ponctuées A Gallica of unknown origin, distinct in its finely spotted flowers. Vigorous growth with few prickles and brownish wood, up to 1.5 m high, and lush leaves. Sepals often foliolate.

Anaïs Ségales A Gallica hybrid, probably with a Centifolia, raised by Vibert in 1837. Thorny stems form a small bush up to 1 m high, with deep pink flowers, becoming pale at the edges.

Jenny Duval A Gallica of unknown origin, known since 1821. Growth up to 1.5 m high. Flowers well scented, fading to pale lilac at the edges and in the centre a blend of crimsons, purples, brown and grey, varying with the temperature.

47

Néron

Gloire de France

Pompon Panaché

Perle des Panachées

Tricolor de Flandres

July 3rd, from Mottisfont

Néron   A Gallica raised by Laffay in 1841. A much branched shrub of vigorous growth up to 1.5 m high. Flowers slightly marked, later reflexing.

Gloire de France (Fanny Bias)   A Gallica known since 1819. An upright shrub of sturdy growth up to 2 m high. Almost thornless, apart from tiny bristles. Flowers fading to pale lilac at the edges.

Pompon Panaché   An old Gallica of unknown origin, which makes a small shrub up to 1 m high, with wiry branches and small leaves.

Perle des Panachés (La Rubanée)   A dwarf Gallica raised by Vibert in 1845. There is also a Centifolia called La Rubanée (see p. 59)

Tricolor de Flandres   A Gallica raised by Van Houtte in 1846. A small dense floppy shrub up to 1 m high. Flowers with a fresh scent.

Complicata   A Gallica, or Gallica hybrid with *R. canina*, of unknown origin, forming a large shrub up to 1.6 m high, or up to 3 m if supported, i.e. in an old apple tree as shown here. The single flowers may be up to 12 cm wide.

Duchesse de Buccleugh   A Gallica of unknown origin from around 1846. A robust, twiggy shrub with leafy stems up to 2 m high and large flowers produced later than other Gallicas. Some scent. Like a fully double sport of *R. gallica* 'Officinalis'.

***Rosa gallica* Officinalis** (*R. gallica* 'Maxima', *R. rubra* Blackw., Apothecary's Rose, Red Rose of Lancaster)   This is probably the oldest form of *R. gallica* in cultivation, having been brought from Damascus to France by Thibaut Le Chansonnier in the 13th century, according to some. It is shown in the famous altarpiece in Ghent Cathedral painted in about 1430. It forms a spreading, suckering bush, up to 1.3 m high, well furnished with semi-double flowers.

Complicata growing into an old apple tree

Complicata

R. gallica 'Officinalis'

Duchesse de Buccleugh

Ipsilante

Jeanne de Montfort

Cosimo Ridolfi

Duc de Guiche

Alain Blanchard

Marie Louise

Duchesse d'Angoulême

July 1st, from Mottisfont

Duchesse d'Angoulême at Mottisfont

Mme Plantier

Boule de Nanteuil

Ipsilante A Gallica known since 1821, which makes a moderately prickly bush up to 1.3 m high, with lush bright green leaves and sweetly scented flowers which fade to lilac pink. Later flowering than most Gallicas.

Jeanne de Montfort A Moss known since 1851, making a large shrub up to 2 m high, with well-scented, semi-double flowers.

Cosimo Ridolfi A Gallica raised by Vibert in 1842. Height about 1 m. Flowers well scented, fading to violet.

Duc de Guiche (Sénateur Romain) A Gallica known since 1835. Arching stems up to 1.6 m high, with well-scented flowers, veined with purple in hot weather.

Alain Blanchard A Gallica raised by Vibert in 1839, with thin, wiry growth to about 1.3 m high, then flopping, with well-scented semi-double flowers, the petals becoming purple mottled with crimson.

Marie Louise A Damask raised in 1813 in the garden at Malmaison. Lax, arching growth up to 1.3 m high, weighed down by the huge flat flowers with a strong, sweet scent.

Duchesse d'Angoulême (Duc d'Angoulême) A Gallica hybrid, probably with an Alba, known since 1827, making a low bush about 1 m high, with arching branches and nodding flowers with delicate, almost transparent petals.

Camaieux A Gallica known since 1830. It makes a bush about 1.3 m high, with white flowers striped red, the stripes fading to magenta, then lilac grey, often showing a green centre. (Not illustrated.)

Mme Plantier An Alba hybrid, possibly with *R. moschata*, raised by Plantier in 1835. It can make a sprawling shrub up to 1.6 m high, or reach 4 m if trained up an old tree, with well-scented flowers opening rich cream before turning white.

Boule de Nanteuil A Gallica known since 1848. Growth up to 1 m high, spreading, twiggy. Good scent. Liable to get mildew.

Leda

Petite Lisette

St Nicholas

Trigintipetala

Madame Hardy

Omar Khayyam

Hebe's Lip

Ispahan

June 25th, from The Gardens of the Rose

St Nicholas A Damask or cross with *R. gallica* which appeared in the garden of the Hon. Robert James at St Nicholas in Richmond, Yorkshire, in 1950. It forms an erect bush up to 1.3 m high. Semi-double flowers with some scent followed by conspicuous orange hips.

Omar Khayyam A damask raised from seeds collected by Mr William Simpson, one of the artists of the *Illustrated London News*, from a bush growing over the grave of Omar Khayyam at Nashapur in Iran, and raised at Kew where it flowered first in June 1894. A plant from Kew was put on Edward FitzGerald's grave at Boulge churchyard, near Woodbridge in Suffolk. From here it was rescued when all but dead by Frank Knight in 1947 and propagated by Messrs Notcutts. It makes a rather erect shrub up to 2 m high with very sweetly scented flowers.

Hebe's Lip (Rubrotincta, Margined Hip or Reine Blanche) A Damask hybrid, probably with *R. rubiginosa* raised by Paul in 1912, which makes a bush up to 1.6 m high. Beautiful buds and semi-double flowers with a strong musky scent, closing at night. The stems have particularly long downward-curving thorns. It has a good crop of hips in autumn.

Petite Lisette A Damask raised by Vibert in 1817. It makes a bushy plant up to 1.3 m high, with downy-grey leaves and fragrant flowers.

Madame Hardy A Damask, possibly crossed with an Alba, raised in 1832 by Hardy. It makes a strong bush, with long shoots up to 2 m high, and lush green leaves.

Trigintipetala (Kazanluk) An ancient Damask and one of the varieties grown in Bulgaria, around Kazanluk, for the production of attar of roses. It makes an upright bush about 2 m high, with very sweetly scented flowers.

Ispahan (Pompon des Princes) A Damask known since 1832. It makes an upright bush up to 2 m high, with well-scented flowers over a longer period than most Damasks, around mid summer.

Leda (Painted Damask) A Damask known since 1827. It makes a small bush up to 1 m high with very lush dark green foliage. Main flowering in summer, but some flowers produced in autumn.

Alba Maxima (background); *St Nicholas* (foreground)

Leda

Omar Khayyam

Oeillet Parfait

Mme Zoetmans

Celsiana

Gloire de Guilan

Portland Rose

Quatre Saisons Blanc Mousseux

Botzaris

Quatre Saisons

July 3rd, from Mottisfont

Mme. Zoetmans

Celsiana

Quatre Saisons Blanc Mousseux reverting

Oeillet Parfait   A Damask raised by Foulard in 1841. It makes a neat bush up to 1.3 m high.

Mme Zoetmans   A Damask raised by Marest in 1830. A low-spreading bush up to 1.3 m high, with bright green leaves.

Celsiana   A Damask known since around 1732. It makes a lax shrub up to 1.6 m high, with grey green leaves and semi-double flowers in small clusters.

Gloire de Guilan   A Damask introduced by Miss Nancy Lindsay in 1949 from Iran where it was said to have been grown for making attar of roses. It makes a sprawling bush up to 1.3 m across.

Portland Rose (*R.* × *portlandica*)   A hybrid between the Autumn Damask and *Rosa gallica*

'Officinalis', known since 1782. It has been said to have come from Italy and to have *R. chinensis* 'Semperflorens' in its parentage, but neither is likely, and it was probably raised by or popularized through Margaret Bentinck, 2nd Duchess of Portland, after whom it is named. It makes a small bushy shrub, less than 1 m high, flowering in summer and again in autumn.

Botzaris   A Damask known since 1856. It makes a bush up to 1 m high, with pale green leaves and sweetly scented flowers.

Quatre Saisons Blanc Mousseux (*R.* × *damascena* 'Bifera Alba Muscosa', Perpetual White Moss, Rosier de Thionville)   A white mossy sport of the Autumn Damask 'Quatre Saisons' known since 1835. Graham Thomas records that it first reverted in 1950 and it continues to do so, as can be seen from the

photographs here. It makes a stiff bush up to 1.6 m high.

Quatre Saisons (Autumn Damask, *R.* × *damascena* 'Bifera')   This is a very ancient rose which probably originated in the Middle East as a hybrid between *R. gallica* and *R. moschata*. It is thought by some to be the rose mentioned by Herodotus in the 5th century BC, growing in the gardens of Midas, and more sweetly scented than all other roses, and by Virgil (*c.* 30 BC) as flowering twice a year at Paestum. It makes a rather upright bush up to 1.3 m high, with pale green leaves and very well-scented flowers, from June to October. The rather untidy double flowers and long thin sepals are characteristic.

Amadis

Blush Boursault

Amy Robsart

L'Héritierana

R. × damascena 'Versicolor'

La Ville de Bruxelles

Blush Damask

June 25th, from The Gardens of the Rose

La Ville de Bruxelles

R. × richardii

Dupontii

R. × richardii

Amadis (Crimson Boursault)   A Boursault rose raised by Laffay in 1829. It makes long, arching thornless canes, up to 5 m long, with dark green leaves, purplish when young, set with double or semi-double flowers which are almost scentless.

Blush Boursault (Calypso)   A Boursault raised in 1848. It makes thornless canes up to 2–5 m long, with dark green leaves, and almost scentless flowers.

L'Héritierana (*R. × l'heritierana* Thory)   The original Boursault rose, said to be a hybrid with *R. pendulina* or some related species and *R. chinensis*, raised before 1820.

Amy Robsart   A *R. rubiginosa* hybrid raised by Lord Penzance in 1894. It makes an arching bush, with stems up to 3 m high, and one flush of slightly scented flowers. Tolerant of poor chalky soil and of some shade.

Rosa × damascena Versicolor (York and Lancaster)   A Damask known since 1551 which is easily recognized by its unstable flower colour, the flowers deep pink, very pale pink, or some combination of the two, occasionally with some striped petals carried in loose clusters. The long sepals are also typical. It makes a bush about 2 m high and as much across and is said to need a rich soil to grow and flower well. It has often been confused with 'Rosa Mundi' (p. 41) but that has much more brightly coloured flowers with many red and white striped petals.

La Ville de Bruxelles   A Damask raised by Vibert in 1849. It makes a rounded, very leafy, prickly bush about 1.6 m high with lax sprays of large, flat, fully double, well-scented flowers. It is in all ways outstanding among the old roses.

Blush Damask   A Damask, or possibly a hybrid with *R. pimpinellifolia*, of unknown origin. It makes a very twiggy, prickly bush, suckering freely, up to 2 m high, with well-scented flowers.

Rosa × richardii Rehder (*R. sancta* Richard) St John's Rose, The Holy Rose   This is an ancient Damask-type rose described from Tigré in Ethiopia in 1847 and introduced to Europe in around 1895 by the firm of Dammann of Naples, from the collections of the botanist Terraciano in Abyssinia, where it was grown around churches and monasteries. Remains of it, or a very similar rose were found forming chaplets on the heads of mummies in Egypt, dating from between the 2nd and 5th centuries AD. It makes a rounded bush up to 1.3 m high with spreading branches. The flowers are produced in loose clusters and have conspicuously exserted styles, indicating that one parent was probably a member of the *synstylae* roses such as *R. arvensis*, the other probably *R. gallica*.

Dupontii   This rose has been known since the early 19th century in France and is probably a hybrid between *R. gallica* and *R. moschata* or *R. arvensis*, in some combination. It makes a large bush up to 2.3 m high or can be trained as a low climber. The large flowers, up to 7.5 cm across, are well scented and show the united styles of the *synstylae* section. They are followed by a good crop of orange hips.

R. centifolia 'Parvifolia'

The Bishop

Blanchefleur

Armide

R. centifolia 'Variegata'

Spong

White Provence

West Green

Tour de Malakoff

de la Grifferaie

July 1st, from Mottisfont

Bullata

Petite de Hollande

Blanchefleur

Rosa centifolia **Parvifolia** (Pompon de Bourgogne)   A dwarf Centifolia, long cultivated and known since 1664. It makes an upright, suckering, twiggy bush with small leaves, up to 1 m high. To flower at all freely this rose should be grown in full sun.

The Bishop (L'Evêque)   A Gallica hybrid of unknown origin illustrated by Redouté in 1821. It makes a rather upright bush up to 1.1 m high, with well-scented flowers opening cerise and fading at the edges to grey purple.

Rosa centifolia **Variegata** (Village Maid, Cottage Maid, Belle des Jardins, La Rubanée).   A mutant of Centifolia introduced in 1845 from Angers. It makes a strong, thorny bush up to 2 m high, with delicate, rounded flowers, easily spoiled by rain. It has been known to revert to ordinary Centifolia. This should not be confused with the Gallica 'Perle des Panachées' (p. 48) which shares the synonym of La Rubanée.

Blanchefleur   A Damask raised by Vibert in 1835. It makes a spreading bush up to 2 m high, with spiny growth and pale green leaves. The flowers which open palest pink are very sweetly scented and are borne in bunches.

Armide   A Damask–China cross raised at Angers (by Vibert?) and introduced in 1847. Very well scented, and autumn – as well as summer – flowering. Armide was a sorceress in Tasso's *Jerusalem Delivered*, and the title of an opera by Glück, 1777.

Spong   A small Centifolia known since 1805. It makes an upright bush, up to 1.3 m high, with very rounded leaflets. The dead flowers have the ugly habit of staying on the plant. Well scented and with a long flowering season. The unusual name comes from that of a gardener who raised large numbers of this rose.

Tour de Malakoff   A Gallica–China hybrid raised by Soupert and Notting in 1856. It makes a large bush up to 2.3 m high, with long shoots which need support. The huge flowers fade to a greyish mauve.

White Provence (Unique Blanche)   A Centifolia mutant first noted at Needham, Suffolk, in 1775, making a bush up to 1.6 m high. Flowers well scented, with petals of a thin, delicate texture, appearing late in the rose season, and extending into early autumn.

West Green   A Damask from West Green

House (?) grown in the collection at Mottisfont. It makes a healthy bush up to 1.6 m high with lush leaves and slightly flopping flowers.

de la Grifferaie   A hybrid between a Gallica and possibly *R. multiflora* raised by Vibert in 1846. It makes a tall shrub up to 2 m high and across, with few thorns. The flowers are well scented, in small bunches. This rose was often used as an understock, and so has in many places outlived the rose which was budded on to it. Nonetheless it deserves to be grown for its own good qualities.

Bullata (Rose à Feuilles de Laitue)   A mutant of Centifolia known since about 1801. It is mainly notable for its leaves which are reddish brown on top when young, pale green in the wrinkles. The flowers are well scented and similar to Centifolia, produced in big trusses.

Petite de Hollande (Pompon des Dames)   A miniature Centifolia known since the end of the 18th century. It makes a bush up to 1.3 m high, with well-scented flowers, freely produced.

Cristata

Henri Martin

Capitaine John Ingram

Fantin-Latour

Ombrée Parfaite

Juno

R. centifolia

Paul Ricault

July 3rd, from Mottisfont

Juno

Cristata

Paul Ricault

Capitaine John Ingram   A Damask Moss rose raised by Laffay in 1854. It makes a dense bush up to 1.3 m high, with very well-scented flowers which vary from deep crimson to purple depending on the temperature.

Cristata (Chapeau de Napoléon, Crested Moss)   A Centifolia mutant introduced by Vibert in 1826. It is said to have been found about 1820 growing on the wall of an old convent at Fribourg in Switzerland. It makes a lax, rather prickly bush up to 1.3 m high, with well-scented flowers. The curious buds are formed by outgrowth on the edges of the sepals, a mutation unique to this plant.

Henri Martin   A Damask Moss rose raised by Laffay in 1863. It makes a tall shrub, up to 2 m, recommended by Graham Thomas for its grace, and for doing well on a north wall. Flowers semi-double, in loose clusters, often bright red in colour, with bright yellow stamens.

Ombrée Parfaite   A Gallica–China hybrid usually classed as a Centifolia, raised by Vibert in 1823. It makes a spreading bush up to 1 m high.

Fantin-Latour   A China or HT hybrid, probably crossed with a Gallica, dating from around 1900. It makes a large spreading shrub up to 2 m high, with well-scented flowers produced only at midsummer, in large clusters, at first cup-shaped, later with the outer petals reflexing.

Juno   A Gallica–China hybrid raised by Laffay in 1832. It forms a spreading, lax bush about 1.3 m across and high, with well-scented flowers, produced only at midsummer, on gracefully hanging branches.

Rosa centifolia (Provence Rose, Cabbage Rose, Rose des Peintres)   This, the original Centifolia rose, has been known since the early 17th century. It makes a lax bush up to 1.6 m high, with varied thorns, lush, coarsely toothed leaves and drooping, richly scented flowers, borne singly or in large bunches.

Paul Ricault   A China hybrid raised by Portemer in 1845. It makes an upright bush, suckering when on its own roots, up to 2 m high, with lax branches weighed down by well-scented flowers. Flowers often a rich cerise in colour.

Louis Gimard

Comtesse de Murinais

Little Gem

Lanei

James Mitchell

Duchess de Verneuil

Général Kléber

Soupert et Notting

July 1st, from Mottisfont

Comtesse de Murinais A Damask Moss raised by Vibert in 1843. It makes a tall, vigorous shrub up to 2.5 m high. The flowers open palest pink and fade to white, often with a button eye. The flowers are well scented; so is the moss.

Little Gem (Valide) A miniature Damask Moss raised by Paul in 1880. It makes a small bush up to 1.1 m high. Once-flowering.

Louis Gimard A Damask–China Moss raised by Pernet (Père) in 1877. A small bush up to 1.1 m high with dark green leaves and well-scented flowers.

James Mitchell A Damask Moss raised by Verdier in 1861. A bush up to 1.2 m high, with very well-scented flowers, freely produced.

Duchesse de Verneuil A Damask Moss, possibly crossed with a China, raised by Portemer in 1856, making a bush up to 1.6 m high.

Lanei A Gallica–hybrid Moss raised by Laffay in 1846. A lanky, prickly bush up to 1.6 m, heavily mossed. Once-flowering. Like 'William Lobb', but shorter, with the flowers fading less when mature.

Général Kléber A Damask–Hybrid Moss raised by Robert in 1856. A vigorous, upright shrub, up to 1.6 m. Once-flowering with large, well-scented flowers. Named after the French general who commanded Napoleon's army in Egypt and was assassinated in Cairo in 1800.

Soupert et Notting An Autumn Damask Moss raised by Pernet in 1874. A low, dense bush up to 1 m high. Well scented, perpetual-flowering and often considered the best of its type. Named after the nursery firm from Luxembourg.

Mme Delaroche-Lambert An Autumn Damask Moss raised by Robert in 1856. It makes an upright bush, with vigorous healthy foliage. Repeat-flowering and similar in appearance to a mossy 'Rose de Resht'; well scented, with sticky moss.

Baron de Wassenaer (see over)

Little Gem

Mme Delaroche Lambert

Centifolia Muscosa

René d'Anjou

Nuits de Young

Baron de Wassenaer

Shailer's White Moss

Striped Moss

Salet

Maréchal Davoust

July 1st, from Mottisfont

Centifolia Muscosa (Common Moss, Old Moss)   The original mossy mutant of *Rosa × centifolia* was known at the end of the 17th century. An open bush up to 1.6 m high, with coarsely toothed leaves, and wonderfully scented flowers, over a season of about two months.

René d'Anjou   A Damask Moss raised by Robert in 1853. A bush up to 1.6 m high, with bronzy young leaves and brownish moss. The pale pink flowers fade to lilac pink and are sweetly scented.

Nuits de Young   A Damask Moss raised by Laffay in 1845. It makes a compact, erect, suckering bush, up to 1.6 m high, with small dark leaves, dark moss and rather small flowers, the darkest of all the old roses, which when fully open show some stamens. Graham Thomas suggests that the unusual name was based on the poem 'Night Thoughts' by Edward Young (pub. 1742–46).

Baron de Wassenaer   A Damask–Hybrid Moss raised by Verdier in 1854. An upright, open shrub with dark brown moss, up to 1.3 m high. The rather cup-shaped flowers are well scented, in very large trusses, with a long flowering season.

Shailer's White Moss (*Centifolia Muscosa Alba*, White Bath)   This rose occurred as a sport of Common Moss in 1788 and has been known to revert to the pink form. It makes a lax bush up to 1.3 m high, with very well-scented flowers, often with a button eye.

Striped Moss (Oeillet Panaché)   A Damask Moss raised by Du Pont in 1880. This is similar to one of the smaller Gallicas but mossy. It makes a bush up to 1.3 m high.

Salet   An Autumn Damask Moss raised by Lacharme in 1854. It makes a strong bush up to 1.6 m high, and is repeat flowering, with well-scented blooms. The most dependable of the perpetual mosses.

Maréchal Davoust   A Damask Moss raised by Robert in 1853. It makes a bush up to 1.3 m high, with rather narrow leaves and is particularly free flowering. Named after Napoleon's Marshal in the Russian campaign, Duc d'Auerstadt, 1770–1823.

Centifolia Muscosa

Shailer's White Moss

Shailer's White Moss

65

Blanche Moreau

Gloire des Mousseux

William Lobb

Cécile Brunner

Mme Pierre Oger

White
Cécile Brunner

Bloomfield Abundance

Mme Isaac Pereire

Zigeuner Knabe

Mousseline

July 10th, from Wisley

La Reine Victoria

Louise Odier

Grüss an Aachen

Gloire des Mousseux

William Lobb (Old Velvet Moss) A Damask Moss with a quarter China in its ancestry, raised by Laffay in 1855. It makes a tall, lank shrub up to 3 m high, suitable for training on a pillar or pergola. Flowers well scented, purple fading to greyish mauve, only produced at midsummer.

Gloire des Mousseux (Mme Alboni) A Damask Moss raised by Laffay in 1852. It makes a stiff, rather upright, bush up to 1.3 m high. The flowers are sweetly scented, produced at midsummer with the occasional one appearing in autumn.

Blanche Moreau A Damask Moss raised by Moreau–Robert in 1880. It makes a vigorous bush up to 2 m high. The sweetly scented flowers are produced at midsummer, with a few appearing later. Parentage: 'White Quatre Saisons' × 'Comtesse de Murinais'.

Mme Pierre Oger This is probably the most popular of the Bourbon roses, found by Oger of Caen in 1874 as a sport on 'La Reine Victoria' and introduced by Verdier in 1878. It makes a rather sparse upright bush up to 2 m high, flowering from midsummer till autumn with a good scent. The petals develop a crimson flush in hot weather.

Bloomfield Abundance (Spray Cécile Brunner) A semi-climbing mutation of 'Cécile Brunner' (see below) introduced by Howard in 1941. It makes a dainty, open, almost thornless bush up to 2 m high, with a succession of miniature hybrid tea flowers with long leafy sepals. The buds are often foliose or otherwise deformed at

their centre. An earlier 'Bloomfield Abundance' was a Hybrid Musk raised by Thomas in 1920.

White Cécile Brunner This white mutation of Cécile Brunner (see below) was introduced by Fanque in France in 1909.

Cécile Brunner (Mignon) A miniature hybrid tea raised by Veuve–Ducher in 1881. It makes a small plant up to 1 m high, with a long succession of branching shoots with sweetly scented flowers. Parentage: Seedling Poly-pom × 'Mme de Tartas'.

Zigeuner Knabe (Gypsy Boy) A shrub rose raised by Lambert in 1909. It makes a very prickly, lax bush up to 1.6 m high, with one good show of almost scentless flowers. Parentage: ? a seedling from 'Russelliana' × *rugosa* seedling.

Mousseline (Alfred de Dalmas) An Autumn Damask Moss raised by Portemer in 1855. It makes a wide bush up to 1.3 m high, with spoon-shaped leaves and not very mossy stems. Repeat-flowering with scent, some say like honeysuckle, others like sweet peas.

Mme Isaac Pereire A Bourbon raised by Garçon in 1881. It is rather coarse, making a gawky bush up to 2.3 m high. It can also be grown as a climber. The flowers are richly scented; the early ones sometimes proliferate in the centre but the autumn flowers are wonderful.

Le Reine Victoria A Bourbon raised by Schwartz in 1872. Tall, upright growth up to 2

m. Flowers with good scent, continuously produced.

Louise Odier (Mme de Stella) A Bourbon raised by Margottin in 1851. Strong bushy upright growth up to 1.5 m. Flowers pink, shaded with lilac, richly scented and continuously produced into autumn.

Grüss an Aachen A Hybrid Tea raised by Geduldig in 1909. Growth up to 1 m. Flowers freely produced, well scented, up to 15 cm across. Parentage: 'Frau Karl Druschki' × 'Franz Deegen' (a HT). This is often classed as a Floribunda in spite of its HT parentage and the large size of its flowers. David Austin groups it with his 'English Roses'.

Cramoisi Supérieur

Hermosa

Fellemberg

Single Pink China

Irene Watts

Old Blush

Mutabilis

Le Vésuve

Mme Laurette Messimy

July 1st, from Mottisfont

Fellemberg (La Belle Marseillaise)   A China rose raised by Fellemberg in 1857. It makes a large spreading shrub up to 2.5 m across, with flowers in clusters produced from summer to autumn.

Cramoisi Supérieur (Agrippina)   A China rose raised by Coquereau in 1832. A small bush up to 1 m high, delicate and perpetual flowering but with little scent. There is also a climbing form.

Hermosa (Armosa)   A China rose raised by Marcheseau in 1840. It makes an attractive plant up to 1 m high, constantly in flower, with good scent. There is also a climbing form.

Single Pink China   A China rose of unknown origin though, possibly, by analogy with the single red, a reversion from a double pink China such as 'Old Blush'. It makes a bush up to 1.3 m high.

Irene Watts   A China raised by Guillot in 1896. It makes a low plant up to 50 cm high, with continuous flowering.

Old Blush (Parsons' Pink China)   This is one of the original China roses, first introduced into Sweden in 1752 by Peter Osbeck and again in 1789 from Canton by Sir Joseph Banks. It makes a small bush about 1 m high, or can be trained on a wall to 3 m. The flowers are produced almost continuously from summer to winter and are scented of sweet peas.

Mutabilis (Tipo Ideale)   This China rose first came to the notice of botanists in 1896 when it was given to Henri Correvon of Geneva by Prince Ghilberto Borromeo. It makes a shrub up to 2.5 m high when old, with bronze young leaves and flowers which open yellow before changing to pink and finally to crimson. This deepening of colour is typical of the wild China rose and creates a beautiful effect in 'Mutabilis' as it is an exceptionally graceful plant.

Le Vésuve (Lemesle)   A China rose raised by Laffay in 1825. It makes a branching, spreading thorny shrub to 1.5 m high, with a succession into autumn of nodding scented flowers, opening pale pink and deepening as they age.

Mme Laurette Messimy   A China rose raised by Guillot Fils in 1887. It makes a bush up to 1.3 m high, with flowers which fade as they age. Parentage: 'Rival de Paestum' × 'Mme Falcot'.

Sanguinea (Miss Lowe, Bengal Crimson)   A China rose of unknown origin, probably a reversion from *R. chinensis* 'Semperflorens'. It forms a twiggy bush up to 1.3 m high and has a succession of flowers. 'Miss Lowe' is considered distinct by some authorities in its dwarfer habit and marginally smaller flowers.

***Rosa chinensis* Semperflorens** (Slater's or Miss Willmott's Crimson China)   This is one of the original China roses introduced in 1792. It makes a dwarf bush up to 1.2 m high, with a succession of small, loosely double flowers. Graham Thomas records two forms, a triploid found in Bermuda, and a dwarfer diploid found in a garden in Hertfordshire, which is probably the form shown here, about 50 cm high.

***Rosa chinensis* Viridiflora** (Green Rose 'Monstrosa')   This form of *R. chinensis* 'Old Blush' has permanently deformed flowers, the petals reduced to green scales, later tinged with red. It is an ugly curiosity, said to have been known in gardens since 1843.

Mutabilis

Le Vésuve

Sanguinea

R. chinensis 'Semperflorens'

R. chinensis 'Viridiflora'

Great Western

Prince Charles

Variegata de Bologna

Commandant Beaurepaire

Ferdinand Pichard

Champion of the World

Boule de Neige

Souvenir de St Anne's

July 3rd, from Mottisfont

Souvenir de St Anne's A Bourbon introduced by Graham Thomas through Hillings in 1950. It occurred as a sport on 'Souvenir de la Malmaison' in the garden of Lady Ardilaun, at St Anne's, Clontarf, near Dublin. A robust bush up to 2 m high, with very well-scented flowers produced freely in early autumn as well as summer.

Honorine de Brabant A Bourbon of unknown origin. Strong leafy growth up to 2 m. Very sweet, rich scent with flowers produced well into autumn.

Kronprinzessin Viktoria A Bourbon introduced by Spaeth in 1888, a white sport of 'Souvenir de la Malmaison'. Growth up to 1.3 m. Good scent.

Bourbon Queen (Queen of Bourbons, Reine de l'Île Bourbon) A Hybrid-China raised by Mauget in 1834. Growth up to 2 m, or higher when trained. Free flowering in summer, in clusters along last year's growths.

Mme Ernst Calvat A Bourbon introduced by Schwartz in 1888, a sport from 'Mme Isaac Pereire'. Growth up to 2 m, or higher if trained, with copper coloured young leaves which set off the wonderfully scented pale flowers.

Gloire des Rosomanes (Ragged Robin) A China–Bourbon hybrid raised by Vibert in 1825. Growth to 1.3 m. Continuous flowering and sweetly scented. Often used in the past as an understock and used for hedging in California.

Souvenir de la Malmaison A Bourbon raised by Beluze in 1843 from 'Mme Desprez', a Bourbon crossed with a Tea. Growth up to 1.3 m high and as much across. Flowers well scented, continuously produced. Apart from the white 'Kronprinzessin Viktoria', there is also a red sport known as 'Leweson Gower'.

Great Western A Bourbon raised by Laffay in 1838. Growth up to 1.5 m high. Flowers purplish, well scented but freely produced only in summer.

Prince Charles A Bourbon of unknown origin, known since 1842. Growth up to 1.5 m. Flowers fading lilac, scented, produced only in summer.

Commandant Beaurepaire (Panachée d'Angers) A Bourbon raised by Moreau–Robert in 1874. Growth up to 2 m, thorny. Flowers produced in summer, rarely in autumn.

Variegata de Bologna A Bourbon raised by Lodi–Bonfiglioli in 1909. Growth up to 2.5 m. Flowers mostly produced at midsummer but a few in autumn.

Ferdinand Pichard A Hybrid Perpetual raised by Tanna in 1921, often classed as a Bourbon. Growth up to 2.5 m, bushy. Flowers well scented, produced at midsummer and into autumn as well, in tight clusters.

Champion of the World (Mrs de Graw) A Hybrid Perpetual raised by Woodhouse 1894. Growth arching, to 1.5 m. Flowers well scented, often better in early autumn than in summer. Parentage: 'Hermosa' × 'Magna Charta'.

Boule de Neige A Bourbon raised by Lacharme in 1867. Growth slender, upright, to 1.5 m. Flowers richly scented in clusters, with reflexing petals, produced continuously from midsummer to autumn. Buds crimson.

Honorine du Brabant

Kronprinzessin Viktoria

Bourbon Queen

Mme Ernst Calvat

Gloire des Rosomanes

Souvenir de la Malmaison

July 1st, from Mottisfont

Bourbon Queen

Baronne Prévost

Grüss an Tepliz

Baron Girod de L'Ain

Empereur du Maroc

Frau Karl Druschki

Eugene Fürst

Archiduchesse Elisabeth d'Autriche

Morlettii

Erinnerung an Brod

July 1st, from Mottisfont

Baronne Prévost A Hybrid Perpetual raised by Desprez in 1842, but with many of the characters of a Portland. Growth up to 1.5 m. Thorny stems with upright, strongly scented flowers. Very hardy. Unfortunately liable to 'ball' and rot in wet weather and susceptible to blackspot.

Grüss an Tepliz A China–Bourbon hybrid raised by Lambert in 1897. It makes a tall shrub to 2 or 4 m on a wall or pergola, with richly scented flowers in small or large clusters. Parentage: ('Sir Joseph Paxton' × 'Fellenberg') × ('Papa Gontier' × 'Gloire des Rosomanes').

Baron Girod de l'Ain A Hybrid Perpetual introduced by Reverchon in 1897, a sport of 'Eugène Fürst'. Strong growth up to 1.5 m. Flowers with white wavy edges, well scented, in crowded clusters.

Empéreur du Maroc A Hybrid Perpetual raised by Bertrand–Guinoisseau in 1858. Growth vigorous, up to 1.3 m. Flowers freely produced with a strong rich scent. Seedling of 'Géant des Batailles'.

Frau Karl Druschki (Reine des Neiges, Snow Queen, White American Beauty) A Hybrid Tea, though often classed as a Hybrid Perpetual, raised by Lambert in 1901. A strong bush up to 2 m. Flowers with little scent, often pink tinted in bud. Parentage: 'Merveille de Lyon' × 'Mme Caroline Testout'.

Eugène Fürst (Général Korolkov) A Hybrid Perpetual raised by Soupert et Notting in 1875. Growth up to 1.5 m. Very good scent. A seedling of 'Baron de Bonstetten'.

Archiduchesse Elisabeth d'Autriche A Hybrid Perpetual raised by Moreau–Robert in 1881. Growth up to 1.3 m. Good scent. Liable to 'ball' in wet weather.

Morlettii (*R. pendulina* 'Plena') This is probably a *R. pendulina* hybrid and was raised by Morlet in 1883. It makes a round bush up to 3 m high, without thorns, once-flowering and with good autumn colour.

Erinnerung an Brod (Souvenir de Brod) A Hybrid Perpetual raised by Geschwind in Brod in 1886. Growth up to 2.5 m, flowers well scented, becoming purple as they fade like a Gallica.

Général Jacqueminot (La Brillante) A Hybrid Perpetual raised by Roussel in 1853. Growth up to 2 m, with good foliage and well-scented flowers, fewer in autumn. Parentage: 'Gloire des Rosomanes' × ? 'Géant des Batailles', and itself an ancestor of 'Crimson Glory', 'Etoile de Hollande' and other good roses.

John Hopper A Hybrid Perpetual raised by Ward in 1862. Growth up to 1.5 m, bushy and thorny. Flowers with good scent, becoming mauve on fading. Parentage: 'Jules Margottin' × 'Madame Vidot'.

Fisher Holmes A Hybrid Perpetual raised by Verdier in 1865. Growth up to 1.5 m, free flowering and with good scent. A seedling of 'Maurice Bernadin'. One of the best Hybrid Perpetuals.

Général Jacqueminot
John Hopper
Fisher Holmes
Hugh Dickson
La Reine
Gloire de Ducher

July 3rd, from Mottisfont

Hugh Dickson

Hugh Dickson A Hybrid Perpetual raised by Dickson in 1905. Growth very strong up to 3 m, so the shoots are best pegged down (as with all vigorous HPs) Some scent. A seedling of 'Grüss an Teplitz'.

La Reine A Hybrid Perpetual raised by Laffay in 1842. Growth up to 1.5 m, vigorous. Very hardy. Flowers often shaded with lilac, slightly scented.

Gloire de Ducher (Germania) A Hybrid Perpetual raised by Ducher in 1865. Strong growth up to 2.3 m. Should be trained on a wall or pegged down; susceptible to mildew. Flowers well scented rich purple, freely produced in summer, fewer but magnificent in autumn.

Archiduchesse Elisabeth d'Autriche

*Triomphe
de l'Exposition*

Roger Lambelin

Jules Margottin

Vick's Caprice

Prince Camille de Rohan

Paul Neyron

Le Havre

Reine des Violettes

Ulrich Brunner Fils

July 3rd, from Mottisfont

Arillaga

Roger Lambelin

Ruhm von Steinforth

Candeur Lyonnaise

Mabel Morrison

Jules Margottin A Hybrid Perpetual raised by Margottin in 1853. Height up to 2 m, thorny. Hardy, free flowering but with little scent. Probably a seedling from 'La Reine'.

Roger Lambelin A sport of 'Prince Camille de Rohan', introduced by Schwartz in 1890. Needs good soil, then up to 1.5 m. Good scent.

Triomphe de l'Exposition A Hybrid Perpetual raised by Margottin in 1855. Height up to 1.5 m, with red thorns and good scent.

Prince Camille de Rohan A Hybrid Perpetual raised by E. Verdier in 1861. On good soil up to 1.3 m, fruity scent. Sometimes less good in autumn.

Paul Neyron A Hybrid Perpetual raised by Levet in 1869. One of the largest-flowered roses, up to 2 m high, with few thorns. Very free flowering, highly scented. Parentage: 'Victor Verdier' × 'Anna de Diesbach'.

Vick's Caprice A Hybrid Perpetual, sport of Archiduchesse Elisabeth d'Autriche', found in a Mr Vick's garden in New York in 1897. It makes a bush up to 1.8 m, with very double pink and white striped flowers, liable to 'ball' in wet weather. It tends to revert to its plain pink parent.

Le Havre A Hybrid Perpetual raised by Ende in 1871. It makes a bush up to 1.3 m high. Before the advent of red Hybrid Teas, this rose was valued for its bright colour and perfect shape.

Reine des Violettes A Hybrid Perpetual raised by Millet–Malet in 1860, a seedling of 'Pope Pius IX'. On good soil it makes a tall, almost thornless shrub up to 2 m high. The flowers open carmine or cerise and later develop violet shading. They are very sweetly scented and reminiscent of a Gallica in shape and colour.

Ulrich Brunner Fils A Hybrid Perpetual raised by Levet in 1882. A large bush up to 2.5 m high, with upright, leggy growth. Flowers in bunches, well scented, liable to 'ball' in wet weather.

Arillaga A Hybrid Perpetual raised by Schoener in 1929. Strong growth up to 1.5 m. A popular variety in America.

Candeur Lyonnaise A Hybrid Perpetual raised by Croibier in 1914. Growth up to 2 m. Good in warm climates.

Ruhm von Steinfurth A Hybrid Tea raised by Weigand in 1920. It makes a large bush up to 1.5 m, with a habit more like a Hybrid Perpetual. Parentage: 'Frau Karl Druschki' × 'General McArthur'.

Mabel Morrison A Hybrid Perpetual introduced by Broughton in 1878. It was a sport from 'Baroness Rothschild' (a light pink). It makes a bush up to 1.3 m high, free flowering, with large unscented flowers, white flushed pink in cool weather.

Céline Forestier

Alister Stella Gray

Desprez à Fleur Jaune

Mme Lauriol de Barny

Souvenir de
Mme Léonie Viennot

Auguste Roussel

Blairii No. 1

Fraülein Oktavia Hesse

Blairii No. 2

July 1st, from Mottisfont

Mme Bravy

Mrs John Laing

Georg Arends

Mme Antoine Mari

July 3rd, from Mottisfont

Mme Victor Verdier

Céline Forestier   A Tea–Noisette raised by Trouillard in 1842. A climber up to 5 m in a good warm situation. Continuous flowering, with very good scent.

Alister Stella Gray (Golden Rambler)   A Tea–Noisette raised by Gray and introduced by Paul in 1894. Growth up to 2.5 m as a shrub, to 5 m on a wall. Flowers with good scent, in small clusters at the first flowering; in large clusters later on new, strong shoots.

Desprez à Fleur Jaune (Jaune Desprez)   A Tea–Noisette raised by Desprez in 1830. Growth up to 5.5 m, with few prickles. Flowers single or in small clusters, wonderfully scented, from midsummer into autumn. Parentage: 'Blush Noisette' × 'Park's Yellow Tea-scented China'.

Mme Lauriol de Barny   A Bourbon raised by Trouillard in 1868. Growth up to 2 m or higher if supported. Flowers mainly at midsummer with fewer later flowers, with good, fruity scent.

Souvenir de Mme Léonie Viennot   A climbing Tea rose raised by Bernaix in 1898. Growth up to 6 m on a warm sheltered wall. Good scent and repeat flowering; one of the hardier of the Tea roses.

Auguste Roussel   An unusual hybrid, 'Papa Gontier' × *R. macrophylla*, raised by Barbier in 1913. Growth up to 6 m, climbing or arching. Flowers well scented, in clusters, produced only at midsummer.

Blairii No. 1.   A Bourbon raised by Blair in 1845. Growth up to 2 m. One main flowering, well scented, and with a few flowers in autumn.

Fraülein Oktavia Hesse   A large-flowered Rambler raised by Hesse in 1918. Growth up to 6 m. Sweet scented; repeat flowering. Similar to 'Alberic Barbier' (p. 87)

Blairii No. 2   A China hybrid raised by Blair in 1845. Growth up to 3 m or more. One main flowering, followed by scattered later flowers; good scent. Susceptible to mildew. This is most effective at Mottisfont, trained up a small apple tree. Parentage: a China rose × 'Tuscany'.

Georg Arends (Fortune Besson)   A Hybrid Tea raised by L. W. Hinner in 1910. It makes a bush up to 2 m high. Very good scent, very few thorns. Usually classed with the hybrid perpetuals in spite of its parentage. Parentage: 'Frau Karl Druschki' × 'La France'.

Mrs John Laing   A Hybrid Perpetual raised by Bennett in 1887. It makes a short, sturdy plant up to 1.3 m high, with very small thorns, and well-scented flowers in clusters of 3 or 4. Impervious to rain. Parentage: seedling of 'François Michelon'.

Mme Antoine Mari   A Tea rose raised by Mari in 1901. It makes a bush up to 1.3 m or higher when trained on a wall. Flowers delicately scented. This is one of the hardier Tea roses.

Mme Bravy (*Alba Rosea*, Mme Serat)   A Tea rose raised by Guillot of Pont Cherin in 1846 and introduced by Guillot (of Lyons) in 1848. It makes a low plant up to 1 m high, with large flowers in hanging clusters, freely produced. This is often said to be one of the parents, with 'Mme Victor Verdier' of the first Hybrid Tea 'La France'.

Mme Victor Verdier   A Hybrid Perpetual raised by Verdier in 1863. It makes an upright, almost thornless bush up to 1.6 m, with large well-scented flowers produced through the summer. This is said, with 'Mme Bravy' (above) to be one of the parents of 'La France' (p. 125), the first Hybrid Tea, but was itself a Hybrid Tea if its usually quoted parentage is correct. Parentage: 'Jules Margottin' × ? 'Safrano' (a yellow Tea rose).

Lamarque

Marie van Houtte

Gloire de Dijon

Maréchal Neil

Devoniensis

Duchesse d'Auerstadt

Mme Sancy de Parabère

Souvenir du Dr Jamain

Rival de Paestum

July 1st, from Mottisfont

Lamarque (Thé Maréchal) A Noisette raised by Maréchal in 1830, with many characters of a Tea rose in its quilled petals, nodding flowers (an asset for a climber) which open flat and white, and tea scent. In cool climates, such as England, it grows up to about 3 m and needs the protection of a wall, but in hotter climates can be very robust. Parentage: 'Blush Noisette' × 'Park's Yellow Tea-scented China'.

Marie van Houtte A Tea rose raised by Ducher in 1871. Growth up to 2 m on a sunny wall. Well-scented flowers, gracefully nodding. Parentage: 'Madame de Tartas' × 'Madame Falcot'.

Gloire de Dijon (The Old Glory Rose) A Tea–Bourbon hybrid raised by Jacotot in 1853, by crossing a yellow Tea rose with 'Souvenir de la Malmaison'. This is still one of the best and most often seen of the climbing roses, perfectly hardy in England, and thriving even on a north wall, up to 4–5 m. In warmer weather the pink tones become stronger; the scent is very good.

Maréchal Neil A Tea–Noisette raised by Pradel in 1864, whose nodding flowers have a good tea scent. This rose does better under glass than outdoors in England and was very popular as a climber in Victorian conservatories. A seedling of 'Cloth of Gold'? ('Chromatella').

Devoniensis climbing (Magnolia Rose) A Tea rose introduced by Pavitt in 1858, a climbing sport of the original 'Devoniensis' raised by Foster in 1838. Growth up to 5 m. Flowers produced into autumn, delightfully scented.

Duchesse d'Auerstadt A Noisette raised by Bernaix in 1888. Growth up to 3 m. Flowers well scented, produced into autumn. Parentage: not recorded.

Mme Sancy de Parabère A climbing Boursault raised by Bonnet in 1874. Growth up to 5 m, without thorns. Lush leaves with characteristic coarse teeth. Flowers with little scent, produced only at midsummer. Parentage: not recorded.

Souvenir du Dr Jamain A Hybrid Perpetual raised by Lacharme in 1865. Growth up to 3 m when supported. Flowers richly scented, produced at midsummer and again in autumn. Best planted out of the hottest sun which can spoil the flowers. Parentage: 'Général Jacqueminot' × 'Charles Lefèbvre'.

Rival de Paestum A China rose raised by Paul in 1863. Growth up to 1.3 m with young shoots and leaves purplish. Flowers nodding when open. This plant may be cut back by a cold winter but by early autumn will be back in full flowering form. Parentage: not recorded.

Tea Rose in China I found this Tea rose growing in two villages in the Lijiang area of Yunnan. It is a robust climber up to 6 m, with glossy leaves like *R. gigantea* and slightly nodding, strongly scented flowers about 12 cm across. This is probably an ancient Chinese garden rose, similar to 'Hume's Blush Tea-scented China'.

La Follette A Tea rose raised by Busby, Lord Brougham's gardener at Cannes, about 1910. It is a strong climber, to at least 10 m, with huge loose flowers early in the summer. In England it does best in a greenhouse or on a sheltered wall, it grows easily in the open in the south of France or California. Parentage: *Rosa gigantea* × H.T.

Tea Rose in China

Tea Rose in China

Gloire de Dijon

La Follette in Brittany

Chaplin's Pink Climber

Paul's Scarlet Climber

Zéphirine Drouhin

Lady Hillingdon

Albertine

Mme Grégoire Staechelin

Dr W. van Fleet

Mermaid

Parade

July 10th, from Wisley

Chaplin's Pink Climber A rambler raised by Chaplin in 1928. Growth up to 4 m. Once flowering with very little scent. Flowers in large, dense clusters. Parentage: 'Paul's Scarlet Climber' × 'American Pillar'.

Paul's Scarlet Climber A climber raised by Paul in 1915. Growth up to 6 m. Flowers in clusters with little scent, continuing into late autumn. Very hardy, tough and long lived. There are several flowers open here as I write this, on 15 December. Parentage: *R. wichuraiana* × a Hybrid Tea.

Zéphyrine Drouhin A Bourbon raised by Bizot in 1868. It makes a bush up to 2.5 m, or can be trained as a climber up to 4 m. Almost thornless with sweetly scented flowers produced from summer continuously into autumn. Suffers slightly from mildew and blackspot. Its paler sport, 'Kathleen Harrop' (1919) is equally beautiful (p. 83).

Lady Hillingdon, climbing A climbing sport of the Tea rose, raised by Lowe and Shawyer in 1910 which occurred, and was introduced by Hicks, in 1917. Growth up to 6 m. Flowers richly scented produced from midsummer into winter, contrasting with the reddish-purple young leaves. Parentage: 'Papa Gontier' × 'Madame Hoste'.

Albertine A large-flowered rambler raised by Barbier in 1921. Growth up to 6 m, stiff, most suitable for training along a hedge or a low wall. Flowers well scented, produced in one spectacular display. Parentage: *R. wichuraiana* × 'Mrs A. R. Waddell'.

Mme Grégoire Staechelin (Spanish Beauty) A climbing Hybrid Tea raised by Dot in 1927. Growth up to 6 m, thorny. Flowers produced at midsummer only; well scented of sweet peas and elegantly nodding. Parentage: 'Frau Karl Druschki' × 'Château de Clos Vougeot'.

Dr W. van Fleet A large-flowered rambler raised by van Fleet in 1910. Growth up to 6 m. Flowers in clusters, well scented, produced only at midsummer. 'New Dawn' (p. 93) is a perpetual flowering sport of this rose. Parentage: (*R. wichuraiana* × 'Safrano') × 'Souvenir du Président Carnot'.

Mermaid A *R. bracteata* hybrid raised by Paul in 1918. Growth vigorous, up to 10 m or more. Flowers in clusters, continuously produced after midsummer, with some scent. Not very hardy and cut down in cold winters. Parentage: *R. bracteata* × a Tea rose.

Parade A climbing Floribunda raised by Boerner in 1953. Growth up to 4 m. Repeat flowering; little scent. Parentage: 'New Dawn' seedling × 'World's Fair' climbing.

Pompon de Paris climbing A miniature China climber, a sport of 'Pompon de Paris', raised in 1839. It makes slender growth up to 2 m with small flowers about 3 cm across. Little scent but pretty, as here, growing through *Ceanothus*, and good for its early flowering on a sheltered wall.

Mme Alfred Carrière A Noisette raised by J. Schwartz in 1879. Growth up to 6 m. Flowers well scented, in clusters, produced intermittently after the main crop. Can also be grown as a large shrub. Parentage: not recorded.

Zéphirine Drouhin

Pompon de Paris

Chaplin's Pink Climber

Mme Alfred Carrière

Mme Grégoire Staechelin

Mme Alfred Carrière

Sombreuil

Souvenir de la Malmaison

Mme Jules Gravereaux

Paul's Lemon Pillar

Constance Spry

Mrs Herbert Stevens

Kathleen Harrop

Paul's Single White

Lady Waterlow

July 1st, from Mottisfont

Blush Noisette

Blush Noisette at Longleat House, Wilts

Princesse de Nassau

Ghislaine de Féligonde

Sombreuil A climbing Tea rose raised by Robert in 1850. Growth up to 4 m. Flowers well-scented, continuously produced into autumn. Parentage: 'Gigantesque' × an HP.

Souvenir de la Malmaison climbing A climbing sport of the Bourbon hybrid, introduced by Francis Bennett in 1893. Growth up to 4 m. Flowers produced in two crops, in June and September, well scented but tending to 'ball' in wet weather. Parentage: 'Mme Desprez' × a Tea rose.

Mme Jules Gravereaux A climbing Tea rose raised by Soupert et Notting in 1901. Growth up to 4 m. Once flowering, slightly scented. Parentage: not recorded.

Paul's Lemon Pillar A climbing Hybrid Tea raised by Paul in 1915. Strong growth up to 6 m. Once-flowering but stongly scented and not damaged by wet weather. Parentage: 'Frau Karl Druschki' × 'Maréchal Neil'.

Constance Spry The first of the English Roses raised by David Austin in 1961. It makes a large shrub to 2 m or a climber up to 4 m if trained on a wall. Once-flowering but making an excellent show, and well scented. Parentage: 'Belle Isis' (a Gallica) × 'Dainty Maid' (a single floribunda).

Mrs Herbert Stevens climbing A climbing sport of Mrs Herbert Stevens (McGredy 1910) introduced by Pernet-Ducher in 1922. Growth

up to 6 m, vigorous. Repeat flowering, well scented, but liable to damage by wet weather. Parentage: 'Frau Karl Druschki' × 'Niphetos'.

Kathleen Harrop A pale flowered sport of the Bourbon 'Zéphirine Drouhin', introduced by Dickson in 1919. It makes a thornless bush up to 2 m, or can be trained on a low wall. Flowers well scented, continuously produced. Rarer and less vigorous than its parent.

Paul's Single White A hybrid of *R. moschata* raised by Paul in 1883. Growth up to 3 m, vigorous. Flowers in clusters, well scented, produced throughout the summer.

Lady Waterlow A climbing Hybrid Tea raised by Nabonnard in 1903. Growth up to 4 m. Flowers well scented, mostly at midsummer but sometimes with an excellent second flowering in September. Parentage: 'La France de '89' × 'Mme Marie Lavalley'.

Blush Noisette The original Noisette rose, a seedling of 'Champney's Pink Cluster', the cross between a China and *R. moschata*, raised before 1817 by Noisette. It makes a loose bush up to 2.5 m or can be trained on a wall to 5 m. The flowers are of medium size in clusters, continuously produced and sweetly scented of cloves.

Ghislaine de Féligonde A rambler raised by Turbat in 1916. It makes a large shrub with shoots up to 3m, with few thorns. Repeat-

flowering, scented. Parentage: *R. moschata* hybrid.

Princesse de Nassau (*R. moschata* 'Autumnalis') This is a late-flowering climbing rose, not coming into flower until August or September in a cool summer. It is probably a hybrid of *Rosa moschata* raised by Laffay in 1835 and, Graham Thomas suggests, could be a hybrid with a noisette.

William's Evergreen

Venusta Pendula

Princess Marie

Splendens

Ruga

Adelaïde d'Orléans

Mme d'Arblay

Flora

Russelliana

July 3rd, from Mottisfont

Princess Marie at Nymans, Sussex

Baltimore Belle

Spectabilis

William's Evergreen   A rambler raised in 1855. Growth to 4 m. Once-flowering. Similar to 'Flora' (below) but with creamy-white flowers. Parentage: *R. sempervirens* hybrid.

Venusta Pendula   A rambler of unknown origin, rediscovered by Kordes. Growth up to 5 m. Once-flowering, negligible scent. Parentage: a form or hybrid of *R. arvensis*.

Princesse Marie (Reine des Belges)   A rambler raised by Jacques in 1829. Growth up to 10 m or more. Once-flowering, some scent. Parentage: *R. sempervirens* hybrid.

Splendens (Ayrshire Splendens, Myrrh-Scented Rose)   A rambler of unknown origin. Growth up to 5 m. Once-flowering. Said to be scented of myrrh. For those who have never smelled myrrh, the scent of this rose is like that of fresh distemper. Parentage: *R. arvensis* hybrid.

Ruga   A rambler known since before 1820, originating in Italy and supposed to be a hybrid between a China rose and *R. arvensis*. Growth up to 3 m, hardy. Flowers in loose clusters, very sweetly scented, produced only at midsummer.

Adelaïde d'Orléans   A rambler raised by Jacques in 1826. Growth up to 6 m, evergreen in warm winters and liable to be cut to the ground in an exceptional freeze; susceptible to mildew. Flowers in clusters, scented of primroses, at

midsummer only, though occasionally with the odd flower later. Parentage: *R. sempervirens* hybrid.

Mme d'Arblay   A rambler raised by Wells in 1835. Growth up to 6 m, trailing. Flowers in clusters, well scented, at midsummer only. Parentage: ?*R. multiflora* × *R. moschata*.

Flora (Flore)   A rambler raised by Jacques in 1830. Growth up to 4 m, trailing. Once-flowering. Some scent, of primroses. Parentage: *R. sempervirens* hybrid.

Russelliana (Old Spanish Rose, Russel's Cottage Rose, Souvenir de la Bataille de Marengo)   A rambler of unknown origin, known since 1840. Growth up to 6 m. Flowers heavily scented in a large open cluster, produced only at midsummer, opening cerise crimson, fading purplish.

Baltimore Belle   A rambler raised by Feast in 1843. Growth up to 5 m high and across; very disease resistant. Flowers in large clusters, well scented, produced in late summer. Parentage: said to be a hybrid of *R. setigera* but very similar to the *R. sempervirens* hybrids.

Spectabilis (Noisette Ayez)   A rambler known since 1848. Growth up to 2.5 m. Flowers small, lilac tinted when first open, sweet scented. Late flowering. Parentage: *R. sempervirens* hybrid.

Kew Rambler

Ethel

Lykkefund

Silver Moon

Albéric Barbier

Venusta Pendula

François Juranville

July 16th, from The Gardens of the Rose

Kew Rambler

American Pillar

Francis E. Lester

Blush Rambler

White Flight

Ethel   A small-flowered rambler raised by Turner in 1912. Growth up to 6 m. Once flowering. Parentage: not recorded.

Kew Rambler   A small-flowered climber or rambler raised at Kew in 1912. Growth up to 6 m. Good scent. Once-flowering. The greyish leaves are inherited from *R. soulieana*. Parentage: *R. soulieana* × 'Hiawatha'.

Lykkefund   A small-flowered rambler raised by Olsen in 1930. Growth up to 6 m, without thorns. Scent good. Once-flowering. Parentage: *R. helenae* × 'Zéphirine Drouhin'.

Silver Moon   A climber raised by van Fleet in 1910. Growth up to 10 m, with glaucous stems. Once-flowering. Good scent, of apples. Parentage: *R. laevigata* × ?'Devoniensis'.

Albéric Barbier   A large-flowered rambler raised by Barbier in 1900. Growth to 6 m. Once-flowering but with many later flowers through the season. Very good scent, of apples. Parentage: *R. luciae* × 'Shirley Hibberd' (a yellow Tea rose).

Venusta Pendula   A rambler of unknown origin, rediscovered by Kordes. Growth up to 5 m. Once-flowering. Negligible scent. Parentage: a form or hybrid of *R. arvensis*.

François Juranville   A large-flowered rambler raised by Barbier in 1906. Growth up to 6 m, with long, flexible shoots. Once-flowering. Good scent. Parentage: *R. luciae* × 'Mme Laurette Messimy'.

Francis E. Lester   This rambling Hybrid Musk was introduced by Lester in 1946. It will grow up to about 5 m and can be trained up a post or wall. The flowers, which are pink in bud, fading to white when opened, are very fragrant. Small red hips are produced in the autumn. Parentage: 'Kathleen' × unnamed seedling.

Blush Rambler   A small-flowered rambler raised by Cant in 1903. Growth almost thornless, up to 5 m. Once-flowering. Good scent. The pale green leaves shown here are characteristic but possibly accentuated by a touch of chlorosis. Parentage: 'Crimson Rambler' × 'The Garland'.

White Flight   A small-flowered rambler of unknown origin, about 1900, rescued from oblivion by Humphrey Brooke at Claydon, and put on to the market by Peter Beales. Growth up to 3 m. Once-flowering. Parentage: a seedling of *R. multiflora*?

American Pillar   A small-flowered rambler raised by van Fleet in 1902. Growth up to 5 m. No scent. Once-flowering. Very robust and floriferous. Susceptible to mildew. Parentage: (*R. wichuraiana* × *setigera*) × red Hybrid Perpetual.

Rambling Rector

Snowdrift

Veilchenblau

Rose-Marie Viaud

Purpurtraum

Violette

Goldfinch

Bleu Magenta

July 3rd, from Mottisfont

Rambling Rector A small-flowered climber known since 1912. Growth rampant, very thorny, up to 10 m in trees. Good scent. Once flowering but very floriferous. Parentage: unknown, but probably *R. multiflora* × *R. moschata*.

Snowdrift A rambler raised by Walsh in 1913. Vigorous growth up to 4 m. Once-flowering. Parentage: not recorded.

Rose-Marie Viaud (Amethyste) A small-flowered rambler, a seedling of 'Veilchenblau', raised by Igoult in 1924. Growth almost thornless, up to 5 m. Once flowering. Little scent. Flowers opening reddish and fading through purple to pale mauve grey.

Veilchenblau A small-flowered rambler raised by Schmidt in 1909. Almost thornless, up to 4 m. Once flowering. Good scent, of apples. Flowers fade to greyish mauve. Parentage: 'Crimson Rambler' × 'Erinnerung an Brod'.

Purpurtraum A small-flowered rambler raised by Kayser and Siebert 1922. Once-flowering. The colour is dark crimson, not purple as suggested by the name. Parentage: not recorded.

Violette (Violetta) A small-flowered rambler raised by Turbat in 1921. Growth almost thornless up to 4 m. Once flowering. Little scent. Flowers opening reddish purple, fading to greyish mauve, often with one white-streaked petal. Parentage: not recorded.

Goldfinch A small-flowered rambler raised by Paul in 1907. Growth to 5 m. Once flowering. Good scent and much loved by bees. Flowers yellow on opening, fading in the sun to white. Good trained into old apple trees. Parentage: *R. multiflora* hybrid, a seedling of Hélène, an HT × ('Aglaia' × Crimson Rambler').

Bleu Magenta A small-flowered rambler of unknown origin, but similar in many characters, especially the thornlessness, to 'Veilchenblau'. Growth up to 5 m. No scent. Once flowering, later than other purple ramblers, the flowers maturing to deep mauve and grey. Parentage not recorded.

Dorothy Perkins A small-flowered rambler raised by Jackson & Perkins in 1901. Shoots up to 6 m. Almost no scent. Once flowering. Exceptionally floriferous, but susceptible to mildew on receptacle and pedicels. Parentage: *R.? wichuraiana* × 'Madame Gabriel Luizet'.

Excelsa (Red Dorothy Perkins) A small-flowered rambler raised by Walsh in 1909. Shoots up to 6 m. Almost no scent. Once-flowering. Parentage: not recorded.

Minnehaha A small-flowered rambler raised by Walsh in 1905. Shoots to 4 m. Almost no scent. Once flowering, later than 'Dorothy Perkins', with flowers that remain deep pink. Parentage: *R. ?wichuraiana* × 'Paul Neyron'.

Sander's White A small-flowered rambler raised by Sanders in 1912. Shoots up to 4 m. Once flowering, late. Good scent. Parentage: *R.? wichuraiana* × unknown.

Débutante A small-flowered rambler raised by Walsh in 1902. Shoots up to 4 m. Once flowering. Scent of primroses. Similar to 'Dorothy Perkins' but not prone to mildew, and with curling petals. Parentage: *R. wichuraiana* × 'Baroness Rothschild'.

Dorothy Perkins

Excelsa

Minnehaha

Débutante

Sander's White

Thisbe

Will Scarlet

Felicia

Callisto

Buff Beauty

Cornelia

Trier

Félicité et Perpétue

Penelope

July 10th, from Wisley

Francesca

Moonlight

Thisbe   This Hybrid Musk was raised by Pemberton in 1918. It will grow up to 1.3 m high, with a similar spread, bearing blooms on graceful arching sprays, and buds of a rich yellow. Strongly scented. Parentage: 'Marie Jeanne' × 'Perle des Jardins'.

Will Scarlet   This Hybrid Musk occurred as a sport on a plant of 'Wilhelm', which was spotted by Graham Thomas in 1947 and introduced in 1950 by Hilling. It grows to about 2 m, with a similar spread, and retains shiny orange hips throughout the winter. Delicate scent.

Felicia   This Hybrid Musk was raised by Pemberton in 1928. A strong, bushy plant, growing to about 2 m in height, and more in width. A good hedging plant. Very floriferous, through summer and autumn, with a sweet scent. Parentage: 'Trier' × 'Ophelia'.

Callisto   A Hybrid Musk raised by Pemberton in 1920. The flowers fade from a warm yellow, eventually almost to white. Sweetly scented. This rose will grow up to about 1.4 m. Parentage: a seedling from 'William Allen Richardson'.

Buff Beauty   A Hybrid Musk raised in 1939 by Bentall. This is a vigorous and floriferous rose, making a shrub of about 2 m in height and width. The young foliage is coppery brown turning to dark green later. The flowers, which fade slightly, possess a delicious scent.

Cornelia   This Hybrid Musk was raised by Pemberton in 1925. It is a vigorous spreading bush, growing up to about 2.5 m. The summer blooms are pale pink (as shown here) but those borne in autumn are of a richer hue. 'Cornelia' has a sweet, musky, pervasive scent.

Trier   This was raised in 1904 by a German nurseryman, Peter Lambert, and was descended from a seedling of 'Aglaia', crossed with the Hybrid Tea 'Mrs R. G. Sharman Crawford'. 'Aglaia' itself was a hybrid between *R. multiflora* and 'Reve d'Or', a Noisette. 'Trier' itself is heavily scented and makes a bush or climber up to about 2.5 m (see p. 11).

Félicité et Perpétue   This rambler raised by M. Jacques, head gardener to the Duke of Orléans in 1827, is descended from *R. sempervirens* and is, as a result, semi evergreen. It is barely hardy with strong healthy growth, and can reach up to 6.5 m. It has a delicate scent. Parentage: *R. sempervirens* × *R. chinensis*.

Penelope   A Hybrid Musk raised by Pemberton in 1924. This is a vigorous variety with strong bushy growth up to 1.8 m, producing flowers throughout summer and autumn. On first appearing, the buds are a bright pinky orange. Sweetly scented. The hips are an unusual greenish-pink colour. Parentage: 'Ophelia' × 'Trier'.

Francesca   A Hybrid Musk raised by Pemberton in 1922. This graceful bush produces arching stems bearing the nodding flowers which fade from apricot yellow to a paler shade in hot sun. Richly scented. Parentage: 'Danaë × 'Sunburst'.

Vanity

Wilhelm

Prosperity

Erfurt

Moonlight   A Hybrid Musk raised by Pemberton in 1913. This variety can be allowed to ramble through other shrubs or can be kept shorter, but will grow up to 2 m or more. In summer the flowers are borne in small clusters, whereas in the autumn the clusters are much larger. Sweet musk scent. Parentage: 'Trier' × 'Sulphurea'.

Vanity   This Hybrid Musk was raised by Pemberton in 1920 and is very vigorous, reaching a height of 3–4 m. The flowers, which have a sweet strong scent, are a clear bright pink in summer, lighter in autumn. Parentage: 'Château de Clos Vougeot' × seedling.

Wilhelm (Skyrocket)   A Hybrid Musk raised by Kordes in 1934. A vigorous shrub, up to 3 m.

Small clusters of only slightly scented flowers appear in summer, followed by larger clusters in the autumn, and bright orange-red hips. Parentage: 'Robin Hood' × 'J. C. Thornton'.

Prosperity   A Hybrid Musk raised by Pemberton in 1919. The well-scented flowers are borne in small sprays during the summer, and in wider clusters in later summer. Height up to 2 m. Parentage: 'Marie Jeanne' × 'Perle des Jardins'.

Erfurt   A Hybrid Musk raised by Kordes in 1939. A compact shrub growing up to 1 m; the young foliage is an attractive coppery colour, and the scented flowers are borne throughout summer and autumn. Parentage: 'Eva' × 'Réveil Dijonnais'.

Golden Showers

Masquerade

Compassion

Handel

Danse du Feu

Dreaming Spires

New Dawn

Schoolgirl

Maigold

June 20th, from Eccleston Sq., London

Danse du Feu on a cottage in East Sussex

Maigold

Coral Dawn

Clair Matin

Golden Showers A Floribunda climber raised by Lammerts in 1957. Growth up to 3 m. Repeat flowering. Some scent. Parentage: 'Charlotte Armstrong' × 'Captain Thomas'.

Masquerade climbing A climbing sport of the familiar Floribunda 'Masquerade', introduced by Dillon in 1958. Growth to 4 m. Little scent. Once-flowering, some later flowers. Parentage: 'Goldilocks' × 'Holiday' (Boerner 1949)

Compassion (Belle de Londres) A climbing Hybrid Tea raised by Harkness 1973. Growth to 3 m. Repeat flowering. Good scent. Parentage: 'White Cockade' × 'Prima Ballerina'.

Handel A Floribunda climber raised by McGredy in 1965. Growth up to 4 m. Repeat flowering. Some scent. One of the most popular climbing roses for its unusually coloured flowers. Parentage: 'Columbine' × 'Heidelberg'.

Danse du Feu (Spectacular) A Floribunda climber raised by Mallerin in 1954. Growth up to 5 m. Repeat flowering. Little scent. May be planted on a north wall. Renowned for its freedom of flowering. Flowers open deep scarlet, and become more purplish as they age. Parentage: 'Paul's Scarlet Climber' × *R. multiflora* seedling.

Dreaming Spires A Hybrid Tea climber raised by Mattock in 1973. Growth up to 4 m. Repeat flowering. Some scent. Parentage: 'Buccaneer' × 'Arthur Bell'.

New Dawn A repeat-flowering sport of the large flowered rambler 'Dr W. van Fleet', introduced by Dreer Somerset in 1930. Growth up to 6 m. Some scent. Parentage: (*R. wichuraiana* × 'Safrano') × 'Souvenir du President Carnot' (Van Fleet 1910).

Schoolgirl A Hybrid Tea climber raised by McGredy in 1964. Growth up to 4 m. Repeat flowering. Some scent. Parentage: 'Coral Dawn' × 'Belle Blonde'.

Maigold A large-flowered climber raised by Kordes 1953. Growth up to 6 m. Once-flowering. Good scent. Parentage: 'Poulsen's Pink' × 'Frühlingstag' (a *R. pimpinellifolia* hybrid).

Coral Dawn A large-flowered climber raised by Boerner in 1952. Growth up to 3 m. Little scent. Repeat flowering. Parentage: 'New Dawn' seedling × (HT × polyantha seedling).

Clair Matin (Meimont) A climbing sport of the Floribunda, introduced by Meilland 1963. Growth up to 3 m. Repeat flowering. Little scent. Parentage: 'Fashion' × [('Independence' × 'Orange Triumph') × 'Phyllis Bide.'].

Meg

White Cockade

Danse des Sylphes

Golden Jubilee

Breath of Life

Sutter's Gold

Sympathie

May Queen

Copenhagen

Elizabeth Harkness

17th July, from R. Harkness & Co.

Mme Caroline Testout

Meg A Floribunda climber raised by Gosset in 1954. Growth to 4 m. Once flowering. Some scent. Parentage: 'Paul's Lemon Pillar' ×? 'Mme Butterfly'.

White Cockade A Floribunda climber raised by Cocker in 1968. Growth up to 3 m. Repeat flowering. Some scent. Parentage: 'New Dawn' × 'Circus'.

Danse des Sylphes A Floribunda Climber raised by Mallerin in 1959. Growth up to 5 m. Repeat flowering. Little scent. Parentage: 'Danse du Feu' × ('Peace' × 'Independence').

Golden Jubilee (Cocagold) A Hybrid Tea raised by Cocker in 1981. Little scent. Parentage: not recorded.

Breath of Life (Harquanne) A Hybrid Tea climber raised by Harkness in 1982. Growth up to 2.3 m. Repeat flowering. Some scent. Parentage: 'Red Dandy' × 'Alexander'.

Sutter's Gold A climbing sport of 'Sutter's Gold' a Hybrid Tea raised by Swim in 1950. Growth to 4 m. Once flowering. Good scent. Parentage: 'Charlotte Armstrong' × 'Signora'.

Sympathie A Kordesii climber raised by Kordes in 1964. Growth up to 4 m. Repeat flowering. Little scent. Parentage: 'Wilhelm Hausmann' × 'Don Juan'.

May Queen A rambler raised by Manda in America in 1898. Growth up to 5 m. Good scent. Once flowering. The flowers become tinged with mauve as they mature. Very free flowering and tolerant of cold sites. Parentage: *R. wichuraiana* × 'Champion of the World'.

Copenhagen A Hybrid Tea climber raised by Poulsen in 1964. Growth up to 2.3 m. Some scent. Repeat flowering. Parentage: seedling × 'Ena Harkness'.

Elizabeth Harkness climbing A sport of 'Elizabeth Harkness' introduced by Harkness in 1975. Growth up to 3 m. Repeat flowering. Some scent. Parentage: 'Red Dandy' × 'Piccadilly' (Harkness 1969).

Mme. Caroline Testout climbing A climbing sport of the Hybrid Tea 'Mme Caroline Testout' introduced by Chauvry in 1901. Growth up to 6 m. Little scent. Once flowering with some further flowers. Parentage: 'Madame de Tartas' × 'Lady Mary Fitzwilliam' (Pernet-Ducher 1890).

Alexander Girault A large-flowered rambler raised by Barbier in 1909. Growth up to 6 m. Good scent, of apples. Once flowering. Parentage: *R. wichuraiana* × 'Papa Gontier'.

Alexander Girault

Alchymist in an apple tree at Sissinghurst Castle

Alchymist

Alchymist A climber raised by Kordes in 1956. Growth up to 4 m. Young leaves bronze. Once flowering. Good scent. Parentage: 'Golden Glow' × *R. rubiginosa* hybrid.

Easlea's Golden Rambler A Floribunda climber raised by Easlea in 1932. Growth up to 5 m. Once flowering. Good scent. Leaves dark green, glossy. Parentage: not recorded.

Emily Gray A large-flowered rambler raised by Williams in 1918. Growth up to 6 m. Once flowering with occasional later flowers. Good scent. Very glossy leaves, reddish when young. Parentage: 'Jersey Beauty' × 'Comtesse du Cayla'. Not very hardy as its parentage (Tea × *R. wichuraiana*) × China would suggest.

Lawrence Johnston A large-flowered climber raised in 1923 by Pernet-Duchet. Growth up to 10 m. Flowers produced intermittently after the main flush. Very good scent. Parentage: 'Madame Eugene Verdier' × *R. foetida* 'Persiana'. Graham Thomas was responsible for introducing this rose and he describes how it was first rejected by Pernet-Ducher in favour of its sister seedling 'Le Rêve' until seen and bought by Lawrence Johnston who planted it at Hidcote. In 1948 Mr Thomas exhibited it at the Royal Horticultural Society under the name 'Lawrence Johnston'.

Auguste Gervais A large-flowered rambler raised by Barbier in 1918. Growth up to 6 m. Once flowering but with a few flowers through the summer. Good scent. Parentage: *R. wichuraiana* × 'Le Progrès', a yellow Hybrid Tea.

Leontine Gervais A large-flowered rambler raised by Barbier in 1903. Growth up to 7 m. Once flowering. Good scent. Parentage: *R. wichuraiana* × 'Souvenir de Catherine Guillot'.

Paul Transon A large-flowered rambler raised by Barbier in 1901. Growth up to 5 m. Good scent, of apples. Once flowering, but with regular later flowers. Parentage: *R. wichuraiana* × 'l'Idéal'.

Elegance A Hybrid Tea climber raised by Brownell in 1937. Growth up to 6 m. Once flowering. Little scent. Parentage: 'Glenn Dale' × ('Mary Wallace' × 'Miss Lolita Armour').

Leontine Gervais

Lawrence Johnston

Easlea's Golden Rambler

Auguste Gervais

Paul Transon

Emily Gray

Elegance

Galway Bay

White Cockade

Autumn Sunlight

Sympathie

Iceberg

Swan Lake

Guinée

Ena Harkness

Casino

Pink Perpetué

June 20th from Eccleston Sq., London

Galway Bay A Floribunda climber raised by McGredy in 1966. Growth up to 3 m. Repeat flowering. Little scent. Parentage: 'Heidelberg' × 'Queen Elizabeth'.

White Cockade A Floribunda climber raised by Cocker in 1968. Growth up to 3 m. Repeat flowering. Some scent. Parentage: 'New Dawn' × 'Circus'.

Autumn Sunlight A Floribunda climber raised by Gregory in 1965. Growth up to 4.5 m. Repeat flowering. Some scent. Parentage: 'Danse du Feu' × climbing 'Goldilocks'.

Sympathie A Kordesii climber raised by Kordes in 1964. Growth up to 4 m. Repeat flowering. Little scent. Parentage: 'Wilhelm Hausmann' × 'Don Juan'.

Iceberg climbing A climbing sport of 'Iceberg', introduced by Cants in 1968. Growth up to 5 m. Repeat flowering. Little scent. A wonderful rose when well grown and trained as can be seen in the accompanying picture.

Swan Lake (Schwanensee) A Hybrid Tea climber raised by McGredy in 1968. Growth up to 3 m. Repeat flowering. Little scent. Susceptible to blackspot. Parentage: 'Memoriam' × 'Heidelberg'.

Guinée A Hybrid Tea climber raised by Mallerin in 1938. Growth up to 5 m. A few flowers through the summer, after the first crop. Excellent scent. This is the darkest red of all roses and can appear almost black. Parentage 'Souvenir de Claudius Denoyel' × 'Ami Quinard'.

Ena Harkness climbing A climbing sport of 'Ena Harkness' introduced by Murrell in 1954. Growth up to 3.5 m. Some scent. Repeat flowering.

Casino (Gerbe d'Or) A Hybrid Tea climber raised by McGredy in 1963. Growth up to 3 m. Repeat flowering. Little scent. Parentage: 'Coral Dawn' × 'Buccaneer'.

Pink Perpetué A Floribunda climber raised by Gregory in 1965. Growth up to 3 m. Repeat flowering. Little scent. Parentage: 'Danse du Feu' × 'New Dawn'.

Joseph's Coat A tall Floribunda which can be trained as a climber, raised by Armstrong in 1964. Growth up to 2.5 m. Repeat flowering. Little scent. Parentage: 'Buccaneer' × 'Circus'.

Étude A Floribunda climber raised by Gregory in 1965. Growth up to 4 m. Repeat flowering. Little scent. Parentage: 'Danse du Feu' × 'New Dawn'.

Étoile de Hollande climbing A climbing sport of the Hybrid Tea 'Étoile de Hollande' introduced by Leenders in 1931. Growth up to 4 m. Repeat flowering. Very good scent. Parentage: 'General MacArthur' × 'Hadley' (1919).

Crêpe de Chine (Deltrop) A Hybrid Tea raised by Delbard in 1970. Parentage: not recorded.

Climbing Iceberg at Cheverell Mill, Wiltshire

Joseph's Coat

Étude

Étoile de Hollande

Crêpe de Chine

R. × rugotida

R. rugosa on dunes by the sea of Okhots in northern Japan

Mrs Anthony Waterer

Rosa rugosa Thunb.　Native of eastern Siberia, northern China, Korea and Japan. It has very prickly stems, leaves with the veins impressed so as to give a wrinkled appearance (*rugosa* = wrinkled), and very fragrant flowers which are produced throughout summer and autumn. Bright red hips are freely produced, often at the same time as the flowers. It is shown here growing wild on sand dunes along the shore of the Sea of Okhotsk, in the north-east of Hokkaido, Japan. It is therefore not surprising that it is found naturalized on similar coastal dunes around the British Isles, from Sandwich Bay in Kent to the north of Scotland. It is also naturalized throughout northern and eastern Europe. Its tolerance of salt winds makes *R. rugosa* and its cultivars a popular plant for hedging in seaside areas.

Rose rugosa Alba　This white form of *R. rugosa* is a strong growing bush, and is particularly notable for its large, shiny, orange-red hips, which appear in late summer making an attractive contrast to the flowers that remain. It can grow up to 2 m in height and width.

Rosa × rugotida　This is a hybrid between *R. rugosa* and the American species *R. nitida*. It makes a low, spreading bush and has the shiny leaves characteristic of *R. nitida*.

Souvenir de Philemon Cochet　A hybrid Rugosa introduced by Cochet-Cochet in 1899. It occurred as a sport of 'Blanc Double de Coubert' (q.v.) and is similar to it, although, as

can be seen from the illustrations, this one has more petals. Height up to 1.5 m.

Nova Zembla　This hybrid Rugosa was introduced by Mees in 1907, having occurred as a sport on 'Conrad F. Meyer' to which it is very similar. It produces a particularly good display of fragrant flowers in late summer or early autumn and grows up to 3 m. Susceptible to rust.

Hollandica　This hybrid Rugosa was used principally as an understock on to which other roses were budded, but, in spite of its great height (up to 2.5 m) and somewhat lanky growth, it is attractive in its own right and is suitable for planting in a hedge or in the wild garden. As the name suggests, it probably originated in Holland, being used by nurserymen there and exported to other countries. It suckers freely and when seen in gardens may not have been deliberately planted.

Mrs Anthony Waterer　This hybrid Rugosa was raised by Waterer in 1898, and makes a fine sight in early summer, when it is covered with fragrant flowers. She seems to exhaust herself with the effort and seldom produces such a good crop in the autumn. Height up to about 1.5 m. Spreading habit. Parentage: Général Jacqueminot' × *R. rugosa* hybrid.

Delicata　A hybrid Rugosa introduced by Cooling in 1898. The beautiful flowers are its best feature as it is not a very strong grower and

can also be difficult to propagate. Height up to about 1 m.

Blanc Double de Coubert　This is one of the most popular of the hybrid Rugosas, and deservedly so, due to its attractive, very fragrant, recurrent blooms. Introduced by Cochet-Cochet in 1892, it usually grows somewhat taller than *R. rugosa* (up to 2 m) but is a little less dense. Parentage: *R. rugosa* × 'Sombreuil' (or sport from *R. rugosa* 'Alba'?).

Paulii Rosea　A hybrid between *R. rugosa* and *R. arvensis* raised by Paul before 1912. It makes a mound of prostrate shoots which may be 4 m long and are very thorny. Once flowering, with the flowers sweetly scented, of cloves, and with characteristic notched, half-folded petals.

Max Graf　A hybrid between *R. rugosa* and *R. wichuraiana* raised by Bowditch in 1919. It makes a dense ground cover of trailing shoots, with shining bright green leaves. Once flowering, but over a long season and with occasional autumn flowers. Good scent, of apples. 'Lady Duncan' is another hybrid of the same parentage. In cultivation at Kordes nursery in Germany, the sterile 'Max Graf' produced, after many failures, three seedlings, one of which proved to be a tetraploid and was, therefore, a new fertile species, *R. kordesii*, the parent of many recent hybrids.

R. rugosa 'Alba'

Delicata

Souvenir de Philemon Cochet

Hollandica

Blanc Double de Coubert

Nova Zembla

Paulii Rosea

Max Graf

F. J. Grootendorst

Pink Grootendorst

Conrad Ferdinand Meyer

Schneezwerg

Fru Dagmar Hastrup

Roseraie de l'Haÿ

Nyveldt's White

Sarah van Fleet

R. rugosa 'Scabrosa'

July 10th, from Wisley

Belle Poiterine

White Grootendorst

Fimbriata

Lady Curzon

Agnes

F. J. Grootendorst A Rugosa hybrid raised by De Goey in 1918. A vigorous, thorny bush, it bears flowers throughout summer and autumn, although these are unfortunately scentless. Height 2–3 m. Parentage: *R. rugosa* 'Rubra' × 'Mme Norbert Levavasseur'.

Pink Grootendorst This Rugosa hybrid occurred as a sport of 'F. J. Grootendorst' and, like that rose, has no scent; it was raised by Grootendorst in 1923. The flower colour is variable, sometimes reverting to a rather darker pink.

Conrad Ferdinand Meyer This hybrid Rugosa was raised by Müller in 1899. A vigorous, thorny plant, it produces a large number of blooms in early summer and in September. Very fragrant. Height up to about 3 m. Parentage: ('Gloire de Dijon' × 'Duc de Rohan') × *R. rugosa* 'Germanica'.

Schneezwerg (Snow Dwarf) A hybrid Rugosa raised by Lambert in 1912. The dense growth of this bush makes it suitable for use as a hedging plant. The flowers are produced repeatedly throughout summer and autumn, the hips appearing at the same time as the later blooms. Height up to 2–5 m. Parentage: *R. rugosa* × *R. bracteata*

Fru Dagmar Hastrup (Frau Dagmar Hartopp) This seedling from *R. rugosa* was raised by Hastrup in 1914. It is suitable for hedging because of its very compact growth, and it bears

attractive bright red hips throughout summer and autumn. Height up to 2 m.

Roseraie de l'Haÿ This Rugosa rose was raised by the passionate rosarian Jules Gravereaux in 1910, and named after the rose garden created by him just south of Paris. The garden still thrives today, with a collection of over three thousand rose varieties. The rose itself is very thorny and makes a dense bush. Height up to 2 m. Parentage:? sport of *R. rugosa*

Nyveldt's White This Rugosa hybrid was raised by Nyveldt in 1955. It makes a large shrub up to 2 m and is suitable for hedging. It has a sweet scent and flowers repeatedly. Parentage: (*R. rugosa* × *R. majalis*) × *R. nitida*.

R. rugosa 'Scabrosa' This form of *R. rugosa* was known prior to 1940 but its origins are unknown. It is very like *R. rugosa*, but tends to be more vigorous, with larger leaves, flowers and hips. It is fragrant and flowers recurrently. Height up to about 2 m.

Sarah van Fleet This hybrid Rugosa was raised by Dr W. van Fleet in 1926. It is tall (up to 3 m), very prickly and often rather bare of foliage at the base. The flowers are produced continuously through summer and autumn and are fragrant. Parentage: *R. rugosa* × 'My Maryland'.

Fimbriata (Phoebe's Frilled Pink, Dianthiflora) This Rugosa hybrid was raised by Morlet in

1891. It makes a largish bush (up to 2 m high) with arching prickly shoots and flowers best in slightly cooler areas. It is sweetly scented and flowers recurrently. Parentage: *R. rugosa* × 'Mme Alfred Carrière'.

Lady Curzon A Rugosa hybrid raised by Turner in 1901. This vigorous, prickly shrub can grow up to about 3 m and can be used to good effect as ground cover or as a climber. The flowers are produced prolifically for a few weeks and are sweetly scented. Parentage: *R. rugosa* × 'Macrantha'.

Belle Poiterine The parentage of this Rugosa hybrid is obscure but it was raised by Bruant in 1894. In addition to its attractive flowers it produces attractively coloured autumn foliage and bright hips. Recurrent flowering. Height up to 2 m.

Agnes A Rugosa hybrid raised by Dr W. Saunders of Ottawa in 1922. It has a graceful habit, with very thorny stems and produces large numbers of heavily scented flowers in early summer, with a second flush later on. Height up to 2 m. Parentage: *R. rugosa* × *R. foetida* 'Persiana'.

White Grootendorst A white sport of 'Grootendorst' introduced by Eddy in 1962. Said to be scented, unlike the other Grootendorst roses.

Andersonii

Golden Wings

Lord Penzance

Frühlingszauber

Lady Penzance

Nevada

Greenmantle

Frühlingsmorgen

Scharlachglut

July 10th, from Wisley

Nevada

Frühlingsgold

Golden Wings

Marguerite Hilling

Andersonii This is a hybrid of *R. canina*, the common Dog Rose, and the resemblance to its parent can be easily seen. The flowers, however, are larger and more brightly coloured; they are sweetly scented. Showy hips are produced in autumn. 'Andersonii' makes a bush which is wider than high, about 2 × 2.8 m.

Golden Wings A hybrid of *R. pimpinellifolia* raised by Shepherd in 1956, this is a compact (up to 2 m tall) bush which produces its sweetly scented flowers almost continuously throughout the season. Parentage: 'Sœur Thérèse' × *R. pimpinellifolia* 'Grandiflora' × 'Ormiston Roy').

Lord Penzance This hybrid of *R. rubiginosa*, introduced in 1894, is named after Lord Penzance, who raised a number of hybrids. The flowers and foliage are sweetly scented. Parentage: *R. rubiginosa* × 'Harrison's Yellow'.

Frühlingszauber A hybrid of *R. pimpinellifolia* 'Grandiflora' raised by Kordes in 1942. It has the same parentage as 'Frühlingsmorgen' (q.v.) but is not normally so vigorous, although it grows up to 2 m. Parentage: ('E. G. Hill' × 'Catherine Kordes') × *R. pimpinellifolia* 'Grandiflora'.

Lady Penzance This *rubiginosa* hybrid was raised by Lord Penzance in 1894. The flowers are scented and the foliage is slightly fragrant too. Parentage: *R. rubiginosa* × *R. foetida* 'Bicolor'.

Nevada This spectacular rose was raised by Dot in 1927; it is very popular for its dramatic appearance during the summer, when it is usually absolutely covered in flowers. During late summer a smaller number of flowers are produced. These open creamy white, becoming pinkish in hot weather, and fading to almost pure white in dull weather. 'Nevada' makes a large, dense bush, with long arching shoots, and grows up to nearly 3 m high, and as wide. A pink sport 'Marguerite Hilling' (q.v.) has occurred on more than one occasion. Parentage: 'La Giralda' (a Hybrid Tea) × *Rosa? pimpinellofolia*.

Greenmantle A *rubiginosa* hybrid raised by Lord Penzance in 1895. The foliage is slightly aromatic.

'Frühlingsmorgen' A hybrid of *R. pimpinellifolia* 'Grandiflora', this was raised by Kordes in 1941, the same year as 'Frühlingszauber' (q.v.) A popular shrub, it

produces a good display of flowers in spring, followed by another crop in late summer. Height up to 2 m. Parentage: ('E. G. Hill' × 'Catherine Kordes') × *R. pimpinellifolia* 'Grandiflora'.

Scharlachglut (Scarlet Fire) A Gallica hybrid raised by Kordes in 1952, which makes a vigorous shrub. The flowers are produced over a long period, and the scarlet hips last throughout the winter. Height up to 2–8 m. Parentage: *R. gallica* form × 'Poinsettia'.

Frühlingsgold (Spring Gold) A *R. pimpinellifolia* hybrid raised by Kordes in 1937 and still extremely popular. It makes a wide, tall (up to 2.5 m) bush, which thrives in any soil and produces sweetly scented blooms during the early summer, with occasionally a second crop in autumn. Parentage: 'Joanna Hill' × *R. pimpinellifolia* 'Hispida'.

Marguerite Hilling A sport from 'Nevada' (q.v.), which has occurred several times in different places. It was introduced by Hilling in 1959. There is still a plant at the entrance to Hillings Nursery in Chobham, Surrey.

Janet's Pride

La Belle Distinguée

R. rubiginosa

Manning's Blush

July 3rd, from Mottisfont

Janet's Pride (Clementine)   This *rubiginosa* hybrid was introduced in 1892 by W. Paul and Sons. The foliage is slightly aromatic, and the stems are less thorny than *rubiginosa*. Height up to 2 m. Parentage:? *R. damascena* × *R. rubiginosa*.

La Belle Distinguée (La Petite Duchesse, Lee's Duchess)   The origins of the 'Double Scarlet Sweetbriar' are obscure, although it is probably a hybrid. Height up to 1.3 m. Non-recurrent. Parentage: *R. eglanteria* × seedling.

Manning's Blush   A hybrid of *R. rubiginosa*, this beautiful old variety has been grown at least since 1797. It makes a dense compact bush, up to 1.6 m. The colour of the flowers fades with age. Parentage: unrecorded.

Rosa rubiginosa (*R. eglanteria*, Eglantine, Sweetbriar)   A native of the British Isles and Europe from southern Scandinavia and Spain eastwards to the Caucasus and western Asia; naturalized in north America. It is usually found on limey soils, especially on chalk downs. Its downland habitat and associated species, although transported to Greece, were perfectly described by Shakespeare in 1594. '. . . a bank whereon the wild thyme blows, Where oxlips and the nodding violet grows/Quite over-canopied with luscious woodbine/With sweet musk-roses, and with eglantine:' (musk roses here = *R. arvensis*). The sweet scent is produced mainly by glands on the underside of the leaves, but also by the flowers. In the garden it makes a shrub up to 2.5 m, with arching branches. The bright red hips last well into the winter. The specimen shown here is a particularly brightly coloured garden form.

Stanwell Perpetual   A *pimpinellifolia* hybrid, this occurred as a chance seedling and was introduced by Lee in 1838. As the name implies, it is perpetual flowering, with its peak in midsummer. Sweetly scented. Height up to 1.6 m. Parentage: *R. damascena* × *R. pimpinellifolia*.

Abbotswood   A seedling of *R. canina*, that occurred at Abbotswood, Gloucestershire, in the 1950s. The head gardener there brought it to the attention of Graham Thomas who named and distributed it. Sweetly scented flowers followed by fine hips. Height up to 2 m.

Cerise Bouquet   A shrub rose introduced by Kordes in 1958. The flowers are sweetly scented and flower in summer and, less freely, in autumn. Height up to 3.3 m. Parentage: *R. multibracteata* × 'Crimson Glory' (an HT).

Fritz Nobis

Raubritter at Mottisfont

Raubritter

Cerise Bouquet at Cheverell Mill, Wilts

Raubritter A low-growing, rather sprawling shrub introduced by Kordes in 1936. The attractive flowers are borne for several weeks during midsummer when the plant is almost smothered, but there is no autumn crop. Susceptible to mildew. Height up to 1 m, and twice as wide. Parentage: 'Macrantha Daisy Hill' × 'Solarium' (a Rambler).

Fritz Nobis A shrub rose introduced by Kordes in 1940. It is vigorous, making a fine bush up to 2 m high, with one magnificent display of flowers in early summer. Good scent. Parentage: 'Joanna Hill' (an HT) × 'Magnifica' (a *R. rubiginosa* seedling).

Abbotswood

Stanwell Perpetual

Ground cover roses at Wisley

Rosy Cushion (Interall)   This bushy shrub, which is useful for ground-covering purposes, was raised by Ilsink in 1979. Height up to 1 m. Parentage: 'Yesterday' × unknown.

Macrantha   This spreading, vigorous shrub has arching, thorny stems on which the sweetly scented flowers are borne in clusters. The blooms open a pale pink, fading to white, as in this photograph. Height up to 3 m. The origins of R. 'Macrantha' are obscure, but it is thought by some to be a seedling of a garden hybrid descended from R. gallica, or possibly R. gallica × R. alba.

Little White Pet (White Pet)   This dwarf perpetual flowering rose, seen here grown as a standard, is a sport of 'Félicité et Perpétue' and was introduced by Henderson in 1970. The flowers are freely produced from midsummer to autumn. Height up to 80 cm.

Euphrates   This unusual hybrid of R. persica was raised by Harkness in 1986. The flowers are borne freely for several weeks during the summer. A low, spreading, bushy plant up to 60 cm high. Parentage: R. persica × unknown.

Chianti   A Shrub rose raised by Austin in 1965. The flowers are fragrant and the colour changes with age to a rich purple; once flowering. Neat habit. Height up to 1.8 m. Parentage: 'Macrantha' × 'Vanity'.

Sea Foam   Raised by Schwartz in 1964, this trailing, semi-prostrate shrub flowers freely throughout the season. Parentage: [('White Dawn' × 'Pinocchio') × ('White Dawn' × 'Pinocchio')] × ('White Dawn' × 'Pinocchio').

Macrantha Daisy Hill   Raised by Smith in Ireland around 1900 and much used by Kordes in his breeding programme. A vigorous grower, it makes a dense shrub wider than high (1.6 × 3.6 m), with arching branches. The well-scented flowers are followed by round hips. Parentage: derived from R. 'Macrantha', (see above).

Cameo   A dwarf Polyantha (height up to 45 cm), raised by De Ruiter in 1932. Repeat flowering, susceptible to mildew. Parentage: sport of 'Orléans Rose'.

Rosy Cushion

Euphrates

Chianti

Cameo

Little White Pet grown as a standard

Sea Foam

Macrantha

Macrantha Daisy Hill

La Sevillana

Pink La Sevillana

Tall Story

Candy Rose

Fiona

Cardinal Hume

Red Blanket

Pink Wave

Save the Children

John Franklin

Champlain

July 18th, from Wisley

Sally Holmes
Anna Zinkeisen
Butterfly Wings
Pearl Drift
Jacquenetta
Rachel Bowes Lyon

July 16th, from Wisley

Fiona

Red Blanket

La Sevillana (Meigekanu)   This Floribunda was introduced by Meilland in 1982. Parentage: [('Meibrim' × 'Jolie Madame') × ('Meialfi' × 'Zambra')] × [('Super Star' × 'Super Star') × ('Meilena' × 'Rusticana')].

Pink La Sevillana (Meigeroka)   A dwarf Floribunda, useful for ground cover, introduced by Meilland in 1985. Parentage: sport of 'La Sevillana'.

Tall Story (Dickooky)   A Shrub Rose introduced by Dickson in 1984. Parentage: not available.

Candy Rose (Meiranovi)   This shrub, which is useful for ground cover, was introduced by Meilland in 1980. Unscented. Parentage: (*R. sempervirens* × 'Mlle Marthe Carron') × seedling.

Cardinal Hume (Harregale)   A low, spreading Shrub Rose, introduced by Harkness in 1984 and named after the present Archbishop of Westminster. The flowers have a slightly musky fragrance. Height up to 1 m. Parentage: seedling × 'Frank Naylor'.

Fiona (Meibeluxen)   A shrub suitable for ground cover, which was introduced by Meilland in 1979. Parentage: 'Sea Foam' × 'Picasso'.

Red Blanket (Intercell)   Useful as ground cover, this shrub was introduced by Dickson in 1979. Height up to almost 1 m. Parentage: 'Yesterday' × unknown seedling.

Pink Wave (Mattgro)   A ground-covering shrub introduced by Mattock in 1983. The prostrate growth extends to about 1 m across, and the flowers are borne throughout the season. Parentage: not available.

Save the Children (Hartred)   This compact (up to 45 cm), bushy Floribunda was introduced by Harkness in 1986. It is named after the Save the Children Fund. Parentage: 'Amy Brown' × 'Red Sprite'.

John Franklin   A shrub introduced by Svejda in 1980. Parentage: 'Marlena' × seedling.

Champlain   A Kordesii hybrid, introduced by Svejda in 1982. Parentage: unnamed seedlings.

Sally Holmes   A modern, repeat-flowering Hybrid Musk introduced by Holmes in 1976. The flowers are borne on tall-growing shoots up to 1.3 m. Parentage: 'Ivory Fashion' × 'Ballerina'.

Anna Zinkeisen (Harquhling)   A Shrub Rose introduced by Harkness in 1983. The flowers have a musky fragrance. Height up to 1.3 m.

Parentage: [(('Chinatown' × 'Golden Masterpiece') × ('Super Star' × 'Piccadilly')) × ('Cläre Grammerstorf' × 'Frühlingsmorgen')] × 'Frank Naylor'.

Butterfly Wings   A Floribunda introduced by Gobbee in 1976. Repeat flowering. Height up to 1.3 m. Susceptible to blackspot. Parentage: 'Dainty Maid' × 'Peace'.

Pearl Drift (Leggab)   A *bracteata* hybrid Shrub Rose introduced by Le Grice in 1980. Produces blooms early and throughout the season. The bushy growth is compact, rather wider (1.3 m) than high (1 m). Parentage: 'Mermaid' × 'New Dawn'.

Jaquenetta   A single-flowered English Rose raised by Austin in 1983. Very floriferous over a long period. Height up to 1.3 m. Parentage: seedling × 'Charles Austin'.

Rachel Bowes Lyon (Harlacal)   A Shrub Rose introduced by Harkness in 1981 and bred from *R. californica*. Height up to 1.8 m. Parentage: 'Kim' × [('Orange Sensation' × 'Allgold') × 'California'].

Fairy Damsel

Ice Fairy

Fairy Prince

Fairy Changeling

International Herald Tribune

Langford Light

Grouse

Red Bells

White Bells

Pink Bells

John Cabot

William Baffin

July 18th, from Wisley

Nozomi

Fairy Damsel (Harneatly) A Polyantha suitable for ground cover, raised by Harkness in 1982. Height up to 45 cm. Free flowering. Parentage: not available.

Ice Fairy (Sanmed) A Shrub Rose, raised by Sanday in 1984. Parentage: not available.

Fairy Prince (Harnougette) A Polyantha suitable for ground cover, raised by Harkness in 1979. Vigorous, spreading growth up to 80 cm. Parentage: 'The Fairy' × 'Yesterday'.

Fairy Changeling (Harnumerous) A Polyantha raised by Harkness in 1979. Dwarf, bushy growth makes a cushion up to 45 cm high. Parentage: 'The Fairy' × 'Yesterday'.

International Herald Tribune (Harquantum, Viorita) A Floribunda raised by Harkness in 1984. Floriferous, with scent in humid weather. Neat, compact growth up to 60 cm. Parentage: not available.

Grouse (Immensee, Kordes' Rose Immensee, Korimro) A dwarf shrub suitable for ground cover raised by Kordes in 1982. Strongly scented. Parentage: 'The Fairy' × *R. wichuraiana* seedling.

Langford Light (Lannie) A Floribunda suitable for ground cover raised by Sealand in 1984. Parentage: not available.

White Bells (Poulwhite) A ground-covering shrub raised by Poulsen in 1980. Parentage: not available.

Pink Bells (Poulbells) A miniature raised by Poulsen in 1983. Parentage: not available.

Red Bells (Poulred) A miniature raised by Poulsen in 1983. Parentage: not available.

John Cabot A Kordesii hybrid raised by Svejda in 1978. This vigorous climber blooms freely. Parentage: *R. kordesii* × unnamed seedling.

William Baffin A Kordesii hybrid raised by Svejda in 1983. Flowers produced repeatedly from early summer to early autumn. Resistant to blackspot and mildew; hardy in cold areas. Parentage: *R. kordesii* × seedling.

Nozomi A miniature climbing rose raised by Onodera in 1968. Very useful for ground cover or the top of a low wall (as illustrated); it can also be grown as a weeping standard. Height up to 45 cm. Parentage: 'Fairy Princess' × 'Sweet Fairy'.

Fairyland (Harlayalong) A Polyantha raised by Harkness in 1979. Spreading habit, up to 80 cm high. Repeat flowering. Parentage: 'The Fairy' × 'Yesterday'.

Dentelle de Malines (Lens Pink) A Shrub Rose raised by Lens and introduced by David Austin in 1983. Graceful arching, spreading growth up to 1.3 m high and more wide. Parentage: not available.

Fairyland

Dentelle de Malines

Simon Robinson

Nikki

Marjorie Fair

Rebecca Claire

News

Sir Lancelot

Chorus Girl

Smarty

Grace Abounding

Lysbeth-Victoria

July 16th, from The Gardens of the Rose

Simon Robinson (Trobwich)   A shrub raised by Robinson in 1982. Parentage: *R. wichuraiana* × 'New Penny'.

Nikki   A Floribunda raised by Bracegirdle in 1981. Bushy growth. Parentage: 'Dusky Maiden' × 'Eye Paint'.

Marjorie Fair (Harhero, Red Ballerina, Red Yesterday)   A Polyantha raised by Harkness in 1978. Repeat flowering. Height up to 1.3 m. Parentage: 'Ballerina' × 'Baby Faurax'.

Rebecca Claire   A Hybrid Tea, raised by Law in 1981. Free flowering. Scented. Upright growth to 1 m. Parentage: 'Blessings' × 'Redgold'

Sir Lancelot   A Floribunda raised by Harkness in 1967. Susceptible to mildew and blackspot. Bushy growth up to 1 m. Parentage: 'Vera Dalton' × 'Woburn Abbey'.

Chorus Girl   A Floribunda raised by Robinson in 1970. Free flowering with a lax habit of growth. Parentage: 'Highlight' × seedling.

News (Legnews)   A Floribunda raised by Le Grice in 1968. Bushy growth up to 1 m. Parentage: 'Lilac Charm' × 'Tuscany Superb'.

Smarty (Intersmart)   A shrub useful for ground cover raised by Ilsink in 1979. Free flowering. Parentage: 'Yesterday' × unknown.

Grace Abounding   A Floribunda raised by Harkness in 1968. Bushy growth. Height up to 1.3 m. Parentage: 'Pink Parfait' × 'Penelope'.

Lysbeth-Victoria   A Floribunda raised by Harkness in 1978. Upright growth, to 1.3 m. Parentage: 'Pink Parfait' × 'Nevada'.

Leverkusen   A Kordesii hybrid raised by Kordes in 1954. Although chiefly known as a climber, this can also be grown as a shrub. It is very hardy and tends to produce one good main crop of flowers, followed by a lesser display later on. Height up to 3 m. Parentage: *R. kordesii* × 'Golden Glow'.

Parkdirektor Riggers   This popular hybrid climber was raised by Kordes in 1957. Repeat flowering. Height up to 4 m. Parentage: *R. kordesii* × 'Our Princess'.

Raymond Chenault   A Kordesii hybrid raised by Kordes in 1960. Vigorous and free flowering. Parentage: *R. kordesii* × 'Montezuma'.

Dortmund   A Kordesii hybrid raised by Kordes in 1955. Repeat flowering. Height up to 2.5 m. Parentage: seedling × *R. kordesii*.

Robusta (Korgosa, Kordes' Rose Robusta)   A shrub raised by Kordes in 1979. Repeat flowering. Wide, bushy growth. Height up to 1.5 m. Parentage *R. rugosa* × seedling.

Raymond Chenault

Leverkusen

Dortmund

Robusta

Parkdirektor Riggers

Simon Robinson

Admired Miranda

Prospero

Red Mary Rose

Gertrude Jekyll

The Squire

Warwick Castle

Sir Clough

Wenlock

Hilda Murrell

July 18th, from David Austin Roses

Charmian

Mary Rose

The Knight

Redcoat

The Yeoman

The Friar

Prospero (Auspero)   An English Rose raised by Austin in 1982, grown for its beautiful scented flowers rather than for overall effect. The rich crimson petals turn to purple with age. Height up to 60 cm. Parentage: 'The Knight' × seedling.

Admired Miranda (Ausmira)   An English Rose raised by Austin in 1982. The habit is similar to a Hybrid Tea and not vigorous. Very fragrant. Height up to 1 m. Parentage: 'The Friar' × 'The Friar'.

Red Mary Rose   A red sport of 'Mary Rose' (q.v.) a vigorous shrub with a long flowering season and marvellous scent. Raised by Austin in 1987. Height up to 1.3 m.

Gertrude Jekyll   An English Rose raised by Austin in 1986. By back-crossing an English rose with 'Comte de Chambord', an Old Portland rose, a new variety with old-fashioned characteristics, notably a strong scent, has been obtained. Rather lanky; height up to 1.6 m.

The Squire   An English Rose raised by Austin in 1977. Vigorous but rather sparse habit. Not particularly free flowering. Good scent. Height up to 1 m. Parentage: 'The Knight' × 'Château de Clos Vougeot'.

Warwick Castle   An English Rose raised by Austin in 1986, this is a seedling of 'Lilian Austin' and is similar to that rose, although the sweetly scented blooms have a more 'old-fashioned' appearance. Hardy and generally disease resistant. Height up to 90 cm.

Sir Clough   A semi-double English Rose raised by Austin in 1983, and named after Sir Clough Williams-Ellis, architect and creator of Portmeirion. Height up to 1.6 m. Parentage: 'Chaucer' × 'Conrad F. Meyer'.

Wenlock (Auswen)   An English Rose raised by Austin in 1984. The well-scented flowers are freely produced on this vigorous shrub. Height up to 1.3 m. Parentage: 'The Knight' × 'Glastonbury'.

Hilda Murrell (Ausmurr)   An English Rose raised by Austin in 1984. The majority of the strongly scented flowers are produced during early summer with some later. Vigorous, bushy growth up to 1.3 m. Parentage: seedling × ('Parade' × 'Chaucer').

Charmian (Ausmian)   An English Rose raised by Austin in 1982. Sweetly scented. Arching habit to 1.2 m. Parentage: unnamed seedling × 'Lilian Austin'.

Mary Rose (Ausmary)   An English Rose raised by Austin in 1983 and named to mark the recovery of Henry VIII's flagship from the Solent. The sweetly scented flowers are produced over a long period. Vigorous growth up to 1.3 m. Good resistance to disease. Parentage: seedling × 'The Friar'.

The Knight   An English Rose raised by Austin in 1969. No longer grown by him but available from Lowe's Nursery in New Hampshire. Free flowering, recurrent. Parentage: 'Chianti' × seedling.

Redcoat   An English Rose raised by Austin in 1973. Flowers produced freely over a long period. Disease resistant. Bushy growth up to 1.6 m. Parentage: unnamed seedling × 'Golden Showers'.

The Yeoman   An English Rose raised by Austin in 1969. The compact bush up to 1 m high bears strongly scented blooms. Parentage: 'Ivory Fashion' × ('Constance Spry' × 'Monique').

The Friar   An English Rose raised by Austin in 1969. The heavily scented flowers are produced freely throughout the season. Parentage: 'Ivory Fashion' × seedling.

Chaucer

Bredon

Tamora

Dove

Troilus

Claire Rose

Belle Story

Proud Titania

Lucetta

July 18th, from David Austin Roses

Chaucer An English Rose raised by Austin in 1970. Strongly scented. Vigorous, bushy growth up to 1 m high and across. Parentage: seedling × 'Constance Spry'.

Bredon An English Rose raised by Austin in 1984. Flowers continuously. Height up to 1 m. Parentage: 'Wife of Bath' × 'Lilian Austin'.

Tamora An English Rose raised by Austin in 1983. Strongly scented. Bushy growth up to 1 m. Parentage: 'Chaucer' × 'Conrad F. Meyer'.

Dove (Ausdove) An English Rose raised by Austin in 1984. Spreading growth up to 90 cm high and 1 m across. Parentage: 'Wife of Bath' × 'Iceberg' seedling.

Troilus An English Rose raised by Austin in 1983. The large blooms have a sweet honey-like scent and are produced throughout the season. Strong growth up to 1.3 m. Parentage: seedling crosses.

Claire Rose An English Rose raised by Austin in 1986. Repeat flowering, scented. Height up to 1.3 m. Parentage: 'Charles Austin' × (seedling × 'Iceberg').

Belle Story An English Rose raised by Austin in 1984. Very large, well-scented blooms are produced intermittently throughout the summer. Strong growing, up to 1.3 m. Parentage: ('Chaucer' × 'Parade') × ('The Prioress' × 'Iceberg').

Proud Titania (Austania) An English Rose raised by Austin in 1982. Scented. Vigorous, up to 1.3 m high. Parentage: unnamed seedlings.

Lucetta An English Rose raised by Austin in 1983. The pink flowers fade to almost white; fragrant. Strong, arching growth makes a shrub up to 1.3 m high and across. Can also be used as a climber, when it will reach up to 3 m. Parentage: unknown.

Moonbeam An English Rose raised by Austin in 1983. Free flowering. Vigorous growth up to 1.3 m high. Parentage: unknown.

Wild Flower An English Rose raised by Austin in 1986. The simple flowers recur throughout the summer. Low, spreading growth up to about 45 cm high and about twice as wide. Parentage: 'Lilian Austin' × ('Canterbury' × 'Golden Wings').

Dapple Dawn An English Rose raised by Austin in 1983. Flowers are produced continuously. Height up to 1.6 m. Parentage: sport of 'Red Coat'.

Windrush An English Rose raised by Austin in 1984. The fragrant flowers are produced continuously throughout the season. Vigorous, branching growth up to 1.3 m. Parentage: seedling × ('Canterbury' × 'Golden Wings').

Scintillation A modern shrub rose raised by Austin in 1968, especially useful for ground cover. Well scented. Blooms once only, but for several weeks. Height up to 1.3 m. Parentage: *R.* 'Macrantha' × 'Vanity'.

The Prioress An English Rose raised by Austin in 1969. Scented. Good display of flowers in late summer. Vigorous growth, up to 1.3 m. Parentage: 'La Reine Victoria' × seedling.

Moonbeam

Wild Flower

Windrush

Scintillation

Dapple Dawn

Claire Rose

Chaucer

The Prioress

The Wife of Bath

Fair Bianca

Hero

Cymbelene

Leander

Cressida

Graham Thomas

Pretty Jessica

July 16th, from Wisley

The Wife of Bath An English Rose: raised by Austin in 1969. Repeat flowering, fragrant. Height up to 1 m. Parentage: 'Mme Caroline Testout' × ('Ma Perkins' × 'Constance Spry').

Fair Bianca (Ausca) An English Rose raised by Austin in 1982. Scented. Strong, upright growth, up to 1 m high. Parentage: unrecorded.

Hero (Aushero) An English Rose raised by Austin in 1982. The later flowers tend to be semi-double rather than double. Strongly scented. Strong growth up to 1.3 m. Parentage: 'The Prioress' × unnamed seedling.

Cymbelene (Auslean) An English Rose raised by Austin in 1982. Strongly-scented flowers produced intermittently throughout the summer. Spreading and arching shrub up to 1.3 m high and more wide. Good disease resistance. Parentage: unnamed seedling × 'Lilian Austin'.

Leander (Auslea) An English Rose raised by Austin in 1982 and suitable for growing as a shrub (up to 2 m) or as a climber (up to 4 m). Scented. Vigorous, open growth. Parentage: 'Charles Austin' × seedling.

Cressida A vigorous, thorny English Rose raised by Austin in 1983 and suitable for cultivation as a shrub (up to 1.6 m) or as a climber (up to 4 m). Strongly scented. Parentage: seedling × 'Conrad F. Meyer'.

Graham Thomas An English Rose raised by Austin in 1983, and named after the most influential of the old rose enthusiasts. The strongly tea-scented flowers are produced continuously throughout the season. Vigorous, bushy growth up to 1.3 m high and across. Parentage: 'Charles Austin' × seedling.

Pretty Jessica An English Rose raised by Austin in 1983. Strongly scented flowers produced repeatedly. Compact growth up to 1 m. Parentage: seedling crosses.

Mary Webb (Auswebb) An English Rose raised by Austin in 1984. Repeat-flowering. Scented. Vigorous, bushy growth up to 1.3 m. Parentage: seedling × 'Chinatown'.

Yellow Button An English Rose raised by Austin in 1975. Scented flowers produced intermittently through the summer. Good disease resistance. Height up to 1 m. Parentage: 'Wife of Bath' × 'Chinatown'.

Yellow Charles Austin An English Rose raised by Austin in 1981. Well-scented flowers produced repeatedly if pruned firmly. Height up to 1.6 m. Parentage: sport of 'Charles Austin'.

Allux Symphony An English Rose raised by Austin in 1986. Bushy growth up to 1 m. Parentage: 'The Friar' × seedling.

Charles Austin An English Rose raised by Austin in 1973. The very large blooms have a fruity scent. To obtain repeat-flowering, prune more firmly than usual. Vigorous, bushy growth up to 1.6 m. Parentage: 'Chaucer' × 'Aloha'.

Mary Webb *Yellow Button* *Yellow Charles Austin* *Allux Symphony*

July 18th, from David Austin Roses

Leander

Graham Thomas

Charles Austin

English Garden

Emanuel

The Reeve

Lilian Austin

Sir Walter Raleigh

Abraham Darby

Othello

Wise Portia

Heritage

July 18th, from David Austin Roses

Constance Spry trained on a wall at Mottisfont

Perdita

Ellen

Emanuel   An English Rose raised by Austin in 1985 and named after the dress designers responsible for the Princess of Wales's wedding dress. Free-flowering and sweetly scented. Height up to 1.3 m. Parentage: ('Chaucer' × 'Parade') × (seedling × 'Iceberg').

English Garden   An English Rose raised by Austin in 1986. Free flowering over a long period. Upright growth, up to 1 m. Parentage: 'Lilian Austin' × (seedling × 'Iceberg').

The Reeve   An English Rose raised by Austin in 1979. Strongly scented. A spreading, arching shrub, with prickly stems, up to 1.3 m. Parentage 'Lilian Austin' × 'Chaucer'.

Abraham Darby   An English Rose raised by Austin in 1985 and named after Abraham Darby, one of the leading lights of the Industrial Revolution. As a shrub it grows up to about 1.6 m but its long, arching stems make it suitable also for use as a climber, when it will grow up to about 3 m. Fragrant. Parentage: 'Aloha' × 'Yellow Cushion'.

Lilian Austin   An English Rose raised by Austin in 1973. Free flowering and sweetly scented over a long period. Arching habit, up to 1.3 m. Parentage: 'Aloha' × 'The Yeoman'.

Sir Walter Raleigh   An English Rose raised by Austin in 1985. Larger flowers than many other roses of this type, with a strong fragrance. Dense, bushy growth up to 1.3 m. Parentage: 'Lilian Austin' × 'Chaucer'.

Othello   An English Rose raised by Austin in 1986. The strongly scented flowers are freely produced and turn purple with age. Vigorous, upright, prickly growth up to 1.2 m high. Parentage: 'Lilian Austin' × 'The Squire'.

Heritage   An English Rose raised by Austin in 1984. Repeat flowering with strong, slightly lemony scent. Vigorous, bushy growth up to 1.3 m. Parentage: seedling × 'Iceberg' seedling.

Wise Portia (Ausport)   An English Rose raised by Austin in 1982. Strongly scented. Height up to 1 m. Parentage: 'The Knight' × seedling.

Constance Spry   The first of the English Roses, raised by Austin in 1961. The large, very fragrant flowers are produced only once, in midsummer, when the display is spectacular. The open, arching growth is suited to growing as a shrub (up to 2 m tall and wide) or a climber (up to 5 m high). Parentage: 'Belle Isis' (a Gallica) × 'Dainty Maid' (a Floribunda).

Ellen (Auscup)   An English Rose raised by Austin in 1984. Strongly scented. Vigorous, bushy shrub up to 1.3 m. Parentage: unknown.

Perdita   A strongly scented English Rose raised by Austin in 1983. Repeat flowering. Vigorous, bushy growth up to 1.2 m. Disease resistant. Parentage: seedling crosses.

Souvenir de Claudius Denoyel

Michèle Meilland

Shot Silk

Westfield Star

Mme Butterfly

La France

Comtesse Vandal

Jenny Wren

Grace de Monaco

July 18th, from David Austin Roses

White Wings

Dainty Maid

Isobel

Ellen Willmott

Dusky Maiden

Mrs Oakley Fisher

July 18th, from David Austin Roses

Shot Silk A Hybrid Tea raised by Dickson in 1924. Good scent. Height up to 1.3 m. Parentage: 'Hugh Dickson' seedling × 'Sunstar'.

Souvenir de Claudius Denoyel A climbing Hybrid Tea raised by Chambard in 1920. Parentage: 'Château de Clos Vougeot' × 'Commander Jules Gravereux'.

Michèle Meilland A Hybrid Tea raised by Meilland in 1945. Height up to 1.3 m. Good as a cut flower. Parentage: 'Joanna Hill' × 'Peace'.

Westfield Star A Hybrid Tea introduced by Morse in 1922. Scented. Parentage: sport of 'Ophelia'.

La France A Hybrid Tea raised by Guillot Fils in 1867. Very good scent. Vigorous growth up to 1.3 m. Described by some as the first hybrid tea. Very free flowering. Parentage: unrecorded.

Mme. Butterfly A Hybrid Tea introduced by Hill in 1918. Good scent. Height up to 1.3 m. Parentage: sport of 'Ophelia'.

Grace de Monaco (Meimit) A Hybrid Tea raised by Meilland and introduced by Universal Rose Selection in 1956. Scented. Height up to about 2 m. Parentage: 'Peace' × 'Michèle Meilland'.

Jenny Wren A Floribunda raised by Ratcliff in 1957. Height up to 1 m. Parentage: 'Cécile Brunner' × 'Fashion'.

Comtesse Vandal A Hybrid Tea raised by Leenders and introduced by Jackson and Perkins in 1932. Scented. Height up to 1 m. Parentage: ('Ophelia' × 'Mrs Aaron Ward') × 'Souvenir de Claudius Pernet'.

Isobel A Hybrid Tea raised by McGredy in 1916. Parentage: unrecorded.

White Wings A Hybrid Tea raised by Krebs and introduced by Howard and Smith in 1947. Some scent. Parentage: 'Dainty Bess × seedling.

Dainty Maid A Floribunda raised by Le Grice in 1940. Height up to 1.3 m. Parentage: 'T Poulsen' × seedling.

Mrs Oakley Fisher A Hybrid Tea raised by Cant in 1921. Scented. Bronzy leaves. Height up to 80 cm. Parentage: unrecorded.

Dusky Maiden A Floribunda raised by Le Grice in 1947. Parentage: ('Daily Mail Scented Rose' × 'Etoile de Hollande') × 'Else Poulsen'.

Ellen Willmott A Hybrid Tea raised by Archer in 1936. Parentage: 'Dainty Bess' × 'Lady Hillingdon'.

Diamond Jubilee

Lady Sylvia

Evensong

Josephine Bruce

Ophelia

Rose Gaujard

Silver Wedding

Royal Highness

Blue Moon

17th July, from R. Harkness & Co.

Dainty Bess

Irish Elegance

Comtesse du Cayla

Mrs Henry Bowles

Mme V. Dimitriu

Diamond Jubilee   A Hybrid Tea raised by Boerner and introduced by Jackson and Perkins in 1947. Good scent. Bushy growth, up to 1.3 m. Parentage: 'Marechal Niel' × 'Feu Pernet-Ducher'.

Lady Sylvia   A Hybrid Tea introduced by Stevens in 1925. Good scent. Height up to 1.3 m. Parentage: Sport from 'Ophelia'.

Evensong   A Hybrid Tea raised by Arnot and introduced in 1963. Parentage: 'Ena Harkness' × 'Sutter's Gold'.

Josephine Bruce   A Hybrid Tea raised by Bees and introduced in 1953. Good scent. Spreading growth up to about 1 m. Susceptible to mildew. Parentage: 'Crimson Glory' × 'Madge Whipp'.

Ophelia   A Hybrid Tea introduced by Paul in 1912. Scented. Height up to 1.3 m. Parentage: unrecorded.

Rose Gaujard (Gaumo)   A popular Hybrid Tea raised by Gaujard and introduced by Armstrong in 1957. Some scent. Height up to 1.3 m. Parentage: 'Peace' × 'Opera' seedling.

Silver Wedding   A Hybrid Tea introduced by Amling in 1921. Parentage: sport of 'Ophelia'.

Royal Highness (Konigliche Hoheit)   A Hybrid Tea raised by Swim and Weeks and introduced by Conard-Pyle in 1962. Flowers easily spoilt by rain. Good scent. Height up to 1.3 m. Susceptible to mildew. Parentage: 'Virgo' × 'Peace'.

Blue Moon (Blue Monday, Mainzer Fastnacht, Sissi, Tannacht)   A Hybrid Tea introduced by Tantau in 1965. Very fragrant. Upright growth to about 1.5 m. Parentage: 'Sterling Silver' seedling × seedling.

Irish Elegance   A Hybrid Tea introduced by Dickson in 1905. Parentage: unrecorded.

Comtesse du Cayla   A China hybrid raised by Guillot in 1902. Scented. Flowers regularly throughout the season. Height up to 1 m. Parentage: unknown.

Mrs Henry Bowles   A Hybrid Tea introduced by Chaplin in 1921. Good scent. Parentage: 'Lady Pirrie' × 'Georgeous'.

Dainty Bess   A Hybrid Tea introduced by Archer in 1925. Scented. Height up to 80 cm. Exceptionally hardy (as befits a rose raised in East Kent, U.K.!) in Britain and U.S.A. Parentage: 'Ophelia' × 'K of K'.

Mme V. Dimitriu (Delcrip)   A Floribunda raised by Delbard in 1967. Leaves glossy, reddish. Parentage: 'Chic Parisien' × 'Provence'.

Antigone   A Hybrid Tea raised by Gaujard in 1969. Flowers well scented. Parentage: 'Rose Gaujard' × 'Guitare'.

Red Lady (Lapacil)   A Hybrid Tea raised by Laperrière in 1977. Parentage: not recorded.

Antigone

Red Lady

Eden Rose

Leigh-Lo

Mischief

Gail Borden

Pascali

Blessings

Super Sun

Blesma Soul

Flaming Peace

July 18th, from Wisley

Wendy Cussons

Piccadilly

Virgo

Pink Favorite

Polly

July 16th, from Wisley

Eden Rose   A Hybrid Tea raised by Meilland and introduced by Universal Rose Selection in 1950. Good scent. Height up to 2 m. Parentage: 'Peace' × 'Signora'.

Leigh-Lo (Harpurl)   A Hybrid Tea raised by Harkness in 1979. Parentage: 'Elizabeth Harkness' × 'Red Devil'.

Mischief (Macmi)   A Hybrid Tea raised and introduced by McGredy in 1961. Some scent. Height up to 1.3 m. Susceptible to rust. Parentage: 'Peace' × 'Spartan'.

Gail Borden   A Hybrid Tea raised by Kordes and introduced by Jackson & Perkins in 1957. Height up to 1.3 m. Parentage:? 'Mrs H. A. Verschuren' × 'Viktoria Adelheid'.

Pascali (Lenip)   A Hybrid Tea raised by Lens and introduced by Dickson in 1963. Height up to 2 m. Parentage: 'Queen Elizabeth' × 'White Butterfly'.

Blessings   A Hybrid Tea raised by Gregory in 1967. Some scent. Upright growth, to 1.3 m. Parentage: 'Queen Elizabeth' × seedling.

Super Sun   A Hybrid Tea raised by Bentley in 1967. Height up to about 1 m. Susceptible to blackspot. Parentage: sport from 'Piccadilly'.

Blesma Soul   A Hybrid Tea raised by Andersons in 1982. Scented. Free-flowering. Parentage: 'Pascale' × 'Fragrant Cloud'.

Flaming Peace (Maccbo, Kronenbourg) A Hybrid Tea raised by McGredy in 1966. Height up to 1.5 m. Parentage: sport of 'Peace'.

Wendy Cussons   A Hybrid Tea raised by Gregory and introduced by Ilgenfritz in 1963. Height up to 2 m. Good scent. Parentage: seedling of 'Independence' × ?'Eden Rose'.

Piccadilly   A Hybrid Tea raised and introduced by McGredy in 1960. Height up to

1 m. Susceptible to blackspot. Parentage: 'McGredy's Yellow' × 'Karl Herbst'.

Pink Favorite   A Hybrid Tea raised by Von Abrams and introduced by Peterson and Dering in 1956. Height up to 1.3 m. Parentage: 'Juno' × ('Georg Arends' × 'New Dawn').

Polly   A Hybrid Tea raised by Beckwith in 1927. Good scent. Rather feeble growth, up to about 1 m. Parentage: 'Ophelia' seedling × 'Mme Colette Martinet'.

Virgo (Virgo Liberationem)   A Hybrid Tea raised by Mallerin and introduced by Meilland–Richardier in 1947. Height up to 1.3 m. Susceptible to mildew. Parentage: 'Pole Nord' × 'Neige Parfum'.

Ernest H. Morse

Alpine Sunset

King's Ransom

Adolf Horstmann

Apricot Silk

Silver Jubilee

Mister Lincoln

Sunblest

Alec's Red

July 16th, from Wisley

Lafter

Silva

Feuerwerk

Mrs Pierre S. du Pont

King's Ransom A Hybrid Tea raised by Morey and introduced by Jackson and Perkins in 1961. Height up to 1.3 m. Parentage: 'Golden Masterpiece' × 'Lydia'.

Alpine Sunset A Hybrid Tea raised by Roberts and introduced by Cants in 1973. Sweetly-scented. Height up to 75 cm. Parentage: 'Grandpa Dickson' × 'Dr A. J. Verhage'.

Ernest H. Morse A popular Hybrid Tea raised by Kordes and introduced by Morse in 1964. Some scent. Flowers fade with age. Height up to 1.8 m. Parentage: unrecorded.

Apricot Silk A Hybrid Tea introduced by Gregory in 1965. Vigorous, upright growth, up to 1.3 m. Susceptible to disease. Parentage: 'Souvenir de Jacques Verschuren' × seedling.

Silver Jubilee A Hybrid Tea introduced by Cocker in 1978. Height up to 1.3 m. Good as a cut flower. Parentage: 'Mischief' × seedling.

Adolf Horstmann (Adolph Horstmann) A Hybrid Tea raised and introduced by Kordes in 1971. Vigorous, upright growth. Parentage: 'Colour Wonder' × 'Dr A. J. Verhage'.

Mister Lincoln A Hybrid Tea raised by Swim and Weeks and introduced by Conard-Pyle in 1964. Good scent. Height up to 2 m. Parentage: 'Chrysler Imperial' × 'Charles Mallerin'.

Sunblest (Landora) A Hybrid Tea introduced by Tantau in 1970. Height up to 1.3 m. Parentage: seedling × 'King's Ransom'.

Alec's Red (Cored) A Hybrid Tea introduced by Cocker in 1973. Vigorous, upright growth, up to 1.3 m. Good scent. Parentage: 'Fragrant Cloud' × 'Dame de Coeur'.

Mrs Pierre S. du Pont A Hybrid Tea raised by Mallerin and introduced by Conard-Pyle in 1929. Fruity scent. Parentage: ('Ophelia' × 'Rayon d'Or') × ['Ophelia' × ('Constance' × 'Souvenir de Claudius Pernet')].

Lafter A Hybrid Tea introduced by Brownell in 1948. Scented. Parentage: ['V for Victory' × ('General Jacqueminot' × 'Dr W. van Fleet')] × 'Pink Princess'.

Mme Louis Laperrière A Hybrid Tea raised by Laperrière and introduced by ?Editions Francaise in 1951. Good scent. Parentage: 'Crimson Glory' × seedling.

Silva (Meicham) A Hybrid Tea raised by Meilland and introduced by Universal Rose Selection in 1964. Vigorous growth up to 1 m. Parentage: 'Peace' × 'Confidence'.

Feuerwerk (Magneet) A shrub rose raised by Tantau in 1962. Height up to 1.6 m. Parentage: not recorded.

Mme Louis Laperrière

Fred Edmunds

French Lace

Mojave

White Masterpiece

Lemon Spice

Sweet Afton

Tiffany

Honor

First Love

October 13th, from Portland, Oregon

Lucky Piece

Royal Sunset

Red Lion

Summer Sunshine

Garden Party

Fred Edmunds (L'Arlesienne)   A Hybrid Tea raised by Meilland and introduced by Conard-Pyle in 1943. Scented. Parentage: 'Duquesa de Penaranda' × 'Marie-Claire'.

French Lace   A Floribunda raised by Warriner in 1980. Tender. Has a light, spicy scent and flowers continuously. Parentage: 'Golden Wave' × 'Bridal Pink'.

Mojave   A Hybrid Tea raised by Swim and introduced by Armstrong in 1954. Height up to 1.3 m. Scented. Parentage: 'Charlotte Armstrong' × 'Signora'.

White Masterpiece   A Hybrid Tea raised by Boerner and introduced by Jackson and Perkins in 1969. Parentage: unrecorded.

Lemon Spice   A Hybrid Tea introduced by Armstrong in 1966. Scented. Spreading growth up to 80 cm. Parentage: 'Helen Traubel' × seedling.

Sweet Afton   A Hybrid Tea introduced by Armstrong and Swim in 1964. Good scent. Bushy, spreading habit up to 2 m. Parentage: ('Charlotte Armstrong' × 'Signora') × ('Alice Stern' × 'Ondine').

Tiffany   A Hybrid Tea raised by Lindquist and introduced by Howard in 1954. Good scent. Parentage: 'Charlotte Armstrong' × 'Girona'.

Honor (Jacolite)   A Hybrid Tea raised by Warriner and introduced by Jackson and Perkins in 1980. Parentage: unrecorded.

First Love (Premier Amour)   A Hybrid Tea raised by Swim and introduced by Burr in 1961. Parentage: 'Charlotte Armstrong' × 'Show Girl'.

Red Lion   A Hybrid Tea raised by McGredy and introduced by Spek in 1964. Some scent. Height up to 1.5 m. Parentage: 'Perfecta' × 'Brilliant'.

Summer Sunshine (Soleil d'Ete)   A Hybrid Tea raised by Swim and introduced by Armstrong in 1962. Rather weak, leggy growth up to 1.3 m. Parentage: 'Buccaneer' × 'Lemon Chiffon'.

Garden Party   A Hybrid Tea raised by Swim and introduced by Armstrong in 1959. Height up to 2 m. Good scent. Parentage: 'Charlotte Armstrong' × 'Peace'.

Lucky Piece   A Hybrid Tea raised by Gordon and introduced by Wyant in 1962. Scented. Parentage: unrecorded.

Don Juan   A climbing Hybrid Tea raised by Malandrone in 1958. Good scent. Height up to 3 m. Parentage: 'New Dawn' seedling × 'New Yorker'.

Royal Sunset   A climbing Hybrid Tea raised by Morey in 1960. Has a fruity scent. Parentage: 'Sungold' × 'Sutter's Gold'.

Tequila (Meigavesol)   A Floribunda raised by Meilland in 1982. Parentage: 'Poppy Flash' × ('Rumba' × seedling).

Don Juan

Photo Meilland

Tequila

Bewitched

Carrousel

Anne Letts

Chrysler Imperial

Memoriam

El Capitan

Crimson Glory

Camelot

Grand Masterpiece

October 13th, from Portland, Oregon

Bewitched A Hybrid Tea raised by Lammerts and introduced by Germain's in 1967. Good scent. Very vigorous. Parentage: 'Queen Elizabeth' × 'Tawny Gold'.

Carrousel A Floribunda raised by Duehrsen in 1950. Scented. Parentage: seedling × 'Margy'.

Anne Letts A Hybrid Tea raised by Letts in 1954. Scented. Bushy growth. Parentage: 'Peace' × 'Charles Gregory'.

Chrysler Imperial A Hybrid Tea raised by Lammerts and introduced by Germain's in 1952. Scented. Growth up to 1 m. Susceptible to mildew. Parentage: 'Charlotte Armstrong' × 'Mirandy'.

Memoriam A Hybrid Tea raised by Von Abrams and introduced by Peterson and Dering in 1961. Good scent. Height up to 80 cm. Susceptible to blackspot. Parentage: ('Blanche Mallerin' × 'Peace') × ('Peace' × 'Frau Karl Druschki').

El Capitan A Floribunda raised by Swim in 1959. Scented. Height up to 1.5 m. Parentage: 'Charlotte Armstrong' × 'Floradora'.

Crimson Glory A Hybrid Tea raised by Kordes and introduced by Dreer and Jackson and Perkins in 1935. Good scent. Bushy growth up to 1 m. Parentage: 'Catherine Kordes' seedling × 'W. E. Chaplin'.

Camelot A Floribunda raised by Swim and Weeks in 1964. Spicy scent. Parentage: 'Circus' × 'Queen Elizabeth'.

Grand Masterpiece A Hybrid Tea raised by Warriner and introduced by Jackson and Perkins in 1978. Parentage: seedling × 'Tonight'.

Miss All-American Beauty (Meidaud, Maria Callas) A Hybrid Tea raised by Meilland and introduced by Wheatcroft in 1965. Height up to 2 m. Parentage: 'Chrysler Imperial' × 'Karl Herbst'.

Color Magic A Hybrid Tea raised by Warriner and introduced by Jackson and Perkins. Parentage: seedling × 'Spellbinder'.

Broadway (Burway) A Hybrid Tea raised by Perry in 1985. Parentage: not yet available.

Friendship (Linrick) A Hybrid Tea raised by Lindquist and introduced by Conard–Pyle in 1978. Scented. Parentage: 'Fragrant Cloud' × 'Maria Callas'.

Folklore (Korlore) A Hybrid Tea raised by Kordes and introduced by Barni–Kordes in 1977. Good scent. Parentage: 'Duftwolke' × seedling.

Oregold (Anneliesse Rothenberger, Miss Harp, Silhouette) A Hybrid Tea raised by Tantau and introduced by Jackson and Perkins in 1975. Some scent. Vigorous growth up to 2 m. Parentage: 'Piccadilly' × 'Colour Wonder'.

Broadway

Miss All-American Beauty

Folklore

Oregold

Color Magic

Friendship

Great News

Black Beauty

Papa Meilland

White Knight

Diorama

Lady Belper

Soraya

Harry Wheatcroft

Pink Peace

July 18th, from David Austin Roses

Papa Meilland (Meicesar)   A Hybrid Tea raised by Meilland and introduced by Universal Rose Selection and Wheatcroft in 1963. Good scent. Height up to 1 m. Parentage: 'Chrysler Imperial' × 'Charles Mallerin'.

Great News   A Hybrid Tea raised by Le Grice in 1973. Height up to 1.3 m. Scented. Parentage: 'Rose Gaujard' × 'City of Hereford'.

Black Beauty   A Hybrid Tea raised by Delbard and introduced by Bees in 1973. Free flowering. Parentage: 'Gloire de Rome' × 'Impeccable'.

Lady Belper   A Hybrid Tea raised by Verschuren and introduced by Gregory in 1948. Scented. Parentage: 'Mev. G. A. van Rossem' × seedling.

White Knight (Meban, Message)   A Hybrid Tea raised by Meilland and introduced in America by Universal Rose Selection in 1955. Parentage: ('Virgo' × 'Peace') × 'Virgo'.

Diorama   A Hybrid Tea introduced by De Ruiter in 1965. Some scent. Bushy growth to 1.3 m. Parentage: 'Peace' × 'Beauté'.

Soraya (Mejenor)   A Hybrid Tea raised by Meilland and introduced by Universal Rose Selection in 1955. Parentage: ('Peace' × 'Floradora') × 'Grand'mère Jenny'.

Harry Wheatcroft (Caribia)   A Hybrid Tea introduced by Wheatcroft in 1972. Height up to about 1 m. Susceptible to blackspot. Parentage: sport from 'Piccadilly'.

Pink Peace (Meibil)   A Hybrid Tea raised by Meilland and introduced by Universal Rose Selection and Conard–Pyle in 1959. Some scent. Height up to 1.5 m. Parentage: ('Peace' × 'Monique') × ('Peace' × 'Mrs John Laing').

Peace (Gioia, Gloria Dei, Mme A. Meilland) A popular Hybrid Tea raised by Meilland and introduced by Conard–Pyle in 1945. Height up to 2 m. Good as a cut flower. Parentage: seedling × 'Margaret McGredy'.

John Waterer   A Hybrid Tea raised and introduced by McGredy in 1970. Scented. Height up to about 2 m. Parentage: 'King of Hearts' × 'Hanne'.

Visa (Meired)   A Hybrid Tea raised by Meilland in 1972. Strong, upright growth. Very popular in France for the cut flower trade. Parentage: ('Baccara' × 'Queen Elizabeth') × 'Lolita'.

Summer Holiday   A Hybrid Tea raised by Gregory in 1967. Some scent. Spreading growth up to 2 m. Parentage: 'Super Star' × unknown.

Roundelay   A Floribunda raised by Swim in 1954. Scented. Repeats well. Height up to 1 m. Parentage: 'Charlotte Armstrong' × 'Floradora'.

Peace

Visa

John Waterer

Summer Holiday

Roundelay

Manou Meilland

Charlie's Aunt

Santa Fé

Red Devil

Ginger Rogers

Fyvie Castle

Dr Barnardo

Stephen Langdon

Gallant

Troika

Precious Platinum

Rosy Cheeks

Bonsoir

Santa Fé   A Hybrid Tea raised and introduced by McGredy in 1967. Vigorous growth up to 1 m. Parentage: 'Mischief' × 'Super Star'.

Manou Meilland (Meitulimon)   A Hybrid Tea raised and introduced by Meilland in 1979. Very free flowering. Parentage: ('Meigriso' × 'Baronne Edmond de Rothschild') × ('Ma Fille' × 'Love Song').

Charlie's Aunt   A Hybrid Tea raised by McGredy and introduced by Geest in 1965. Upright growth to 2 m. Parentage: 'Golden Masterpiece' × 'Karl Herbst'.

Red Devil (Coeur d'Amour)   A Hybrid Tea raised by Dickson and introduced in America by Jackson & Perkins in 1970. Good scent. Height up to 2 m. Blooms liable to be spoilt by rain. Parentage: 'Silver Lining' × 'Prima Ballerina' seedling.

Ginger Rogers (Salmon Charm)   A Hybrid Tea raised and introduced by McGredy in 1969. Height up to about 1 m. Parentage: 'Super Star' × 'Miss Ireland'.

Fyvie Castle (Cocbamber)   A Hybrid Tea raised by Cocker in 1985. Compact growth up to 80 cm. Parentage: 'Silver Jubilee' × seedling.

Dr Barnardo   A Floribunda raised by Harkness in 1968. Parentage: 'Vera Dalton' × 'Red Dandy'.

Stephen Langdon   A Floribunda raised by Sanday in 1969. Height up to 1.3 m. Parentage: 'Karl Herbst' × 'Sarabanda'.

Gallant   A Floribunda raised by Dickson in 1968. Scented. Parentage: 'Tropicana' × 'Barbecue'.

Troika (Royal Dane)   A Hybrid Tea raised by Poulsen in 1971. Good scent. Height up to about 1.5 m. Parentage: unrecorded.

Bonsoir (Dicbo)   A Hybrid Tea raised by Dickson in 1968. Fragrant. Bushy growth up to 1.3 m. Petals tend to be easily spoilt by rain. Parentage: unrecorded.

National Trust (Bad Nauheim)   A Hybrid Tea raised and introduced by McGredy in 1970. Bushy growth up to 75 cm. Parentage: 'Evelyn Fison' × 'King of Hearts'.

Precious Platinum (Opa Potschke, Red Star)   A Hybrid Tea raised by Dickson in 1974. Height up to about 1.5 m. Scented. Parentage: 'Red Planet' × 'Franklin Engelmann'.

Rosy Cheeks   A Hybrid Tea raised by Andersons in 1975. Good scent. Height up to 1.3 m. Parentage: 'Beauty of Festival' × 'Grandpa Dickson'.

Whisky Mac (Whisky)   A Hybrid Tea raised by Tantau in 1967. Good scent. Susceptible to mildew and frost damage. Height up to 1.3 m. Parentage: unrecorded.

National Trust

Whisky Mac

Duet

Chicago Peace

Dolce Vita

Madame Violet

Admiral Rodney

Sonia

Peter Frankenfeld

Revival

Silver Lining

Rose Parade

October 14th, from Fred Edmunds Inc, Wilsonville, Oregon

Neue Revue *Bobby Charlton* *Duftzauber*

Eva Gabor *Crimson Tide* *Osiria*

October 14th, from Fred Edmunds Inc, Wilsonville, Oregon

Grand Siècle

Magicienne

Louqsor

Duet A Hybrid Tea raised by Swim and introduced by Armstrong in 1960. Scented. Parentage: 'Fandango' × 'Roundelay'.

Chicago Peace (Johnago) A Hybrid Tea raised by Johnston and introduced by Conard–Pyle and Universal Rose Selection in 1962. Upright, bushy growth, to 2 m. Parentage: sport of 'Peace' discovered in Chicago.

Dolce Vita (Deldal) A Hybrid Tea raised by Delbard in 1971. Scented. Hardy. Height up to 2 m. Parentage: 'Voeux de Bonheur' × seedling.

Madame Violet A Hybrid Tea raised by Teranishi in 1981. Scented. Susceptible to mildew. Height up to 2 m. Parentage: 'Lady X' × unknown.

Sonia (Meihelvet, Sonia Meilland, Sweet Promise) A Floribunda raised by Meilland in 1974. Fruity scent. Good under glass. Height up to 1.3 m. Parentage: 'Zambra' × ('Baccara' × 'Message').

Peter Frankenfeld A Hybrid Tea raised by Kordes and introduced by Dickson in 1966. Good as a cut flower. Height up to 1.3 m. Parentage: unrecorded.

Admiral Rodney A Hybrid Tea raised by Basildon Rose Gardens and introduced by Warley Rose Gardens in 1973. Vigorous. Height up to 1.3 m. Good scent. Parentage: unrecorded.

Revival A Hybrid Tea raised by Barni–Pistoia in 1979. Parentage: mutation of 'Folklore'.

Silver Lining A Hybrid Tea raised by Dickson in 1958. Good scent. Height up to 1.3 m. Parentage: 'Karl Herbst' × 'Eden Rose' seedling.

Rose Parade A Floribunda raised by Williams in 1974. Scented. Tolerant of hot sun. Height up to 1 m. Parentage: 'Sumatra' × 'Queen Elizabeth'.

Neue Revue A Hybrid Tea raised by Kordes in 1962. Good scent. Parentage: 'Königin der Rosen' × seedling.

Bobby Charlton A Hybrid Tea raised and introduced by Fryer's in 1974. Spicy fragrance. Upright growth to 2 m. Parentage: 'Royal Highness' × 'Prima Ballerina'.

Duftzauber (Kordu, Fragrant Charm) A Hybrid Tea raised and introduced by Kordes in 1969. Good scent. Parentage: 'Prima Ballerina' × 'Kaiserin Farah'.

Eva Gabor (Poultal, Sentimental) A Hybrid Tea raised by P. and M. Olesen and introduced by Fred Edmunds in 1983. Some scent. Good as a cut flower. Height up to 2 m. Parentage: unnamed seedlings.

Crimson Tide (Macmota) A Hybrid Tea raised by McGredy and introduced by Edmunds in 1983. Flowers are of particularly good substance. Good as a cut flower. Parentage: unnamed seedlings.

Osiria A Hybrid Tea raised by Kordes and introduced by Willemse in 1978. Good scent. Parentage: 'Snowfire' × seedling.

Grand Siècle (Delegran) A Hybrid Tea raised by Delbard-Chabert in 1977. Parentage: not recorded.

Magicienne 78 (Laponda) A Hybrid Tea raised by Laperrière in 1978. Parentage: not recorded.

Louqsor (Delcraf, Louksor) A Hybrid Tea raised by Delbard-Chabert in 1967. Leaves glossy. Parentage: 'Dr. Albert Schweitzer' × 'Provence'.

Flaming Peace

Ambassador

Electron

Ivory Tower

Lady X

Heirloom

Medallion

Sweet Surrender

Helen Traubel

October 13th, from Portland, Oregon

Flaming Beauty

Guadalajara

Gitte

Lolita

Embassy

Die Welt

October 14th, from Fred Edmunds Inc, Wilsonville, Oregon

Flaming Peace (Macbo, Kronenbourg)
A Hybrid Tea raised by McGredy in 1966.
Height up to 1.5 m. Parentage: sport of 'Peace'.

Ambassador (Meinuzeten) A Hybrid Tea
raised by Meilland and introduced by Conard–
Pyle in 1979. Parentage: seedling × 'Whisky
Mac'.

Electron (Mullard Jubilee) A Hybrid Tea
raised and introduced by McGredy in 1970.
Scented. Bushy and compact, up to 1.3 m.
Parentage: 'Paddy McGredy' × Prima Ballerina'.

Ivory Tower A Hybrid Tea raised by Kordes
and introduced in America by Armstrong in
1979. Scented Parentage: 'Colour Wonder' ×
'King's Ransom'.

Lady X (Meifigu) A Hybrid Tea raised by
Meilland and introduced in America by
Conard–Pyle in 1965. Height up to 80 cm.
Parentage: seedling × 'Simone'.

Heirloom A Hybrid Tea raised by Warriner
and introduced by Jackson & Perkins in 1972.
Good scent. Parentage: unnamed seedlings.

Medallion A Hybrid Tea raised by Warriner
and introduced by Jackson & Perkins in 1973.
Rather leggy growth, up to 80 cm. Parentage:
'South Seas' × 'King's Ransom'.

Sweet Surrender A Hybrid Tea raised by
Weeks in 1983. Good tea scent. Free flowering.
Parentage: seedling × 'Tiffany'.

Helen Traubel A Hybrid Tea raised by Swim
and introduced by Armstrong in 1951. Some
scent. Height up to about 1.5 m. Parentage:
'Charlotte Armstrong' × 'Glowing Sunset'.

Flaming Beauty A Hybrid Tea raised by
Winchel and introduced by Kimbrew–Walter
in 1978. Parentage 'First Prize' × 'Piccadilly'.

Guadalajara (Macdeepo) A Hybrid Tea raised
by McGredy in 1984. Height up to 1.3 m.
Hardy. Parentage: 'New Day' × 'Yellow Bird'.

Gitte (Korita, Peach Melba) A Hybrid Tea
raised by Kordes in 1978. Good scent.
Parentage: ('Fragrant Cloud' × 'Peer Gynt') ×
[('Dr A. J. Verhage' × 'Colour Wonder') ×
'Zorina'].

Lolita (Korlita, Litakor) A Hybrid Tea raised
by Kordes in 1973. Some scent. Rather leggy
growth up to 2 m. Parentage: 'Colour Wonder'
× seedling.

Embassy A Hybrid Tea raised by Sanday in
1967. Some scent. Height up to 1.3 m.
Parentage: 'Gavotte' × ('Magenta' × ? 'Spek's
Yellow').

Die Welt (The World) A Hybrid Tea raised
by Kordes in 1976. Parentage: seedling × 'Peer
Gynt'.

143

Birmingham Post

Red Queen

Adair Roche

Kalahari

Fred Gibson

Interflora

Astral

Eroica

Devotion

July 16th, from The Gardens of the Rose

Duke of Windsor

Caramba

Grandpa Dickson

Photo Meilland   *Baron E. de Rothschild*

Rainer Maria Rilke

Photo Meilland   *Baccará*

Lancôme

Birmingham Post A Floribunda raised by Watkins Roses in 1968. Good scent. Parentage: 'Queen Elizabeth' × 'Wendy Cussons'.

Red Queen (Liebestraum) A Hybrid Tea raised by Kordes and introduced by Buisman and McGredy in 1968. Parentage: 'Konigin der Rosen' × 'Liberty Bell'.

Adair Roche A Hybrid Tea raised by McGredy in 1968. Parentage: 'Paddy McGredy × 'Femina' seedling.

Kalahari A Hybrid Tea raised and introduced by McGredy in 1971. Height up to 80 cm. Parentage: 'Uncle Walter' × ('Hamburger Phoenix' × 'Danse de Feu').

Fred Gibson A Hybrid Tea introduced by Sanday in 1966. Height up to 2 m. Good as a cut flower. Parentage: 'Gavotte' × 'Buccaneer'.

Interflora (Interview) A Hybrid Tea introduced by Meilland in 1968. Vigorous growth up to 2 m. Parentage: [('Baccara' × 'White Knight') × ('Baccara' × 'Jolie Madame')] × ('Baccara' × 'Paris-Match').

Astral A Hybrid Tea introduced by Bees in 1976. Good scent. Vigorous growth. Parentage: 'Super Star' × 'Pink Favorite'.

Eroica (Erotika) A Hybrid Tea introduced by Tantau in 1968. Good scent. Height up to 1.3 m. Parentage: unrecorded.

Devotion A Floribunda introduced by

Harkness in 1971. Scented. Parentage: 'Orange Sensation' × 'Peace'.

Grandpa Dickson (Irish Gold) A popular Hybrid Tea raised by Dickson and introduced by Jackson and Perkins in 1966. Growth up to about 1 m. Parentage: ('Perfecta' × 'Governador Braga de Cruz') × 'Piccadilly'.

Duke of Windsor (Herzog von Windsor) A Hybrid Tea by Tantau in 1969. Good scent. Height to 1.3 m. Susceptible to mildew. Parentage: 'Prima Ballerina' × seedling.

Caramba A Hybrid Tea introduced by Tantau in 1966. Bushy growth up to 1.5 m. Parentage: unrecorded.

Baronne Edmond de Rothschild (Meigriso) A Hybrid Tea raised by Meilland and introduced by Universal Rose Selection in 1968. Good scent. Height up to 1.3 m. Parentage: ('Baccara' × 'Crimson King') × 'Peace'.)

Rainer Maria Rilke (Uwe Seeler, Orange Vilmorin, Gitte Grummer, Korsee) A Floribunda raised by Kordes in 1970. Leaves glossy, reddish. Parentage: 'Queen Elizabeth' × 'Königin der Rosen'.

Baccará (Meger) A Hybrid Tea raised by Meilland in 1954. Leaves dark green. Parentage: 'Happiness' × 'Independence'.

Lancôme (Delbolp) A Hybrid Tea raised by Delbard-Chabert in 1973. Parentage: not recorded.

Sparkling Scarlet

Mary Mine

Altissimo

Rosy Mantle

Highfield

Malaga

Compassion

Grand Hotel

Horizon

July 16th, from Wisley

Orangeade

Bantry Bay

Morning Jewel

Orfeo

Copacabana

July 16th, from Wisley

Sparkling Scarlet (Iskra)   A climbing Floribunda raised by Meilland in 1970. Growth up to 3 m. Repeat flowering. Parentage: 'Danse des Sylphes' × 'Zambra'.

Mary Mine   A Floribunda raised by Harkness in 1971. Parentage: unrecorded.

Altissimo   A climbing Floribunda raised by Delbard–Chabert in 1966. Growth up to 4 m. Repeat flowering. Parentage: 'Tenor' × unknown.

Rosy Mantle   A climbing Hybrid Tea raised by Cocker in 1968. Growth up to 3 m. Repeat flowering. Parentage: 'New Dawn' × 'Prima Ballerina'.

Highfield (Harcomp)   A climbing Hybrid Tea, raised by Harkness in 1981. Growth up to 3 m. Repeat flowering. Good scent. Parentage: sport of 'Compassion'.

Malaga   A climbing Hybrid Tea raised by McGredy in 1972. Growth up to 3 m. Repeat flowering. Some scent. Parentage: ('Danse du Feu' × 'Hamburger Phoenix') × 'Copenhagen'.

Compassion (Belle de Londres)   A climbing Hybrid Tea raised by Harkness in 1973. Growth up to 3 m. Repeat flowering. Good scent. Parentage: 'White Cockade' × 'Prima Ballerina'.

Grand Hotel   A climbing Hybrid Tea, raised by McGredy in 1972. Growth up to 4 m. Repeat flowering. Parentage: 'Brilliant' × 'Heidelberg'.

Horizon   A Floribunda raised by Tantau in 1956. Scented. Parentage: 'Crimson Glory' × 'Cinnabar'.

Orangeade   A Floribunda raised by McGredy in 1959. Growth up to 2 m. Repeat flowering. Susceptible to blackspot. Parentage: 'Orange Sweetheart' × 'Independence'.

Bantry Bay   A climbing Floribunda raised by McGredy in 1967. Growth up to 5 m. Repeat flowering. Parentage: 'New Dawn' × 'Korona'.

Orfeo, climbing   A large-flowered climber raised by Leenders in 1963. Parentage: 'Curly Pink' × 'Guinée'.

Morning Jewel   A climbing Floribunda raised by Cocker in 1968. Growth up to 3 m. Some later flowers. Little scent. Parentage: 'New Dawn' × 'Red Dandy'.

Copacabana   A climbing Floribunda raised by Dorieux in 1967. Growth up to 2.5 m. Repeat flowering. Parentage: 'Coup de Foudre' × seedling.

Laura

Tenerife

With Love

Johnnie Walker

Helmut Schmidt

Peer Gynt

Mala Rubinstein

Champion

Alexander

July 18th, from Wisley

Velvet Hour

Evening Star

Prima Ballerina

Cheshire Life

Goya

Super Star

July 12th, from Wisley

Laura (Meidragelac) A Hybrid Tea raised by Meilland in 1981. Parentage: unrecorded.

With Love (Andwit) A Hybrid Tea raised by Andersons in 1983. Parentage: 'Grandpa Dickson' × 'Daily Sketch'.

Tenerife A Hybrid Tea raised by Timmermans in 1972. Good scent. Height up to 1.3 m. Parentage: 'Fragrant Cloud' × 'Piccadilly'.

Johnnie Walker (Frygram) A Hybrid Tea raised by Fryers in 1982. Good scent. Height up to 1.3 m. Parentage: 'Sunblest' × seedling.

Helmut Schmidt (Korbelma, Simba) A Hybrid Tea raised by Kordes in 1979. Some scent. Parentage: 'Mabella' × seedling.

Peer Gynt A Hybrid Tea raised by Kordes and introduced by McGredy in 1968. Height up to 1.3 m. Parentage: 'Colour Wonder' × 'Golden Giant'.

Mala Rubinstein A Hybrid Tea raised by Dickson in 1971. Good scent. Height up to 1.3 m. Susceptible to rust. Parentage: 'Sea Pearl' × 'Fragrant Cloud'.

Champion A Hybrid Tea raised and introduced by Fryer in 1976. Scented. Bushy growth up to 1 m. Susceptible to blackspot. Parentage: 'Grandpa Dickson' × 'Whisky Mac'.

Alexander (Harlex) A Hybrid Tea raised by Harkness in 1972. Height up to 2 m. Good for hedging. Parentage: 'Super Star' × ('Ann Elizabeth' × 'Allgold').

Velvet Hour A Hybrid Tea raised by Le Grice in 1978. Some scent. Parentage: unrecorded.

Prima Ballerina (Première Ballerine) A Hybrid Tea raised by Tantau in 1957. Good scent. Height up to about 1.3 m. Susceptible to mildew. Parentage: seedling × 'Peace'.

Evening Star A Floribunda raised by Warriner in 1974. Height up to 1.5 m. Parentage: 'White Masterpiece' × 'Saratoga'.

Cheshire Life A Hybrid Tea raised and introduced by Fryer in 1972. Upright growth, to 1.3 m. Parentage: 'Prima Ballerina' × 'Princess Michiko'.

Goya A Floribunda raised by Bees in 1976. Parentage: 'Mildred Reynolds' × 'Arthur Bell'.

Super Star (Tropicana, Tanorstar) A Hybrid Tea raised by Tantau and introduced by Jackson & Perkins in 1960. Good scent. Height up to 1.5 m. Some susceptibility to mildew. Parentage: (seedling × 'Peace') × (seedling × 'Alpine Glow').

Brocade

Journey's End

Fine Fare

Rachel Crawshay

Deep Secret

Cinderella's Midnight Rose

Dutch Gold

Summer Days

Tynwald

Julia's Rose

Doris Tysterman

July 12th, from Wisley

Yorkshire Bank

Dream Time

Dr Darley

Pristine

Purple Beauty

Princess Margaret of England

July 12th, from Wisley

Journey's End A Hybrid Tea raised by Gandy 1978. Parentage: 'Doreen' × 'Vienna Charm'.

Brocade (Jeune Fille) A Hybrid Tea raised by Combe in 1960. Good scent. Parentage: 'Charlotte Armstrong' × 'Baiser'.

Fine Fare A Hybrid Tea raised by Bees in 1978. Some scent. Parentage: 'Fragrant Cloud' × 'Mildred Reynolds'.

Rachel Crawshay A Hybrid Tea raised by Harkness in 1977. Parentage: 'Fragrant Cloud' × 'Mary Mine'.

Deep Secret (Mildred Scheel) A Hybrid Tea raised by Tantau and introduced by Wheatcroft in 1977. Good scent. Parentage: unrecorded.

Cinderella's Midnight Rose A Hybrid Tea raised by Bernard in 1976. Parentage: unrecorded.

Dutch Gold A Hybrid Tea raised by Wisbech Plant Co. in 1978. Some scent. Height up to 1.3 m. Parentage: 'Peer Gynt' × 'Whisky Mac'.

Summer Days A Hybrid Tea raised by Bees in 1976. Some scent. Parentage: 'Fragrant Cloud' × 'Dr A. J. Verhage'.

Tynwald (Mattwyt) A Hybrid Tea raised by Mattock in 1979. Scented. Parentage: 'Peer Gynt' × 'Isis'.

Julia's Rose A Hybrid Tea introduced by Wisbech Plant Co. in 1976. Bushy growth, up to 75 cm. Parentage: 'Blue Moon' × 'Dr A. J. Verhage'.

Doris Tysterman A Hybrid Tea introduced by Wisbech Plant Co. in 1975. Upright growth, to 1.3 m. Susceptible to mildew. Parentage: 'Peer Gynt' × seedling.

Yorkshire Bank (Rutrulo, True Love) A Hybrid Tea raised by De Ruiter in 1979. Parentage: 'Pascali' × 'Peer Gynt'.

Dream Time A Hybrid Tea raised by Bees in 1977. Good scent. Parentage: 'Kordes' Perfecta' × 'Prima Ballerina'.

Dr Darley (Harposter) A Hybrid Tea raised by Harkness in 1982. Upright growth to 1 m. Parentage: 'Red Planet' × ('Carina' × 'Pascali').

Princess Margaret of England (Meilista) A Hybrid Tea raised by Meilland and introduced by Universal Rose Selection in 1968. Height up to 1.3 m. Parentage: 'Queen Elizabeth' × ('Peace' × 'Michèle Meilland').

Pristine (Jacpico) A Hybrid Tea raised by Warriner and introduced by Jackson & Perkins in 1978. Good scent. Height up to 1.3 m. Parentage: 'White Masterpiece' × 'First Prize'.

Purple Beauty A Hybrid Tea raised by Gandy in 1979. Some scent. Parentage: 'Eminence' × 'Tyrius'.

Lakeland Princess

Sunset Song

Fosse Way

Anna Pavlova

Innoxa Femille

Cleo

Sandringham Centenary

Can Can

Pacemaker

Camphill Glory

July 12th, from Wisley

Fosse Way   A Hybrid Tea raised by Langdale in 1980. Height up to 2 m. Parentage: 'Colour Wonder' × 'Prima Ballerina'.

Lakeland Princess (Vintage Wine, Pollak) A climbing Hybrid Tea raised by Poulsen and introduced by Edmunds in 1983. Height up to 3.3 m. Scented. Parentage: 'Troika' × 'Arthur Bell'.

Sunset Song (Cocasun)   A Hybrid Tea raised by Cocker in 1981. Height up to 1.3 m. Parentage: ('Sabine' × 'Circus') × 'Sunblest'.

Innoxa Femille (Harprincely)   A Hybrid Tea raised and introduced by Harkness in 1983. Scented. Parentage: 'Red Planet' × 'Eroica'.

Cleo (Beebop)   A Hybrid Tea raised and introduced by Bees in 1981. Parentage: 'Kordes' Perfecta' × 'Prima Ballerina'.

Anna Pavlova   A Hybrid Tea raised by Beales in 1981. Very good scent. Height up to 1.3 m. Parentage: unrecorded.

Sandringham Centenary   A Hybrid Tea introduced by Wisbech Plant Co. in 1980. Height up to 2 m. Parentage: 'Queen Elizabeth' × 'Baccara'.

Can Can (Legglow)   A Hybrid Tea raised by Le Grice in 1982. Good scent. Bushy growth up to 75 cm. Parentage: 'Just Joey' × seedling.

Pacemaker (Harnoble)   A Hybrid Tea raised by Harkness in 1981. Good scent. Parentage: 'Red Planet' × 'Wendy Cussons'.

Camphill Glory (Harkreme)   A Hybrid Tea raised by Harkness in 1980. Height up to 1.3 m. Parentage: 'Elizabeth Harkness' × 'Grandpa Dickson' (or ? 'Perfecta')

Fragrant Cloud (Duftwolke, Nuage Parfumé, Tanellis)   A Hybrid Tea raised by Tantau and introduced by Jackson and Perkins in 1967. Flower colour fades a little a few days after opening. Good scent. Height up to 1.3 m. Susceptible to blackspot. Parentage: seedling × 'Prima Ballerina'.

Neville Gibson (Harportly)   A Hybrid Tea raised and introduced by Harkness in 1982. Height up to 80 cm. Parentage: 'Red Planet' × seedling.

Remember Me (Cocdestin)   A Hybrid Tea raised by Cocker in 1984. Height up to 1 m. Parentage: not yet available.

Double Delight   A Hybrid Tea raised by Swim and Ellis and introduced by Armstrong in 1977. Good scent. Upright growth to 1.3 m. Susceptible to mildew. Parentage: 'Granada' × 'Garden Party'.

Freedom (Dicjem)   A Hybrid Tea raised by Dickson and introduced by Harkness in 1984. Some scent. Height up to 1.3 m. Parentage: ('Eurorose' × 'Typhoon') × 'Bright Smile'.

Isobel Harkness   A Hybrid Tea raised by Norman and introduced by Armstrong and Harkness in 1957. Scented. Height up to 1 m. Susceptible to blackspot. Parentage: 'Phyllis Gold' × 'McGredy's Yellow'.

Piccadilly   A Hybrid Tea raised by McGredy in 1960. Susceptible to blackspot. Height up to 2 m. We have illustrated a full-blown specimen which has faded to orange; when first open it is red with yellow on the reverse of the petals. Parentage: 'McGredy's Yellow' × 'Karl Herbst'.

Hot Pewter (Crucenia)   A Hybrid Tea raised by Harkness in 1978. Height up to 1.3 m. Susceptible to mildew. Parentage: 'Alec's Red' × 'Red Dandy'.

Canadian White Star (Dr Wolfgang Poschl) A Hybrid Tea raised by Mander in 1980. Carries on flowering until the first frost. Parentage: 'Blanche Mallerin' × 'Pascali'.

Fragrant Cloud   *Neville Gibson*
Remember Me   *Freedom*
Double Delight
Isobel Harkness   *Piccadilly*   *Hot Pewter*

July 17th, from R. Harkness & Co.

Canadian White Star

The Coxswain

Big Chief

Babylon

Susan Hampshire

Elida

Roaming

City of Gloucester

Guinevere

New Day

July 16th, from The Gardens of the Rose

Fragrant Hour

Fleet Street

Stephanie Diane

Nana Mouskouri

Kiskadee

Royal Show

July 18th, from Wisley

The Coxswain (Cocadilly) A Hybrid Tea raised by Cocker in 1983. Height up to 1 m. Parentage: ('Highlight' × 'Colour Wonder') × ('Parkdirektor Riggers' × 'Piccadilly').

Big Chief (Portland Trailblazer) A Hybrid Tea raised by Dickson and introduced by Edmunds in 1975. Growth upright, to 2 m. Parentage: 'Ernest H. Morse' × 'Red Planet'.

Babylon A Hybrid Tea raised by Bees in 1976. Good scent. Parentage: 'Super Star' × 'Pink Favorite'.

Susan Hampshire (Meinatac) A Hybrid Tea raised by Paolino in 1972. Some scent. Height up to 1.3 m. Parentage: ('Monique' × 'Symphonie') × 'Maria Callas'.

Elida A Hybrid Tea raised by Tantau in 1966. Scented. Parentage: unrecorded.

Roaming A Hybrid Tea raised by Sanday in 1970. Parentage: 'Vera Dalton' × 'Super Star'.

City of Gloucester A Hybrid Tea raised by Sanday in 1969. Upright growth, up to 2 m. Good as a cut flower. Parentage: 'Gavotte' × 'Buccaneer'.

Guinevere A Hybrid Tea raised by Harkness in 1967. Parentage: 'Red Dandy' × 'Peace'.

New Day (Korgold, Mabella) A Hybrid Tea raised by Kordes and introduced by Jackson & Perkins in 1977. Good scent. Parentage: 'Arlene Francis' × 'Roselandia'.

Stephanie Diane A Hybrid Tea raised by Bees in 1971. Parentage: 'Fragrant Cloud' × 'Cassandra'.

Fragrant Hour A Hybrid Tea raised by McGredy in 1973. Good scent. Parentage: 'Arthur Bell' × ('Spartan' × 'Grand Gala').

Fleet Street A Hybrid Tea raised and introduced by McGredy in 1972. Scented. Height up to 80 cm. Parentage: 'Kronenbourg' × 'Prima Ballerina'.

Kiskadee A Floribunda raised by McGredy in 1973. Parentage: 'Arthur Bell' × 'Cynthia Brooke'.

Royal Show A Hybrid Tea raised by Gregory in 1973. Height up to 2 m. Parentage: 'Queen Elizabeth' × seedling.

Nana Mouskouri A Floribunda raised by Dickson in 1975. Height up to 75 cm. Parentage: 'Red Gold' × 'Iced Ginger'.

L'Oreal Trophy

Flamingo

Torville and Dean

Rosemary Harkness

Wimi

Maritime Bristol

Pink Panther

Selfridges

Sheila's Perfume

July 16th, from Wisley

Chablis

Rosemary Harkness

Brandy

Blue Nile

Pounder Star

Charles De Gaulle

Sweet Mimi

L'Oreal Trophy (Harlexis) A Hybrid Tea introduced by Harkness in 1981. Growth up to 2 m. Parentage: sport of 'Alexander'.

Flamingo (Margaret Thatcher, Porcelain, Veronica, Korflug) A Hybrid Tea introduced by Kordes in 1979. Some scent. Parentage: seedling × 'Ladylike'.

Torville and Dean (Lantor) A Hybrid Tea introduced by Sealand in 1984. Parentage: not available.

Rosemary Harkness (Harrowbond) A Hybrid Tea introduced by Harkness in 1985. Scented. Good as a cut flower. Spreading growth up to 1 m high and as much wide. Parentage: 'Compassion' × ('Basildon Bond' × 'Grandpa Dickson').

Wimi (Tanrowisa) A Hybrid Tea introduced by Tantau in 1982. Parentage: not available.

Maritime Bristol (Santang) A Hybrid Tea raised and introduced by Sanday in 1983. Scented. Parentage: 'City of Gloucester' × seedling.

Pink Panther (Meicapinal) A Hybrid Tea raised and introduced by Meilland in 1981. Height up to about 1.5 m. Parentage: 'Meigurami' × 'Meinaregi'.

Selfridges (Korpriwa) A Hybrid Tea introduced by Kordes in 1984. Good scent. Parentage: seedling × 'Korgold'.

Sheila's Perfume (Harsherry) A Hybrid Tea introduced by Sheridan in 1985. Good scent. Parentage: 'Peer Gynt' × seedling.

Chablis A Hybrid Tea introduced by Weeks in 1983. Parentage: not available.

Brandy (Arocad) A Hybrid Tea raised by Swim and Christensen and introduced by Armstrong in 1981. Height up to 1.5 m. Parentage: 'First Prize' × 'Golden Wave'.

Blue Nile (Delnible, Nil Bleu) A Hybrid Tea raised by Delbard and introduced by Armstrong in 1981. Good scent. Spreading growth, up to about 1.5 m. Parentage: ('Holstein' × 'Bayadere') × ('Prelude' × 'Saint Exupery').

Pounder Star (Macnic, Karma) A Hybrid Tea raised by McGredy and introduced by Edmunds in 1981. Scented. Height up to 1.3 m. Parentage: 'John Waterer' × 'Kalahari'.

Charles de Gaulle (Meilanein, Katherine Mansfield) A Hybrid Tea raised by Meilland in 1974. Well scented. Parentage: ('Sissi' × 'Prélude') × ('Kordes Sondermeldung' × 'Caprice').

Sweet Mimi (Haumi) A Hybrid Tea raised by Hauser in 1981. Growth to 80 cm. Good scent. Parentage: 'Super Star' × 'Elizabeth Harkness'.

Paul Shirville

Abbeyfield Rose

Showman

Melinda

Royal Romance

Madame Georges
Delbard

Goldstar

Ruth Harker

Loving Memory

Paul Shirville

July 16th, from Wisley

Abbeyfield Rose (Cocbrose) A Hybrid Tea raised by Cocker in 1985. Height up to 80 cm. Parentage: 'National Trust' × 'Silver Jubilee'.

Showman (Mattjo) A Hybrid Tea raised by Mattock in 1983. Parentage: not yet available.

Melinda (Rulimpa, Impala) A Hybrid Tea raised by De Ruiter and introduced by Fryer in 1980. Scented. Height up to 90 cm. Parentage: 'Whisky Mac' × 'Criterion'.

Royal Romance (Liselle, Rulis) A Hybrid Tea raised by De Ruiter in 1980. There is a lemon-yellow rose, raised by Fryer, with the same name. Parentage: unrecorded.

Madame Georges Delbard (Deladel) A Hybrid Tea raised by Delbard–Chabert in 1959. Parentage: 'Impeccable' × 'Mme Robert Joffet'.

Goldstar (Candide, Point de Jour) A Hybrid Tea raised by Cants in 1983. Good as a cut flower. Height up to 1 m. Parentage: 'Yellow Pages' × 'Dr A. J. Verhage'.

Ruth Harker (Harpooh) A Hybrid Tea raised by Harkness in 1981. Sweet scent. Parentage: 'Fragrant Cloud' × 'Compassion'.

Paul Shirville (Harqueterwife, Heart Throb) A Hybrid Tea raised by Harkness in 1983. Good scent. Height up to 1 m. Parentage: 'Compassion' × 'Mischief'.

Loving Memory (Korgund '81) A Hybrid Tea raised by Kordes in 1981. Good scent. Bushy growth up to 2 m. Parentage: unrecorded.

Brasilia A Hybrid Tea raised by McGredy in 1968. Parentage: 'Perfecta' × 'Piccadilly'.

Sarah Arnott A Hybrid Tea raised by Croll in 1957. Some scent. Parentage: 'Ena Harkness' × 'Peace'.

Summer Love (Franluv) A Floribunda raised by Cowlishaw in 1986. Bushy growth up to 1.3 m. Good scent. Parentage: 'Pink Parfait' × 'Cynthia Brooke'.

Tombola A Floribunda raised by De Ruiter in 1966. Height up to 75 cm. Parentage: 'Amor' × seedling.

Typhoon (Taifun) A Hybrid Tea raised by Kordes, introduced by McGredy 1972. Scented. Height to 1 m. Free flowering. Parentage: 'Colour Wonder' × 'Dr A. J. Verhage'.

Tombola

Brasilia

Sarah Arnott

Typhoon

Summer Love

Voodoo

Yellow Pages

Shreveport

Portrait

Gold Medal

Mon Chéri

Olympic Torch

Maid of Honour

Love

October 13th, from Portland, Oregon

October 14th, from Fred Edmunds Inc, Wilsonville, Oregon

Voodoo (Aromiclea)   A Hybrid Tea raised by Christensen in 1986. Parentage: not yet available.

Yellow Pages   A Hybrid Tea raised and introduced by McGredy in 1971. Some scent. Height up to 1.3 m. Parentage: 'Arthur Bell' × 'Peer Gynt'.

Shreveport   A Floribunda raised by Kordes and introduced by Armstrong in 1981. Scented. Parentage: 'Zorina' × 'Ulve Seeler'.

Portrait (Meypink, Stephanie de Monaco)   . A Hybrid Tea raised by Meyer and introduced by Conard–Pyle in 1971. Some scent. Height up to 1 m. Parentage: 'Pink Parfait' × 'Pink Peace'.

Gold Medal (Aroyquelia, Aroyqueli) A Floribunda raised by Christensen and introduced by Armstrong in 1982. The young buds are sometimes suffused with pale pink.

Parentage: 'Yellow Pages' × ('Granada' × 'Garden Party').

Mon Chéri (Arocher)   A Hybrid Tea raised by Christensen and introduced by Armstrong in 1981. Flowers early, repeating rapidly. Flower colour darkens with age. Parentage: Seedling × 'Double Delight'.

Olympic Torch (Sei-ka)   A Hybrid Tea raised by Suzuki and introduced by Keisei Rose Nursery and Country Garden Nursery. Parentage: 'Rose Gaujard' × 'Crimson Glory'.

Maid of Honour   A Hybrid Tea raised by Weddle in 1986. Parentage: unrecorded.

Love (Jactwin)   A Floribunda raised by Warriner and introduced by Jackson & Perkins in 1980. Lasts well into winter. Parentage: seedling × 'Redgold'.

Swarthmore (Meitaras)   A Hybrid Tea raised by Meilland and introduced by Conard–Pyle in 1963. Parentage: ('Independence' × 'Happiness') × 'Peace'.

Las Vegas (Korgane)   A Hybrid Tea raised by Kordes in 1981. Blooms intermittently. Parentage: 'Ludwigshafen am Rhein' × 'Feuerzauber'.

Angelique (Ankori)   A Hybrid Tea raised by Kordes in 1982. Parentage: unrecorded.

Chiyo   A Hybrid Tea raised by Ota and introduced by Eastern Roses in 1975. Parentage: 'Karl Herbst' × 'Chrysler Imperial'.

Wini Edmunds   A Hybrid Tea raised by McGredy and introduced by Edmunds in 1973. Some scent. Parentage: 'Red Lion' × 'Hanne'.

Modern Art (Poulart)   A Hybrid Tea raised by Poulsen in 1984. Parentage: not yet available.

Australian Gold

Ruby Wedding

Derek Nimmo

Paradise

Malmesbury

Sweetheart

Keepsake

Midas

Congratulations

July 12th, from Wisley

Conqueror's Gold   *Funkhur*

Geraldine   Photo Meilland   *Catherine Déneuve*

Dolly Parton

Derek Nimmo (Macwhenu, Macwhe)   A Hybrid Tea raised by McGredy and introduced by Mattock in 1981. Some scent. Parentage: unnamed seedlings.

Ruby Wedding   A Hybrid Tea introduced by Gregory in 1979. Spreading growth. Parentage: 'Mayflower' × ?

Australian Gold (Kormat)   A Floribunda raised by Kordes and introduced by Mattock in 1980. Some scent. Repeat-flowering. Parentage: unrecorded.

Malmesbury   A Hybrid Tea introduced by Sanday in 1980. Compact growth. Parentage: 'Vera Dalton' × 'Parasol'.

Paradise (Wezeip)   A Hybrid Tea raised by Weeks and introduced by Conard-Pyle in 1978. Some scent. Height up to 1.3 m. Flowers verging on mauve. Parentage: 'Swarthmore' × seedling.

Sweetheart (Cocapeer)   A Hybrid Tea introduced by Cocker in 1980. Good scent. Height up to 2 m. Parentage: 'Peer Gynt' × ('Fragrant Cloud' × 'Gay Gordons').

Keepsake (Esmeralda, Kormalda)   A Hybrid Tea introduced by Kordes in 1981. Growth up to 1.3 m. Parentage: Seedling × 'Red Planet'.

Midas (Dorothe, Legga)   A Hybrid Tea

introduced by Le Grice in 1980. Height up to 1.3 m. Parentage: 'Grandpa Dickson' × 'Dr A. J. Verhage'.

Congratulations (Korlift, Sylvia)   A Hybrid Tea introduced by Kordes in 1979. Upright growth to 2 m. Good as a cut flower and for hedging. Parentage: 'Carina' × seedling.

Conqueror's Gold (Hartwiz)   A Floribunda introduced by Harkness in 1986. Parentage: not available.

Dolly Parton   A Hybrid Tea introduced by Winchel in 1983. Good scent. Parentage: 'Fragrant Cloud' × 'Oklahoma'.

Funkhur (Korport, Golden Summers)   A Hybrid Tea raised by Kordes in 1984. Parentage: not available.

Geraldine (Peahaze)   A Floribunda raised by Pearce and introduced by Limes in 1983. Parentage: unnamed seedlings.

Catherine Déneuve (Meipraserpi)   A Hybrid Tea raised by Meilland in 1981. Parentage: not recorded.

Bettina (Mepal)   A Hybrid Tea raised by Meilland in 1953. Well-scented. Leaves glossy, reddish. Parentage: 'Peace' × ('Mme Joseph Perraud' × 'Demain').

Photo Meilland   *Bettina*

163

Manou Meilland

Colorama

Hidalgo

Orient Express

Pot O' Gold

Forgotten Dreams

Marion Harkness

Ace of Hearts

Marijke Koopman

July 12th, from Wisley

Manou Meilland (Meitulimon)   A Hybrid Tea raised and introduced by Meilland in 1979. Very free flowering. Parentage: ('Meigriso' × 'Baronne Edmond de Rothschild') × ('Ma Fille' × 'Love Song').

Colorama (Meirigalu)   A Hybrid Tea raised by Meilland and introduced by Conard-Pyle in 1968. Bushy growth up to 1.3 m tall. Parentage: 'Suspense' × 'Confidence'.

Hidalgo (Meitulandi)   A Hybrid Tea raised and introduced by Meilland in 1979. Good scent. Parentage: ('Queen Elizabeth' × 'Karl Herbst') × ('Meifiga' × 'Pharaon') × ('Meicesar' × 'Papa Meilland').

Orient Express   A Hybrid Tea introduced by Wheatcroft in 1978. Good scent. Parentage: 'Sunblest' × seedling.

Pot O' Gold (Dicdivine)   A Hybrid Tea introduced by Dickson in 1980. Some scent. Height up to 1.3 m. Parentage: 'Eurorose' × 'Whiskey Mac'.

Forgotten Dreams   A Hybrid Tea raised by Bracegirdle and introduced by Higgs in 1981. Good scent. Parentage: 'Fragrant Cloud' × 'Tenerife'.

Marion Harkness (Harkantibil)   A Hybrid Tea introduced by Harkness in 1979. Parentage: ('Manx Queen' × 'Prima Ballerina') × ('Chanelle' × 'Piccadilly').

Ace of Hearts (Asso di Cuori, Korred, Toque Rouge)   A Hybrid Tea introduced by Kordes in 1981. Parentage: not recorded.

Marijke Koopman   A Hybrid Tea raised and introduced by Fryer in 1979. Some scent. Height up to 1.3 m. Parentage: not recorded.

Agéna   A Hybrid Tea raised by Delbard-Chabert in 1966. Leaves glossy, leathery. Parentage: 'Chic Parisien' × ('Michele Meilland' × 'Mme Joseph Perraud').

Domila (Lapnat)   A Hybrid Tea raised by Laperrière in 1971. Parentage: not recorded.

Anne de Bretagne (Meituraphar, Décor Rose)   A shrub rose raised by Meilland in 1976. Tall growing. Parentage: ('Malcair' × 'Danse des Sylphes') × ('Meialfi' × 'Zambra').

Gilbert Bécaud (Meiridorio)   A Hybrid Tea raised by Meilland in 1984. Parentage: not recorded.

Centenaire de Lourdes (Delge, Mrs. Jones)   A Hybrid Tea raised by Delbard-Charbert in 1958. Parentage: derived originally from 'Frau Karl Druschki'.

Porthos (Lapad)   A Floribunda raised by Laperrière in 1971. Parentage: not recorded.

Agena

Domila

Photo Meilland   *Anne de Bretagne*

Photo Meilland   *Gilbert Bécaud*

Centenaire de Lourdes

Porthos

Heidi Jayne

Rosemary Harkness

Mary Donaldson

Remember Me

Polar Star

Sexy Rexy

Princess Alice

Marion Foster

Red Brigand

July 14th, from Wisley

Heidi Jayne A Hybrid Tea raised by Esser in 1986. Scented. Height up to 1.3 m. Parentage: ('Piccadilly' × 'Queen Elizabeth') × ('Fragrant Cloud' × seedling).

Rosemary Harkness (Harrowbond) A Hybrid Tea raised by Harkness in 1985. Scented. Good as a cut flower. Spreading growth up to 1 m high and as much wide. Parentage: 'Compassion' × ('Basildon Bond' × 'Grandpa Dickson').

Mary Donaldson (Canmiss, Canana) A Hybrid Tea raised by Cants in 1984. Good scent. Height up to about 80 cm. Parentage: 'English Miss' × seedling.

Remember Me (Cocdestin) A Hybrid Tea raised by Cocker in 1984. Height up to 1 m. Parentage: not yet available.

Polar Star (Polarstern, Tanlarpost) A Hybrid Tea raised by Tantau and introduced by Wheatcroft in 1982. Good scent. Bushy growth up to 1.3 m. Parentage: unrecorded.

Sexy Rexy (Macrexy) A Floribunda raised by McGredy and introduced by Sealand in 1984. Bushy growth up to 1.3 m. Parentage: 'Seaspray' × 'Dreaming'.

Princess Alice (Hartanna, Zonta Rose) A Floribunda raised and introduced by Harkness in 1985. Height up to 1.1 m. Parentage: 'Judy Garland' × 'Anne Harkness'.

Marion Foster (Meicapula) A Floribunda raised by Meilland in 1984. Parentage: not yet available.

Red Brigand (Santor) A Floribunda raised by Sanday in 1984. Parentage: not yet available.

Anastasia A Hybrid Tea raised by Greff in 1980. Very vigorous. Parentage: 'John F. Kennedy' × 'Pascali'.

Captain Cook A Floribunda raised by McGredy and introduced by Mattock in 1977. Scented. Parentage: 'Irish Mist' × seedling.

Glengarry A Floribunda raised by Cocker in 1969. Height up to 1.3 m. Parentage: 'Evelyn Fison' × 'Wendy Cussons'.

Intrigue (Korlech, Lavaglut, Lavaglow) A Floribunda raised by Kordes in 1978. Height up to 1 m. Parentage: 'Grüss an Bayern' × seedling.

Sheer Bliss (Jactro) A Hybrid Tea raised by Warriner and introduced by Jackson & Perkins in 1987. Scented. Height up to 1.3 m. Parentage: 'White Masterpiece' × 'Grand Masterpiece'.

Stroller A Floribunda raised by Dickson in 1969. Bushy growth up to 75 cm. Parentage: 'Manx Queen' × 'Happy Event'.

Touch of Class (Kricarlo, Maréchal le Clerke) A Hybrid Tea raised by Kriloff in 1980. Parentage: unrecorded.

Anastasia

Intrigue

Captain Cook

Glengarry

Touch of Class

Sheer Bliss

Stroller

Café

Jocelyn

Lavender Pinocchio

Plentiful

Orange Sensation

Tip Top

Allgold

Paddy McGredy

Chanelle

July 18th, from David Austin Roses

Frensham

Lavender Pinocchio

Natalie Nypels

Rosemary Rose

Irene of Denmark

Kathleen Ferrier

Café A Floribunda raised by Kordes in 1956. Tall growth. Good scent. Parentage: ('Golden Glow' × R. × *kordesii*) × 'Lavender Pinocchio'.

Jocelyn A Floribunda raised by Le Grice in 1970. Medium height. Parentage: unrecorded.

Lavender Pinocchio A Floribunda raised by Boerner in 1948. Short to medium height. Good scent. Parentage: 'Pinocchio' × 'Grey Pearl'.

Plentiful A Floribunda raised by De Ruiter in 1960. Medium height. Good scent. Susceptible to mildew and blackspot. Parentage: 'Amor' × 'Fashion'.

Orange Sensation A Floribunda raised by de Ruiter in 1960. Medium height. Good scent. Susceptible to mildew and blackspot. Parentage 'Amor' × 'Fashion'.

Tip Top A Floribunda raised by Tantau in 1963. Very short growth. Susceptible to blackspot. Parentage: seedling × seedling.

Allgold A Floribunda raised by Le Grice in 1956. Short growth. Colour very stable. Parentage: 'Goldilocks' × 'Ellinor Le Grice'.

Paddy McGredy A Floribunda raised by McGredy in 1962. Short growth. Susceptible to blackspot but exceptionally floriferous. Parentage: 'Spartan' × 'Tzigane'.

Chanelle A Floribunda raised by McGredy in 1958. Medium height. Some scent. Parentage:

'Ma Perkins' × ('Mrs William Sproth' × 'Fashion').

Frensham A Floribunda raised by Norman in 1946. Tall growth. Slightly susceptible to mildew. Formerly a very popular rose and common in old gardens. Parentage: seedling × 'Crimson Glory'.

Natalie Nypels (Mevrouw Natalie Nypels) A Polyantha hybrid raised by Leenders in 1919. Short growth. Good scent. Parentage: 'Orléans Rose' × ('Comtesse du Cayla' × R. *foetida* 'Bicolor').

Rosemary Rose A Floribunda raised by De Ruiter in 1955, with flat, old-rose-like flowers of a particularly virulent colour. Medium height. Young growth purplish. Somewhat susceptible to mildew. Parentage: 'Grüss an Teplitz' × seedling.

Irene of Denmark A Floribunda raised by Poulsen in 1948. Short growth. Some scent. Parentage: 'Orléans Rose' × ('Mme Plantier' × 'Edina').

Kathleen Ferrier A Floribunda raised by Buisman in 1952. Medium height. Some scent. Parentage: 'Gartenstolz' × 'Shot Silk'.

Dusky Maiden A Floribunda raised by Le Grice in 1947. Medium height. Good scent. Parentage: ('Daily Mail Scented Rose' × 'Etoile de Holland') × 'Else Poulsen'.

Dusky Maiden

Westerland

Prominent

Queen Elizabeth

Ice White

Evelyn Fison

Escapade

Sea Pearl

Copper Pot

Dearest

July 16th, from Wisley

Magenta

Goldbusch

Lavender Lassie

Nymphenburg

Saga

Sparrieshoop

July 10th, from Wisley

Westerland   A Floribunda raised by Kordes in 1969. Medium height. Good scent. Parentage: 'Friedrich Wörlein' × 'Circus'.

Prominent (Korp)   A Floribunda raised by Kordes in 1970. Medium to tall growth. Parentage: 'Colour Wonder' × 'Zorina'.

Queen Elizabeth (The Queen Elizabeth Rose) A Floribunda raised by Lammerts in 1955. Very tall upright growth, up to 3 m. The commonest pink Floribunda. Parentage: 'Charlotte Armstrong' × 'Floradora'.

Ice White   A Floribunda raised by McGredy in 1966. Medium height. Parentage: 'Mme Leon Cuny' × ('Orange Sweetheart' × 'Tantua's Triumph').

Evelyn Fison (Irish Wonder)   A Floribunda raised by McGredy in 1962. Short to medium height. Very bushy and a popular bedding rose. Parentage: 'Moulin Rouge' × 'Corona'.

Escapade   A Floribunda raised by Harkness in 1967. Medium to tall growth. Good scent. Parentage: 'Pink Parfait' × 'Baby Faurax'.

Sea Pearl (Flower Girl)   A Floribunda raised by Dickson in 1964. Tall growth. Some scent. Parentage: 'Perfecta' × 'Montezuma'.

Copper Pot   A Floribunda raised by Dickson in 1968. Medium to tall growth. Parentage: seedling × 'Spek's Yellow'.

Dearest   A Floribunda raised by Dickson in 1960. Short to medium growth. Good scent. Susceptible to blackspot and to damage by rain. Parentage: seedling × 'Spartan'.

Lavender Lassie   A Hybrid Musk raised by Kordes in 1959. Medium height. Repeat flowering. Good scent. Parentage: 'Hamburg' × 'Mme Norbert Levavasseur'.

Magenta (Kordes' Magenta)   A Floribunda

raised by Kordes in 1955. Short semi-prostrate growth. Good scent. Parentage: seedling × 'Lavender Pinocchio'.

Goldbusch   A modern Shrub Rose raised by Kordes in 1954. Repeat flowering. Growth tall. Good scent. Parentage: 'Golden Glow' × *R. eglanteria* seedling.

Nymphenburg   A Hybrid Musk raised by Kordes in 1954. Tall growth. Repeat flowering. Good scent. Parentage: 'Sangerhausen' × 'Sun Mist'.

Saga   A Floribunda raised by Harkness in 1974. Short to medium height. Some scent. Parentage 'Rudolph Timm' × ('Chanelle' × 'Piccadilly').

Sparrieshoop   A modern Shrub Rose raised by Kordes in 1953. Medium to tall growth. Some scent. Parentage: ('Baby Château' × 'Else Poulsen') × 'Magnifica' (a *rubiginosa* hybrid).

Lilli Marlene

Pink
Elizabeth Arden

Europeana

Vera Dalton

Elizabeth of Glamis

Pink Parfait

Paprika

Woburn Abbey

Dorothy Wheatcroft

July 18th, from Wisley

Glenfiddich

Sunsprite

Southampton

Margaret Merrill

Satchmo

Elizabeth Philp

July 18th, from Wisley

Lilli Marlene A Floribunda raised by Kordes in 1959. Medium height. Susceptible to mildew. Parentage: ('Our Princess' × 'Rudolph Timm') × 'Anna'.

Pink Elizabeth Arden (Geisha) A Floribunda raised by Tantau in 1964. Medium height. Parentage: unrecorded.

Europeana A Floribunda raised by De Ruiter in 1963. Medium height. Susceptible to mildew. Parentage: 'Ruth Leuwevak' × 'Rosemary Rose'.

Vera Dalton A Floribunda raised by Norman in 1961. Medium height. Parentage: 'Paul's Scarlet Climber' selfed × ('Mary' × 'Queen Elizabeth').

Elizabeth of Glamis (Irish Beauty) A Floribunda raised by McGredy in 1964. Medium height. Good scent. Parentage: 'Spartan' × 'Highlight'.

Pink Parfait A Floribunda raised by Swim in 1960. Medium height. Parentage: 'First Love' × 'Pinocchio'.

Paprika A Floribunda raised by Tantau in 1958. Medium height. Parentage: 'Marchenland' × 'Red Favourite'.

Woburn Abbey A Floribunda raised by Sidey and Cobley in 1962. Medium height. Susceptible to mildew and rust. Parentage: 'Masquerade' × 'Fashion'.

Dorothy Wheatcroft A Floribunda raised by Tantau in 1960. Medium height. Parentage: unrecorded.

Glenfiddich A Floribunda raised by Cocker in 1976. Medium height. Some scent. Parentage: 'Arthur Bell' × ('Sabine' × 'Circus').

Sunsprite (Korresia, Friesia) A Floribunda raised by Kordes in 1974. Short to medium

height. Some scent. Parentage: 'Friedrich Worlein' × 'Spanish Sun'.

Southampton (Susan Ann) A Floribunda raised by Harkness in 1972. Tall to medium height. Some scent. Parentage: ('Ann Elizabeth' × 'Allgold') × 'Yellow Cushion'.

Margaret Merrill A Floribunda raised by Harkness in 1978. Medium height. Susceptible to blackspot. Strong scent. Parentage: ('Rudolph Timm' × 'Dedication') × 'Pascali'.

Satchmo A Floribunda raised by McGredy in 1970. Medium height. Parentage: 'Evelyn Fison' × 'Diamant'.

Elizabeth Philp A Floribunda raised by J. B. Philp & Son in 1976. Parentage: sport of 'Liverpool Echo'.

Olé

Aquarius

Happy Wanderer

Nearly Wild

Viva

Betty Prior

Tony Jacklin

Redgold

Impatient

October 13th, from Portland, Oregon

Charisma

Gene Boerner

Angel Face

John S. Armstrong

Elmshorn

Moonraker

Olé   A Hybrid Tea raised by Armstrong in 1964. Tall to medium height. Good scent. Parentage: 'Roundelay' × 'El Capitan'.

Aquarius (Armaq)   A Hybrid Tea raised by Armstrong in 1971. Medium height. Parentage: ('Charlotte Armstrong' × 'Contrast') × [('Fandango' × ('World's Fair' × 'Floradora')].

Happy Wanderer   A Floribunda raised by McGredy in 1972. Medium height. Parentage: seedling × 'Marlena'.

Nearly Wild   A Floribunda raised by Brownwell in 1941. Good scent. Parentage: 'Dr van Fleet' × 'Leuchtstern'.

Viva   A Floribunda raised by Warriner in 1974. Tall growth. Parentage: unnamed seedlings.

Betty Prior   A Floribunda raised by Prior in 1935. Medium height. Good scent. Parentage: 'Kirsten Poulsen' × seedling.

Tony Jacklin   A Floribunda raised by McGredy in 1972. Medium to tall growth. Parentage: 'City of Leeds' × 'Irish Mist'.

Redgold (Dicor, Rouge et Or)   A Floribunda raised by Dickson in 1971. Tall growth. Parentage: [('Karl Herbst' × 'Masquerade') × 'Faust'] × 'Piccadilly'.

Impatient (Jacdew)   A Floribunda raised by Warriner in 1984. Medium height. Very thorny. Parentage: 'Climbing America' × seedling.

Charisma   A Floribunda raised by Hill in 1977. Medium height. Parentage: 'Gemini' × 'Zorina'.

Gene Boerner   A Floribunda raised by Boerner in 1968. Medium to tall growth. Parentage: 'Ginger' × ('Ma Perkins' × 'Garnette Supreme').

Angel Face   A Floribunda raised by Swim and Weeks in 1968. Medium height. Good scent. Parentage: ('Circus' × 'Lavender Pinocchio') × 'Sterling Silver'.

John S. Armstrong   A Hybrid Tea raised by Swim in 1961. Tall growth. Parentage: 'Charlotte Armstrong' × seedling.

Elmshorn   A modern Shrub Rose raised by Kordes in 1951. Repeat flowering. Parentage: 'Hamburg' × 'Verdun'.

Moonraker   A Floribunda raised by Harkness in 1968. Medium height. Parentage: 'Pink Parfait' × 'Highlight'.

Yellow Queen Elizabeth   A yellow sport of 'Queen Elizabeth' introduced by Vlaeminck in 1958.

Prince Igor climbing (Frenzy, Meihigor)   A climbing sport of a Floribunda raised by Meilland 1970. Well-scented. Parentage: ('Sarabande' × 'Dany Robin') × 'Zambra'.

Yellow Queen Elizabeth

Photo Meilland

Prince Igor

Variety Club

Michelle

Mellow Yellow

Ville de Zürich

Lorna Doone

Texas

Summer Meeting

Merlin

Beauty Queen

Irish Rover

July 16th, from The Gardens of the Rose

Taora   *King Arthur*   *Shepherdess*

Dorrit   *Bonfire Night*   *Lively Lady*

July 16th, from The Gardens of the Rose

Variety Club A Floribunda raised by McGredy in 1965. Parentage: 'Columbine' × 'Circus'.

Michelle (Michele) A Floribunda raised by De Ruiter in 1970. Medium height; good scent. Parentage: seedling × 'Orange Sensation'.

Mellow Yellow A Hybrid Tea raised by Waterhouse Nurseries in 1968. Medium height. Parentage: a sport of 'Piccadilly'.

Ville de Zürich A Floribunda raised by Gaujard in 1967. Medium height. Parentage: 'Miss France' × 'Nouvelle Europe'.

Lorna Doone A Floribunda raised by Harkness in 1970. Medium height. Parentage: 'Red Dandy' × 'Lilli Marlene'.

Texas (Poultex, Golden Piccolo) A Floribunda raised by Poulsen in 1984. Parentage: 'Mini-Poul' × seedling.

Summer Meeting A Floribunda raised by Harkness in 1968. Low growth. Parentage: 'Allgold' × 'Circus'.

Merlin A Floribunda raised by Harkness in 1967. Medium height. Parentage: 'Pink Parfait' × 'Circus'.

Beauty Queen (Canmiss) A Floribunda raised by Cants in 1984. Good scent. Parentage: not yet available.

Irish Rover A Hybrid Tea raised by McGredy in 1970. Medium height. Parentage: 'Violet Carson' × 'Super Star'.

Taora (Tanta) A Floribunda raised by Tantau in 1968. Tall growth. Parentage: 'Fragrant Cloud' × 'Schweitzer Grüss'.

King Arthur A Floribunda raised by Harkness in 1967. Medium height. Parentage: 'Pink Parfait' × 'Highlight'.

Shepherdess A Floribunda raised by Mattock in 1967. Medium height. Parentage: 'Allgold' × 'Peace'.

Dorrit A Floribunda raised by Sønderhausen in 1968. Medium height. Parentage: seedling × 'Folie d'Espagne'.

Bonfire Night (Bonfire) A Floribunda raised by McGredy in 1971. Medium height. Parentage: 'Tiki' × 'Variety Club'.

Lively Lady A Floribunda raised by Cocker in 1969. Medium height. Some scent. Parentage: 'Elizabeth of Glamis' × 'Super Star'.

Rainbow

Dublin Bay

Chivalry

Red Rum

Centurion

Minuette

Yorkshire Bank

Black Beauty

Roddy McMillan

Olympiad

July 16th, from The Gardens of the Rose

Rainbow   A modern shrub raised by Mattock in 1974. Repeat flowering. Medium height. Parentage: not yet available.

Dublin Bay   A climbing Floribunda raised by McGredy in 1976. Repeat flowering. Parentage: 'Bantry Bay' × 'Altissimo'.

Chivalry (Macpow)   A Hybrid Tea raised by McGredy in 1977. Tall, upright growth. Parentage: 'Peer Gynt' × 'Brasilia'.

Red Rum   A Floribunda raised by Bees in 1976. Parentage: 'Handel' × 'Arthur Bell'.

Centurion   A Floribunda raised by Mattock in 1975. Medium height. Some scent. Parentage: 'Evelyn Fison' × seedling. Named for the centenary of John Mattock.

Minuette (Laminuette)   A dwarf Floribunda raised by Lammerts in 1969. Medium height. Some scent. Parentage: 'Peace' × 'Rumba'.

Yorkshire Bank (Rutrulo, True Love) A Hybrid Tea raised by De Ruiter in 1979. Medium height. Some scent. Parentage: 'Pascali' × 'Peer Gynt'.

Black Beauty   A Hybrid Tea raised by Delbard in 1973. Short to medium height. Parentage: ('Gloire de Rome' × 'Impeccable') × 'Papa Meilland'.

Roddy McMillan (Cocared)   A Hybrid Tea raised by Cocker in 1982. Parentage: ('Fragrant Cloud' × 'Postillion') × 'Wisbechpold'.

Olympiad (Macauck)   A Hybrid Tea raised by McGredy in 1983. Medium height. Some scent. A particularly good deep red. Parentage: 'Red Planet' × 'Pharoah'.

Iceberg (Fée des Neiges, Schneewittchen) A Floribunda raised by Kordes in 1958. Tall to medium height. Moderately susceptible to blackspot. In cold weather the flowers may be pale pink. Very hardy. This is probably the best and most popular of all white Floribunda roses, and is very graceful when not overfed. For the climbing sport see p. 99. Parentage: 'Robin Hood' (a hybrid musk) × 'Virgo'.

Hamburger Phoenix   A modern Shrub raised by Kordes in 1955. Tall growth, up to 3 m with support. Parentage: *Rosa × kordesii* × seedling.

Sarabande   A Floribunda raised by Meilland in 1957. Short growing. Parentage: 'Cocorico' × 'Moulin Rouge'.

Hakuun   A Floribunda raised by Poulsen in 1962. Short growing. Parentage: seedling × ('Pinocchio' × 'Pinocchio').

Miracle   A Floribunda raised by Verbeek in 1962. Medium to tall growth. Parentage: seedling × 'Fashion'.

Nina Weibull   A Floribunda raised by Poulsen in 1962. Short growth. Parentage: 'Fanal' × 'Masquerade'.

Coronet   A Floribunda raised by De Ruiter in 1947. Medium height. Parentage: 'Independence' × 'Red Wonder'.

Hamburger Phoenix

Iceberg

Hakuun

Sarabande

Miracle

Nina Weibull

Coronet

Coventry Cathedral

Sun Flare

Bahia

Marina

Saratoga

The Sun

Granada

Little Darling

Playboy

October 13th, from Portland, Oregon

FLORIBUNDAS

Orange Silk

Grace Abounding

City of Leeds

Sir Lancelot

Kerryman

Liverpool Echo

July 18th, from Wisley

Coventry Cathedral (Cathedral)   A Floribunda raised by McGredy in 1973. Medium height. Susceptible to blackspot. Parentage: ('Little Darling' × 'Goldilocks') × 'Irish Mist'.

Sun Flare (Jacjem)   A Floribunda raised by Warriner in 1981. Medium height. Parentage: 'Sunsprite' × seedling.

Bahia   A Floribunda raised by Lammerts in 1974. Medium height. Parentage: 'Rumba' × 'Tropicana'.

Marina (Rinakor)   A Floribunda raised by Kordes in 1974. Tall growth. Parentage: 'Colour Wonder' × seedling.

Saratoga   A Floribunda raised by Boerner in 1963. Medium height. Very good scent. Parentage: 'White Bouquet' × 'Princess White'.

The Sun   A Floribunda raised by McGredy in 1973. Medium height. Some scent. Parentage: ('Little Darling' × 'Goldilocks') × 'Irish Mist'.

Granada (Donatella)   A Hybrid Tea raised by Lindquist in 1964. Medium height. Good scent. Parentage: 'Tiffany' × 'Cavalcade'.

Little Darling   A Floribunda raised by Duehrsen in 1956. Tall growth. Good scent. Parentage: 'Capt. Thomas' × ('Baby Château' × 'Fashion').

Playboy (Cheerio)   A Floribunda raised by Cocker in 1976. Medium height. Parentage: 'City of Leeds' × seedling.

Orange Silk   A Floribunda raised by McGredy in 1968. Medium height. Parentage: 'Orangeade' × ('Ma Perkins' × 'Independence').

Grace Abounding   A Floribunda raised by Harkness in 1968. Medium height. Flower colour variable from white, through cream to pink. Some scent. Parentage: 'Pink Parfait' × 'Penelope'.

City of Leeds   A Floribunda raised by McGredy in 1966. Medium height. Parentage: 'Evelyn Fison' × ('Spartan' × 'Red Favourite').

Sir Lancelot   A Floribunda raised by Harkness in 1967. Short to medium height. Susceptible to mildew and blackspot. Parentage: 'Vera Dalton' × 'Woburn Abbey'.

Kerryman   A Floribunda raised by McGredy in 1971. Medium height. Susceptible to blackspot. Parentage: 'Paddy McGredy' × ('Mme Leon Cuny' × 'Columbine').

Liverpool Echo   A Floribunda raised by McGredy in 1971. Medium to tall. Parentage: ('Little Darling' × 'Goldilocks') × 'München'.

Benson and Hedges Gold

Rocky

Regensberg

Poppet

Sue Lawley

Blue Parfum

Everest Double Fragrance

Amanda

Norwich Castle

Gold Bunny

Alpha

July 12th, from Wisley

Amanda

City of Belfast

Busy Lizzie

Fred Loads

Moon Maiden

Anne Cocker

Benson and Hedges Gold (Macgem)   A Hybrid Tea raised by McGredy in 1979. Medium height. Somewhat scented. Parentage: 'Yellow Pages' × ('Arthur Bell' × 'Cynthia Brooke').

Rocky (Mackepa)   A Floribunda raised by McGredy in 1979. Tall growing or can be used as a climber. Parentage: 'Liverpool Echo' × ['Evelyn Fison' × ('Orange Sweetheart' × 'Frühlingsmorgen')].

Regensberg (Macyoumis, Young Mistress, Buffalo Bill).   A Floribunda raised by McGredy in 1979. Short growth. Some scent. Parentage: 'Geoff Boycott' × 'Old Master'.

Poppet   A Floribunda raised by Bees in 1979. Some scent. Parentage: 'Spartan' × 'Arthur Bell'.

Sue Lawley (Kobold, Macspash)   A Floribunda raised by McGredy in 1980. Medium height. Parentage: a complex hybrid involving 'Frühlingsmorgen'.

Blue Parfum (Tanfifum, Blue Parfume)   A Hybrid Tea raised by Tantau in 1978.

Everest Double Fragrance   A Floribunda raised by Beales in 1979. Tall, upright growth. Good scent. Parentage: 'Dearest' × 'Elizabeth of Glamis'.

Amanda (Beesian)   A Floribunda raised by Bees in 1980. Medium height. Parentage: 'Arthur Bell' × 'Zambra'.

Norwich Castle   A Floribunda raised by Beales in 1979. Medium height. Parentage: ('Whisky Mac' × 'Arthur Bell') × seedling.

Gold Bunny (Meigronuri)   A Floribunda raised by Paolino in 1978. Medium height. Susceptible to blackspot. Parentage: 'Poppy Flash' × (Meiridge' × 'Allgold').

Alpha (Meinastur)   A Hybrid Tea raised by Paolino in 1975. Medium height. Parentage: [('Show Girl' × 'Baccara') × 'Romantica'] × ('Romantica' × 'Super Star').

City of Belfast   A Floribunda raised by McGredy in 1968. Short to medium height. Parentage: 'Evelyn Fison' × ('Korona' × 'Circus').

Fred Loads   A Floribunda raised by Holmes in 1967. Medium to tall. Some scent. Parentage: 'Orange Sensation' × 'Dorothy Wheatcroft'.

Moon Maiden   A Floribunda raised by Mattock in 1970. Good scent. Parentage: 'Fred Streeter' × 'Allgold'.

Busy Lizzie (Harbusy)   A Floribunda raised by Harkness in 1971. Medium height. Parentage: ('Pink Parfait' × 'Masquerade') × 'Dearest'.

Anne Cocker   A Floribunda raised by Cocker in 1971. Tall growth. Susceptible to mildew. Parentage: 'Highlight' × 'Colour Wonder'.

Coronation Gold

John Crossley

Memento

Stirling Castle

Wonder of Woolies

Fragrant Delight

Young Venturer

Amsterdam

Tabler's Choice

Harry Edland

Bobby Dazzler

July 12th, from Wisley

Arthur Bell

Baby Bio

Gypsy Moth

Princess Michiko

Fragrant Delight

Coronation Gold A Floribunda raised by Cocker in 1978. Medium height. Parentage: ('Sabine' × 'Circus') × ('Anne Cocker' × 'Arthur Bell').

John Crossley A Hybrid Tea raised by Wheatcroft in 1978. Parentage: unrecorded.

Memento (Dicbar) A Floribunda raised by Dickson in 1978. Medium height. Parentage: 'Bangor' × 'Korbell'.

Stirling Castle A Floribunda raised by Cocker in 1978. Short growth. Parentage: ('Anne Cocker' × 'Elizabeth of Glamis') × ('Orange Sensation' × 'Sweet Repose').

Wonder of Woolies A Floribunda raised by Bees in 1978. Tall growth. Very good scent. Parentage: 'Arthur Bell' × 'Elizabeth of Glamis'.

Fragrant Delight A Floribunda raised by the Wisbech Plant Co. 1978. Medium height. Good scent. Parentage: 'Chanelle' × 'Whisky Mac'.

Young Venturer (Mattsun) A Floribunda raised by Mattock in 1979. Upright growth. Good scent. Parentage 'Arthur Bell' × 'Cynthia Brooke'.

Amsterdam A Floribunda raised by Verschunen in 1972. Medium height. Susceptible to mildew. Parentage: 'Europeana' × 'Parkdirektor Riggers'.

Tabler's Choice A Floribunda raised by Harkness in 1973. Medium height. Parentage: ('Orange Sensation' × 'Allgold') × ('Super Star' × 'Piccadilly').

Harry Edland A Floribunda raised by Harkness 1978. Medium height. Good scent. Parentage: ('Lilac Charm' × 'Sterling Silver') ×

['Blue Moon' × ('Sterling Silver' × 'Africa Star')].

Bobby Dazzler A Floribunda raised by Harkness in 1972. Medium height. Some scent. Parentage: ('Vera Dalton' × 'Highlight') × ('Anne Elizabeth' × 'Circus').

Arthur Bell A Floribunda raised by McGredy in 1965. Tall growth. Good scent. Parentage: 'Clâre Grammerstorf' × 'Piccadilly'.

Princess Michiko A Floribunda raised by Dickson in 1966. Medium height. Susceptible to blackspot. Parentage: 'Spartan' × 'Circus'.

Gypsy Moth A Floribunda raised by Tantau 1968. Medium height. Parentage: unrecorded.

Baby Bio A Floribunda raised by Smith in 1977. Short growth. Parentage: 'Golden Treasure' × seedling.

Purple
Splendour

Rose Warrior

June Aberdeen

Red Sprite

Yellow Ribbon

English Miss

Eye Catcher

Rosedale Farm

Stargazer

Blaze Away

July 12th, from Wisley

FLORIBUNDAS

Megiddo

Burma Star

Ann Aberconway

Eye Paint

Fleur Cowles

Rob Roy

July 16th, from Wisley

June Aberdeen   A Floribunda raised by Cocker in 1977. Medium height. Parentage: 'Anne Cocker' × ('Sabine' × 'Circus').

Rose Warrior   A Floribunda raised by Le Grice in 1977. Low growth. Parentage: 'City of Belfast' × 'Ronde Endiablée'.

Purple Splendour   A Floribunda raised by Le Grice in 1976. Medium height. Some scent. Flowers clear purple colour. Parentage: 'News' × 'Overture'.

Red Sprite   A Floribunda raised by Le Grice in 1974. Low growth. Some scent. Parentage: unrecorded.

Yellow Ribbon (Dicalow)   A Floribunda raised by Dickson in 1977. Growth very short. Parentage: 'Illumination' × 'Stroller'.

English Miss   A Floribunda raised by Cant in 1978. Short to medium height. Good scent. Parentage: 'Dearest' × 'Sweet Repose'.

Eye Catcher   A Floribunda raised by Cant in 1976. Tall growth. Good scent. Parentage: 'Arthur Bell' × 'Permille Poulsen'.

Rosedale Farm   We collected this rose at Wisley, but have been unable to find out anything about it!

Stargazer   A Floribunda raised by Harkness in 1977. Growth short. Parentage: 'Marlena' × 'Kim'.

Blaze Away   A Floribunda raised by Sanday in 1979. Low, bushy growth. Parentage: ('Karl Herbst' × 'Crimson Glory') × 'Sarabande'.

Megiddo   A Floribunda raised by Gandy in 1970. Medium height. Susceptible to blackspot. Parentage: 'Coup de Foudre' × 'S'Agaro'.

Burma Star   A Floribunda raised by Cocker in 1974. Tall growth. Some scent. Parentage: 'Arthur Bell' × 'Manx Queen'.

Ann Aberconway   A Floribunda raised by Mattock in 1976. Medium height. Parentage: 'Arthur Bell' × seedling.

Eye Paint   A Floribunda raised by McGredy in 1976. Growth tall. Susceptible to blackspot. Very hardy; sensitive to drought. Parentage: seedling × 'Picasso'.

Fleur Cowles   A Floribunda raised by Gregory in 1972. Medium height. Spicy scent. Parentage: 'Pink Parfait' × seedling.

Rob Roy   A Floribunda raised by Cocker in 1971. Medium height. Parentage: 'Evelyn Fison' × 'Wendy Cussons'.

Arabesque

High Summer

Fiesta Flame

Judy Garland

Topeka

Mr E. E. Greenwell

Grace Kimmins

Letchworth Garden City

Bright Smile

July 12th, from Wisley

Bonnie Hamilton

Matangi

Crimson Wave

Dame of Sark

Old Master

Philip Harvey

July 12th, from Wisley

Arabesque A Floribunda raised by Sanday in 1978. Tall to medium growth. Parentage: ('Gavotte' × 'Super Star') × 'Super Star'.

High Summer (Dicbee) A Floribunda raised by Dickson in 1978. Medium height. Parentage: 'Zorina' × 'Ernest H. Morse'.

Fiesta Flame A Floribunda raised by Sanday in 1978. Low growth. Parentage: 'Sarabande' × 'Ena Harkness'.

Judy Garland A Floribunda raised by Harkness in 1978. Medium height. Scented. Parentage: [('Super Star' × 'Circus') × ('Sabine' × 'Circus')] × 'Pineapple Poll'.

Topeka A Floribunda raised by Wisbech Plant Co. in 1978. Medium height. Parentage: 'Vera Dalton' × seedling.

Mr E. E. Greenwell A Floribunda raised by Harkness in 1979. Short growth. Parentage: 'Jove' × 'City of Leeds'.

Grace Kimmins A Floribunda raised by Gobbee in 1973. Medium height. Parentage: 'Dainty Maid' × 'Red Dandy'.

Letchworth Garden City (Harkover) A Floribunda raised by Harkness in 1979. Medium height. Parentage: ('Sabine' × 'Pineapple Poll') × ('Circus' × 'Mischief').

Bright Smile (Dicdance) A Floribunda raised by Dickson in 1980. Short growth. Parentage: 'Eurorose' × seedling.

Bonnie Hamilton A Floribunda raised by Cocker in 1976. Medium height. Parentage: 'Anne Cocker' × 'Allgold'.

Matangi (Macman) A Floribunda raised by McGredy in 1974. Medium height. Parentage: seedling × 'Picasso'.

Crimson Wave (Meiperator) A Floribunda raised by Meilland in 1971. Tall growth. Parentage: 'Zambra' × [('Sarabande' × ('Goldilocks' × 'Fashion')].

Dame of Sark A Floribunda raised by Harkness in 1976. Tall to medium height. Parentage: ('Pink Parfait' × 'Masquerade') × 'Tabler's Choice'.

Old Master A Floribunda raised by McGredy in 1974. Tall to medium height. Parentage: 'Maxi' × [('Evelyn Fison') × ('Orange Sweetheart' × 'Frühlingsmorgen')].

Philip Harvey A Floribunda raised by Harkness in 1973. Medium height. Parentage: 'Fragrant Cloud' × 'Circus'.

Jan Spek

Vesper

Snowline

Maestro

Scherzo

Cairngorm

Jubilant

Freedom

Seven Seas

Molde

July 16th, from The Gardens of the Rose

Trumpeter

Bonica

Showbiz

Molly McGredy

Jan Spek A Floribunda raised by McGredy in 1966. Short growth. Parentage: 'Cläre Grammerstorf' × 'Doctor Faust'.

Vesper A Floribunda raised by Le Grice in 1966. Medium height. Parentage: unrecorded.

Snowline (Edelweiss) A Floribunda raised by Poulsen in 1970. Short to medium height. Parentage: unrecorded.

Maestro (Mackinju) A Hybrid Tea raised by McGredy in 1981. Medium height. Parentage: unrecorded.

Scherzo (Meipuma) A Floribunda raised by Paolino in 1975. Medium height. Some scent. Parentage: 'Tamango' × ['Sarabande' × ('Goldilocks' × 'Fashion')].

Cairngorm A Floribunda raised by Cocker in 1973. Tall to medium height. Parentage: 'Anne Cocker' × 'Arthur Bell'.

Jubilant A Floribunda raised by Dickson in 1967. Medium height. Bronze leaves. Parentage: 'Dearest' × 'Circus'.

Freedom (Dicjem) A Hybrid Tea raised by Dickson in 1984. Short growth. Some scent. Flower colour does not change. Parentage: ('Eurorose' × 'Typhoon') × 'Bright Smile'.

Seven Seas A Floribunda raised by Harkness in 1971. Short to medium height. Parentage: 'Lilac Charm' × 'Sterling Silver'.

Molde (Mistigri) A Floribunda raised by Tantau in 1964. Medium height. Parentage: seedling × seedling.

Trumpeter (Mactru) A Floribunda raised by McGredy in 1977. Short growth. Parentage: 'Satchmo' × seedling.

Bonica (Meidomonac, Demon) A modern Shrub rose raised by Meilland in 1982. Spreading, arching growth. Very hardy. Produces abundant orange hips. Foliage is disease resistant. Parentage: (*R. sempervirens* × 'Mlle. Marthe Carron') × 'Picasso'.

Showbiz (Tanweieke, Ingrid Weibull) A Floribunda raised by Tantau in 1981. Medium height. Parentage: unrecorded.

Molly McGredy A Floribunda raised by McGredy in 1969. Medium height. Parentage: 'Paddy McGredy' × ('Mme Leon Cuny' × 'Columbine').

Mary Sumner

Intrigue
(Lavaglut)

Nicola

Kapai

Painted Lady

Greensleeves

Basildon Bond

Regensberg

Anne Harkness

Lovers' Meeting

July 12th, from Wisley

Mary Sumner (Macstra)   A Floribunda raised by McGredy in 1976. Growth tall. Parentage: ('Orangeade' × 'Margot Fonteyn') × [('Elizabeth of Glamis' × ('Little Darling' × 'Goldilocks')].

Intrigue (Korlech, Lavaglut, Lavaglow)   A Floribunda raised by Kordes in 1978. Height up to 1 m. Parentage: 'Grüss an Bayern' × seedling. Do not confuse with the mauve 'Intrigue' (Jacum) raised by Warriner in 1984 (below).

Nicola   A Floribunda raised by Gandy in 1980. Medium height. Parentage: unrecorded.

Kapai (Macgam)   A Floribunda raised by McGredy in 1977. Short growth. Very fragrant. Parentage: 'Madame Bollinger' × 'Tombola'.

Basildon Bond (Harjosine)   A Hybrid Tea raised by Harkness in 1980. Medium height. Flowers early, tolerant of rain. Parentage: ('Sabine' × 'Circus') × ('Yellow Cushion' × 'Glory of Ceylon').

Painted Lady   A Hybrid Tea raised by J. A. Herholdt in 1980. Bronze foliage. Parentage: seedling × seedling.

Intrigue (Jacum)   A Floribunda raised by Warriner in 1984. Medium height. Lemony scent. Parentage: 'White Masterpiece' × 'Heirloom'.

Living Fire   A Floribunda raised by Gregory in 1972. Medium to tall. Parentage: 'Super Star' × unknown.

Greensleeves (Harlenten)   A Floribunda raised by Harkness in 1980. Medium height; some scent. Parentage: ('Rudolph Timm' × 'Arthur Bell') × seedling.

Regensberg (Macyoumis, Young Mistress, Buffalo Bill)   A Floribunda raised by McGredy in 1979. Short growth. Some scent. Parentage: 'Geoff Boycott' × 'Old Master'.

Anne Harkness (Harkararnel)   A Floribunda raised by Harkness in 1979. Growth tall. Parentage: 'Bobby Dazzler' × [('Manx Queen' × 'Prima Ballerina') × ('Chanelle' × 'Piccadilly')].

Lovers' Meeting   A Floribunda raised by Gandy in 1980. Medium to tall. Parentage: seedling × 'Egyptian Treasure'.

Fountain (Fontaine)   A Floribunda raised by Tantau in 1970. Medium height. Some scent. Parentage: unrecorded.

Poppy Flash (Meilena, Rusticana)   A Floribunda raised by Meilland in 1971. Medium height. Parentage: ('Dany Robin' × 'Fire King') × ('Alain' × 'Mutabilis').

Picasso (Macpic)   A Floribunda raised by McGredy in 1971. Short to medium height. Susceptible to blackspot. Parentage: 'Marlena' × ['Evelyn Fison' × ('Orange Sweetheart' × 'Frühlingsmorgen')].

Living Fire

Intrigue (Jacum)

Fountain

Picasso

Anne Harkness

Poppy Flash

Caroline Davison

Iced Ginger

English Holiday

Hiroshima's Children

Harpippin

Gardeners' Sunday

City of Bradford

Lovely Lady

Wandering Minstrel

Rediffusion Gold

July 17th, from R. Harkness & Co.

English Holiday A Floribunda raised by Harkness in 1977. Medium height. Susceptible to blackspot. Parentage: 'Bobby Dazzler' × 'Goldbonnet'.

Caroline Davison A Floribunda raised by Harkness in 1980. Short growth. Some scent. Parentage: 'Tip Top' × 'Kim'.

Iced Ginger A Floribunda raised by Dickson in 1971. Medium height. Parentage: 'Anne Watkins' × unknown.

Hiroshima's Children (Harmark) A Floribunda raised by Harkness in 1985. Medium height. Flower colour varies according to the season. Parentage: not yet available.

Harpippin A climber raised by Harkness in 1984. Up to 2 m high. Parentage: 'Royal Dane' × seedling.

Gardeners' Sunday A Floribunda raised by Harkness in 1975. Medium height. Some scent. Parentage: ('Pink Parfait' × 'Masquerade') × 'Arthur Bell'.

City of Bradford (Harrotang) A Floribunda raised by Harkness in 1986. Medium height. Parentage: seedling cross.

Lovely Lady (Dicjabell) A Hybrid Tea raised by Dickson in 1986. Short growth. Good scent. Parentage: 'Silver Jubilee' × ('Eurorose' × 'Annabel').

Wandering Minstrel A Floribunda raised by Harkness in 1986. Short growth. The colour of the flowers changes according to the season. Parentage: 'Dame of Sark' × 'Silver Jubilee'.

Rediffusion Gold (Harquorgold) A Floribunda raised by Harkness in 1984. Short growth. Parentage: not yet available.

Softly Softly (Harkotur) A Floribunda raised by Harkness in 1977. Tall growth. Parentage: ['White Cockade' × ('Highlight' × 'Colour Wonder')] × ('Parkdirektor Riggers' × 'Piccadilly').

Scented Air A Floribunda raised by Dickson in 1963. Medium height. Good scent. Parentage; 'Spartan' seedling × 'Queen Elizabeth'.

Marlena A Floribunda raised by Kordes in 1964. Very short growth. Parentage: 'Gertrud Westphal' × 'Lilli Marlene'.

Apricot Nectar A Floribunda raised by Boerner in 1965. Medium height. Some scent. Parentage: seedling × 'Spartan'.

Manx Queen (Isle of Man) A Floribunda raised by Dickson in 1963. Medium height. Parentage: 'Shepherds' Delight' × 'Circus'.

Chinatown (Ville de Chine) A Floribunda raised by Poulsen in 1963. Medium height. Good scent. This is still one of the best yellow Floribundas. Parentage: 'Columbine' × 'Cläre Grammerstorf'.

Scarlet Queen Elizabeth A Floribunda raised by Dickson in 1963. Growth tall. Parentage: 'Korona' seedling × 'Queen Elizabeth'.

Scented Air

Softly Softly

Apricot Nectar

Manx Queen

Marlena

Chinatown

Scarlet Queen Elizabeth

195

Mountbatten

Wee Jock

Court Jester

Crathes Castle

Princess Michael of Kent

Pretty Maid

Georgie Anderson

Kumbaya

Hannah Gordon

July 12th, from Wisley

Topsi

Sugar Sweet

Strawberry Ice

Redcliffe

Golden Shot

Mountbatten (Harmantelle) A Floribunda raised by Harkness in 1982. Medium to tall growth. Some scent. Parentage: 'Peer Gynt' × [('Anne Cocker' × 'Arthur Bell') × 'Southampton'].

Wee Jock (Cocabest) A Floribunda raised by Cocker in 1980. Short growth. Parentage: 'National Trust' × 'Wee Man'.

Court Jester A Floribunda raised by Cants in 1980. Tall, upright growth. Parentage: unrecorded.

Crathes Castle (Cocathes) A Floribunda raised by Cocker in 1980. Short growth. Parentage: 'Dreamland' × 'Topsi'.

Princess Michael of Kent (Harlightly) A Floribunda raised by Harkness in 1981. Medium height. Parentage: 'Manx Queen' × 'Alexander'.

Pretty Maid A Floribunda raised by Fryers in 1982. Parentage: unrecorded.

Georgie Anderson (Andgeo) A Floribunda raised by Andersons in 1982. Parentage: 'Elizabeth of Glamis' × seedling.

Kumbaya A Floribunda raised by Sanday in 1981. Low, bushy growth. Parentage: 'Chatterbox' × 'Allgold'.

Hannah Gordon (Korweison) A Floribunda raised by Kordes in 1983. Spreading growth. Parentage: seedling × 'Bordure'.

Topsi A Floribunda raised by Tantau in 1971 Very short growth. Susceptible to blackspot. Parentage: 'Fragrant Cloud' × 'Fire Signal'.

Sugar Sweet A Floribunda raised by Sanday in 1973. Medium height. Good scent. Parentage: 'Wendy Cussons' × 'Prima Ballerina'.

Golden Shot A Floribunda raised by Martin in 1973. Medium height. Parentage: seedling × 'Allgold'.

Sunsilk A Floribunda raised by Fryers in 1974. Medium height. Parentage: 'Pink Parfait' × 'Redgold' seedling.

Strawberry Ice A Polyantha raised by Bees in 1975. Low growth. Parentage: ('Goldilocks' × 'Virgo') × ('Orange Triumph' × 'Yvonne Rabier').

Redcliffe A Floribunda raised by Sanday in 1975. Medium height. Some scent. Parentage: seedling × 'Sarabande'.

Sunsilk

Redland Court

Sweet Nell

Piccolo

Champagne Cocktail

Wishing

Volunteer

Anisley Dickson

Vale of Clwyd

Sonatina

Floral Choice

July 16th, from Wisley

FLORIBUNDAS

Carefree Beauty

Olive

Fervid

Radox Bouquet

Just Joey

July 16th, from Wisley

Piccolo (Tanolokip, Piccola) A Floribunda raised by Tantau in 1983. Parentage: not yet available.

Redland Court A Floribunda raised by Sanday in 1982. Short to medium height. Small leaves. Parentage: 'Red Maid' × 'Sarabande'.

Sweet Nell (Cocavoter) A Floribunda raised by Cocker in 1983. Height up to 80 cm. Parentage: ('Anne Cocker' × 'Mischief') × ('Super Star' × 'Circus').

Wishing (Dickerfuffle) A Floribunda raised by Dickson in 1986. Short growth. Parentage: 'Silver Jubilee' × 'Bright Smile'.

Champagne Cocktail (Horflash) A Floribunda raised by Horner in 1985. Parentage: 'Old Master' × 'Southampton'.

Volunteer (Harquaker) A Floribunda raised by Harkness in 1986. Low growth. Parentage: 'Dame of Sark' × 'Silver Jubilee'.

Anisley Dickson (Dickimono) A Floribunda raised by Dickson in 1985. Medium height. Parentage: 'Coventry Cathedral' × 'Memento'.

Vale of Clwyd (Beeval) A Floribunda raised by Bees in 1983. Short growth. Parentage: 'Handel' × 'Arthur Bell'.

Sonatina A Floribunda raised by Sanday in 1982. Medium height. Parentage: 'Red Maid' × 'Sarabande'.

Floral Choice A Floribunda raised by Fryers in 1982. Parentage: not yet available.

Carefree Beauty (Bucbi) A Floribunda raised by Buck in 1977. Medium height. Good scent.

Parentage: seedling × 'Prairie Princess'.

Olive (Harpillar) A Floribunda raised by Harkness in 1982. Medium height. Flowers rain resistant. Some scent. Parentage: seedling × 'Dublin Bay'.

Fervid A Floribunda raised by Le Grice in 1960. Medium growth. Parentage: 'Pimpernell' × 'Korona'.

Radox Bouquet A Floribunda raised by Harkness in 1981. Medium height. Good scent. Parentage: ('Alec's Red' × 'Piccadilly') × ['Southampton' × ('Cläre Grammerstorf' × 'Frühlingsmorgen')].

Just Joey A Hybrid Tea raised by Cant in 1973. Medium height. Some scent. Parentage: 'Fragrant Cloud' × 'Dr A. J. Verhage'.

Toynbee Hall

Avocet

The Times

G. P. & J. Baker

Glowing Embers

Warley Jubilee

Invincible

Sue Ryder

Bright Eyes

Sunshine Princess

July 16th, from Wisley

FLORIBUNDAS

Toynbee Hall (Korwonder, Bella Rosa) A Floribunda raised by Kordes in 1982 and introduced by Mattock in 1984. Short, spreading growth. Parentage: seedling × 'Traumerei'.

Avocet (Harpluto) A Floribunda raised by Harkness in 1984. Medium height. Parentage: 'Dame of Sark' × seedling.

The Times (Korpeahn) A Floribunda raised by Kordes and introduced in 1985. Medium bushy growth. Parentage: 'Tornado' × 'Redgold'.

Glowing Embers (Andglo) A Floribunda raised by Andersons in 1982. Short bushy growth. Parentage: 'Manx Queen' × 'Daily Sketch'.

G.P. & J. Baker (Harrango) A Floribunda raised by Harkness in 1984. Medium height. Parentage: seedling × 'Marion'.

Invincible A Floribunda raised by De Ruiter in 1983. Medium height. Upright growth. Parentage: 'Rubella' × 'National Trust'.

Warley Jubilee (Warletu) A Floribunda introduced by Warley Rose Gardens in 1985 to celebrate their silver jubilee. Growth bushy, up to 80 cm. Parentage: a sport of 'Warrior'.

Sue Ryder (Harlino) A Floribunda raised by Harkness in 1980. Short to medium height. Parentage: 'Southampton' × seedling.

Bright Eyes A Floribunda raised by Sanday in 1983. Medium height with dark green foliage. Parentage: seedling × 'Circus'.

Sunshine Princess A Floribunda raised by Anderson in 1983. Medium height. Parentage: unrecorded.

Amber Queen (Harrony) A Floribunda raised by Harkness in 1984. Short to medium height. Good scent. Parentage: 'Southampton' × 'Typhoon'. Rose of the Year 1984.

Betty Driver (Gardri) A Floribunda raised by Gandy in 1982. Short, bushy growth. Parentage: seedling × 'Topsi'.

Beautiful Britain (Dicfire) A Floribunda raised by Dickson in 1983. Low to medium height. Parentage: 'Red Planet' × 'Eurorose'. Rose of the Year 1983.

Arcadian (Macnewye, New Year) A Floribunda raised by McGredy in 1982. Medium height. Some scent. Parentage: 'Mary Sumner' × seedling.

Bridgewater Pride A Floribunda raised by Sanday in 1982. Short growth. Good scent. Parentage: 'Vera Dalton' × 'Allgold'.

Alexia (Canlot) A Floribunda raised by Cants in 1984. Medium height. Good scent. Parentage: 'Jubilant' × seedling.

Deb's Delight (Legsweet) A Floribunda raised by Le Grice in 1983. Short growth. Some scent. Parentage: 'Tip Top' × seedling.

Vital Spark (Cocacert) A Floribunda raised by Cocker in 1982. Medium height. Parentage: ['Anne Cocker' × ('Sabine' × 'Circus')] × 'Yellow Pages'.

St Helena (Canlish) A Floribunda raised by Cants in 1983. Medium height. Good scent. Parentage: 'Jubilant' × 'Prima Ballerina'.

Brown Velvet (Maccultra, Color Break) A Floribunda raised by McGredy in 1983. Height up to 1 m. Flowers orange, becoming brownish in cool weather. Parentage: 'Mary Sumner' × 'Kapai'.

Apogée (Delbaf, Delbal) A Hybrid Tea raised by Delbard-Chabert in 1966. Leaves glossy, reddish. Some scent. Parentage: ('Queen Elizabeth' × 'Provence') × ('Sultane seedling' × 'Mme Joseph Perraud').

Amber Queen
Betty Driver
Beautiful Britain
Arcadian
Bridgewater Pride
Alexia
Deb's Delight
Vital Spark
St Helena
Brown Velvet

July 12th, from Wisley

Apogée

201

Amy Brown

Esther's Baby

Len Turner

Yvonne Rabier

Bianco

Fairy Maid

Robin Red Breast

Stacey Sue

Baby Gold Star

The Fairy

Gentle Touch

July 17th, from R. Harkness & Co.

The Fairy

Colibri

Baby Masquerade

Antique Rose

Roulettii

Jean Mermox

Amy Brown (Harkushi) A dwarf Floribunda raised by Harkness and introduced in 1979. Parentage: ['Orange Sensation' × ('Highlight' × 'Colour Wonder')] × ('Parkdirektor Riggers' × 'Piccadilly').

Esther's Baby (Harkinder) A Miniature Floribunda raised by Harkness and introduced in 1979. Parentage: ['Vera Dalton' × ('Chanelle' × 'Piccadilly')] × 'Little Buckaroo'.

Len Turner A miniature Floribunda type raised by Dickson and introduced in 1984. Named in honour of Len Turner, Secretary of the Royal National Rose Society, 1965–83. Parentage: 'Mullard Jubilee' × 'Eye Paint'.

Yvonne Rabier A dwarf Polyantha raised by Turbat and introduced in 1910. Parentage: *Rosa wichuraiana* × a polyantha seedling.

Bianco (Cocblanco) A dwarf Floribunda raised by Cocker and introduced in 1983. Parentage: 'Darling Flame' × 'Jack Frost'.

Fairy Maid (Harlassie) A dwarf Polyantha raised by Harkness and introduced in 1981. Parentage: 'The Fairy' × 'Yesterday'.

Robin Red Breast (Interrob) A miniature raised by Interplant and introduced in 1983. Parentage: unnamed seedling × 'Eye Paint'.

Stacey Sue A miniature raised by Moore and introduced in 1976. Height up to 35 cm. Parentage: 'Ellen Poulsen' × 'Fairy Princess'.

Baby Gold Star (Estrellita de Oro) A miniature raised by Dot and introduced in 1940. Very large blooms. Height up to 35 cm. Parentage: 'Eduardo Toda' × 'Roulettii'.

The Fairy A dwarf Polyantha raised by Bentall and introduced in 1932. Parentage: sport of 'Lady Godiva'.

Gentle Touch (Diclulu) A miniature raised by Dickson. Parentage: not yet available. Rose of the Year 1986.

Colibri A miniature raised by Meilland and introduced in 1959. Very large blooms. Susceptible to blackspot. Parentage: 'Goldilocks' × 'Perla de Montserrat'.

Baby Masquerade (Baby Carnaval) A miniature raised by Tantau and introduced in 1956. Medium height. Bushy growth. Parentage: 'Peon' × 'Masquerade'.

Antique Rose (Morcara) A miniature rose raised by Moore and introduced in 1980. Height up to 45 cm. Parentage: 'Baccara' × 'Little Chief'.

Roulettii This is the parent of many of the cultivated miniature roses. The original plant was discovered in a Swiss village by Dr Roulet, after whom it was named by Henry Correvon of Geneva, who introduced it into cultivation in 1922. When originally found it was growing as a pot plant, but it can also be grown out of doors, and is hardy. The origins of 'Roulettii' are

Beauty Secret

obscure. It is a very small form of *R. chinensis* and Graham Stuart Thomas has discovered that it is a mutant form of the miniature *R. chinensis* 'Pumila'.

Jean Mermox (Jean Marmoz) A dwarf Polyantha raised by Chenault and introduced in 1937. Parentage: *R. wichuraiana* × a Hybrid Tea.

Beauty Secret A miniature raised by Moore and introduced in 1965. Height up to 45 cm. Particularly good for growing indoors. Parentage: 'Little Darling' × 'Magic Wand'.

Avandel

Carnival Parade

Simplex

Valerie Jeanne

Cheerleader

Rainbow's End

White Angel

Magic Carrousel

Ko's Yellow

Minnie Pearl

Cricket

Baby Sunrise

Jet Trail

Mary Marshall

Summer Butter

Donna Faye

China Doll

October 14th, from Justice Mini Roses, Wilsonville, Oregon

Avandel A miniature raised by Moore and introduced in 1977. Parentage: 'Little Darling' × 'New Penny'.

Carnival Parade A miniature raised by E. D. Williams and introduced in 1978. Height up to 45 cm. Parentage: 'Starburst' × 'Over the Rainbow'.

Simplex A miniature raised by Moore and introduced in 1961. Vigorous; needs pinching back. Good resistance to disease. Parentage: (*R. wichuraiana* × 'Floradora') × unnamed seedling.

Valerie Jeanne A miniature raised by Saville and introduced in 1980. Note: in some soils the colour of the flower becomes more mauve. Parentage: 'Sheri Anne' × 'Tamango'.

Cheerleader (Morcheer) A miniature raised by Moore and introduced in 1986. Unscented. Parentage: 'Fairy Moss' × 'Orange Honey'.

White Angel A miniature raised by Moore and introduced in 1971. Parentage: (*R. wichuraiana* × 'Floradora') × ('Little Darling' × red miniature seedling).

Ko's Yellow (Mackosyel) A miniature raised by McGredy and introduced in 1978. Free flowering. Disease resistant. Good in containers. Parentage: ('New Penny' × 'Banbridge') × ('Border Flame' × 'Manx Queen').

Magic Carrousel A miniature raised by Moore and introduced in 1972. Height medium to tall. Rather leggy growth unless pinched back. Parentage: 'Little Darling' × 'Westmont'.

Rainbow's End (Savalife) A miniature raised by Saville and introduced in 1984. Parentage: not yet available.

Minnie Pearl (Savahowdy) A miniature raised

by Saville and introduced in 1982. Disease resistant. Parentage: ('Little Darling' × 'Tiki') × 'Party Girl'.

Cricket (Aroket) A miniature raised by Christensen and introduced in 1978. Height medium to tall. Parentage: 'Anytime' × ('Zorina' × 'Dr A. J. Verhage').

Baby Sunrise (Macparlez) A miniature raised by McGredy and introduced in 1984. Disease resistant. Good in containers. Parentage: not yet available.

Jet Trail A miniature raised by Moore and introduced in 1964. Long flowering season. Height medium to tall. Disease resistant. Parentage: 'Little Darling' × 'Magic Wand'.

Mary Marshall A miniature raised by Moore and introduced in 1970. Parentage: 'Little Darling' × 'Fairy Princess'.

Summer Butter A miniature raised by Saville and introduced in 1979. Disease resistant. Parentage: 'Arthur Bell' × 'Yellow Jewel'.

Donna Faye A miniature raised by Schwartz and introduced in 1976. Good as a pot plant or outdoors. Parentage: 'Ma Perkins' × 'Baby Betsy McCall'.

China Doll A dwarf Polyantha raised by Lammerts and introduced in 1946. Parentage: 'Mrs Dudley Fulton' × 'Tom Thumb'.

Calgold A miniature raised by Moore and introduced in 1977. Parentage: 'Golden Glow' × 'Peachy White'.

Orange Honey A miniature raised by Moore and introduced in 1979. Parentage: 'Rumba' × 'Over the Rainbow'.

Happy Thought A miniature raised by Moore and introduced in 1978. Vigorous, bushy. Parentage: (*R. wichuraiana* × 'Floradora') × 'Sheri Anne'.

Takapuna (Mactenni) A miniature raised by McGredy and introduced in 1978. Parentage: 'New Penny' × [('Cläre Grammerstorf' × 'Cavalcade') × 'Elizabeth of Glamis'].

Wee Barbie (Jaybar) A miniature raised by Jellyman and introduced in 1980. Parentage: unnamed seedling × unnamed seedling.

Lemon Delight A miniature raised by Moore and introduced in 1978. Parentage: 'Fairy Moss' × 'Gold Moss'.

Cupcake A miniature raised by Spies and introduced in 1981. Parentage: 'Gene Boerner' × ('Gay Princess' × 'Yellow Jewel').

Rise 'n' Shine A miniature raised by Moore and introduced in 1977. Large flowers. Height medium to tall. Susceptible to mildew and blackspot. Parentage: 'Little Darling' × 'Yellow Magic'.

Peachy White A miniature raised by Moore and introduced in 1976. Parentage: 'Little Darling' × 'Red Germain'.

Calgold

Orange Honey

Happy Thought

Takapuna

Wee Barbie

Lemon Delight

Cupcake

Rise 'n' Shine

Peachy White

Mighty Mouse

Angela Rippon

Minijet

Bonnie Hamilton

Snow Carpet

Meirov

Dainty Dinah

Sunday Times

Wanaka

Anabell

Travesti

Peek a Boo

Disco Dancer

Seaspray

Little Jewel

July 16th, from The Gardens of the Rose

Mighty Mouse (Magmigmou) A dwarf Floribunda raised by McGredy and introduced in 1980. Parentage: 'Anytime' × 'Eye Paint'.

Angela Rippon (Ocaru, Ocarina) A miniature raised by De Ruiter and introduced in 1978. Height medium. Bushy growth. Parentage: 'Rosy Jewel' × 'Zorina'.

Minijet (Meirotego) A miniature raised by Meilland and introduced in 1977. Parentage: 'Seventeen' × ('Mon petit' × 'Perla de Montserrat')

Bonnie Hamilton A Floribunda raised by Cocker and introduced in 1976. Parentage: 'Anne Cocker' × 'Allgold'.

Meirov (Meillandina) A miniature raised by Paolino and introduced in 1973. Height up to 45 cm. Parentage: 'Rumba' × ('Dany Robin' × 'Fire King').

Snow Carpet (Maccarpe) A miniature raised by McGredy and introduced in 1980. Can be used as ground cover. Parentage: 'New Penny' × 'Temple Bells'.

Wanaka (Longleat, Macinca, Young Cale) A miniature raised by McGredy and introduced in 1978. Parentage: 'Anytime' × 'Trumpeter'.

Anabell (Korbell) A Floribunda raised by Kordes and introduced in 1972. Parentage: 'Zorina' × 'Colour Wonder'.

Sunday Times A dwarf Floribunda raised by McGredy and introduced in 1972. Parentage: not recorded.

Dainty Dinah (Cocamond) A Floribunda raised by Cocker and introduced in 1981. Parentage: 'Anne Cocker' × 'Wee Man'.

Peek a Boo (Dicgrow, Brass Ring) A miniature raised by Dickson and introduced in 1981. Parentage: ('Bangor' × 'Korbell') × 'Nozomi'.

Travesti A dwarf Floribunda raised by De Ruiter and introduced in 1965. Parentage: 'Orange Sensation' × 'Circus'.

Disco Dancer (Dicinfra) A dwarf Floribunda raised by Dickson and introduced in 1984. Parentage: 'Coventry Cathedral' × 'Memento'.

Seaspray (Macnew, Macnewing) A dwarf Floribunda raised by McGredy and introduced in 1982. Parentage: 'Anytime' × 'Moana'.

Little Jewel (Cocabel) A dwarf Floribunda raised by Cocker and introduced in 1980. Low compact growth. Parentage: 'Wee Man' × 'Belinda'.

Little Eskimo (Morwhit) A miniature raised by Moore and introduced in 1981. Parentage: *R. wichuraiana* × 'Floradora'.

Galaxy (Morgal) A miniature raised by Moore and introduced in 1980. Bushy, vigorous growth. Floriferous, with continuous bloom throughout the season. Parentage: 'Fairy Moss' × 'Fire Princess'.

Fairlane A miniature raised by Schwartz and introduced in 1980. Disease resistant. Parentage: 'Charlie McCarthy' × unnamed seedling.

Chipper A miniature raised by Meilland and introduced in 1966. Parentage: ('Dany Robin' seedling × 'Fire King') × 'Perla de Montserrat'.

Baby Katie A miniature raised by Saville and introduced in 1978. Disease resistant. Parentage: 'Sheri Anne' × 'Watercolor'.

Centrepiece (Savapiece) A miniature raised by Saville and introduced in 1984. Parentage: not yet available.

Earthquake (Morquake) A miniature raised by Moore and introduced in 1983. Parentage: not yet available.

Chipper

Fairlane

Earthquake   *Galaxy*

Baby Katie   *Centrepiece*

Little Eskimo

Jelly Bean

Tara Allison

Singles Better

Green Ice

Helen Boehm

Puppy Love

Cherry's Jubilee

Sweet Chariot

Littlest Angel

Red Flush

Baby Betsy McCall

Cuddles

You 'n' Me

Little Sir Echo

Betty Bee

October 14th, from Justice Mini Roses, Wilsonville, Oregon

Jelly Bean (Savabean) A miniature raised by Saville and introduced in 1982. Floriferous. Very dwarf. Parentage: unnamed seedling × 'Poker Chip'.

Tara Allison A miniature raised by McGredy and introduced in 1986. Parentage: not yet available.

Singles Better (Savabet) A miniature raised by Saville and introduced in 1985. In full sun the flowers are red, while in shade they develop a bluish tinge. Disease resistant. Parentage: not yet available.

Green Ice A miniature raised by Moore and introduced in 1971. Very floriferous. Good in hanging baskets. Parentage: (*R. wichuraiana* × 'Floradora') × 'Jet Trail'.

Helen Boehm (Aroprawn) A miniature raised by Christensen and introduced in 1983. Not reliably hardy. Parentage: 'Foxy Lady' × 'Deep Purple'.

Puppy Love A miniature raised by Schwartz and introduced in 1978. Parentage: 'Zorina' × unnamed seedling.

Cherry's Jubilee We collected this exciting striped rose in Justice's nursery near Portland, Oregon, but have not succeeded in finding out anything about it.

Sweet Chariot (Morchari) A miniature raised by Moore and introduced in 1984. Lavender flowers. Some scent. Parentage: not yet available.

Littlest Angel A miniature raised by Schwartz and introduced in 1976. Very dwarf and

compact. Parentage: 'Gold Coin' seedling × unnamed miniature seedling.

Red Flush A miniature raised by Schwartz and introduced in 1978. Parentage: unrecorded.

Baby Betsy McCall A miniature raised by Morey and introduced in 1960. Suitable for containers. Disease resistant. Parentage: 'Cécile Brunner' × 'Rosy Jewel'.

Cuddles A miniature raised by Schwartz and introduced in 1978. Good in containers. Some scent. Disease resistant. Parentage: 'Zorina' × unnamed seedling.

You 'n' Me (Seayou) A miniature raised by McCann and introduced in 1985. Parentage: not yet available.

Little Sir Echo A miniature raised by Schwartz and introduced in 1977. Good scent. Parentage: 'Ma Perkins' × 'Baby Betsy McCall'.

Betty Bee (Blabee) A miniature raised by Blazey and introduced in 1983. Good in containers. Parentage: not yet available.

Hokey Pokey A miniature raised by Saville and introduced in 1980. Disease resistant. Easy to grow. Parentage: 'Rise 'n' Shine' × 'Sheri Anne'.

Holy Toledo (Arobri) A miniature raised by Christensen and introduced in 1978. Tall. Not reliably hardy. Parentage: 'Gingersnap' × 'Magic Carrousel'.

Honest Abe (Aron) A miniature raised by Christensen and introduced in 1978. Vigorous,

bushy. Parentage: 'Fairy Moss' × 'Rubinette'.

Purple Fantasy A miniature raised by Dobbs and introduced in 1982. Parentage: 'Blue Mist' × 'Snow Magic'.

Popcorn A miniature raised by Morey and introduced in 1973. Honey-scented. Parentage 'Katharina Zeimet' × 'Diamond Jewel'.

Pacesetter (Pace Setter) A miniature raised by Schwartz and introduced in 1979. Parentage: 'Ma Perkins' × 'Magic Carrousel'.

Memory Lane A miniature raised by Moore and introduced in 1973. Fragrant. Good indoors. Parentage: 'Pinocchio' × 'William Lobb'.

Anita Charles (Mornita) A miniature raised by Moore and introduced in 1981. Needs pinching back to maintain good habit. Parentage: 'Golden Glow' (Brownell) × 'Over the Rainbow'.

Baby Eclipse A miniature raised by Moore in 1984. Very tall plant with large blooms. Parentage: not yet available.

Angel Darling A miniature raised by Moore and introduced in 1976. Fragrant. Parentage: 'Little Chief' × 'Angel Face'.

Acey Deucy (Savathree) A miniature raised by Saville and introduced in 1982. Spreading habit. Good in containers. Parentage: ('Yellow Jewel' × 'Tamango') × 'Sheri Anne'.

Ada Perry A miniature raised by Bennett and introduced in 1978. Parentage: 'Little Darling' × 'Coral Treasure' seedling.

MINIATURES

Hokey Pokey

Holy Toledo

Honest Abe

Purple Fantasy

Popcorn

Pacesetter

Memory Lane

Anita Charles

Baby Eclipse

Angel Darling

Acey Deucy

Ada Perry

Minuette

Pink Posy

Gold Pin

Fire Princess

Pink Sunblaze

Chelsea Pensioner

Swany

Angela Rippon

Clarissa

Dwarfking

Penelope Keith

Benson and Hedges
Special

Royal Baby

Mood Music

Orange Sunblaze

Baby Faurax

Hula Girl

Fashion Flame

July 18th, from Wisley

MINIATURES

Petit Four

Mini Metro

Little Flirt

Tapis Jaune

Darling Flame

Dreamglo

Pink Posy (Cocanelia)   A Polyantha raised by Cocker and introduced in 1983. Parentage: 'Trier' × 'New Penny'.

Gold Pin   A miniature raised by Mattock and introduced in 1974. Semi-double flowers. Young foliage is bronzy. Susceptible to black spot. Some scent. Parentage: unrecorded.

Minuette (Laminuette)   A dwarf floribunda raised by Lammerts and introduced in 1969. Parentage: 'Peace' × 'Rumba'.

Fire Princess   A miniature raised by Moore and introduced in 1969. Height up to 45 cm. Parentage: 'Baccara' × 'Eleanor'.

Pink Sunblaze (Pink Meillandina, Meijidiro)   A miniature raised by Meilland and introduced in 1982. Parentage: sport of 'Meijikatar'.

Chelsea Pensioner (Mattche)   A miniature raised by Mattock and introduced in 1982. Parentage: 'Gold Pin' seedling × unnamed seedling.

Swany (Meiburenac)   A miniature raised by Meilland and introduced in 1978. Suitable for ground cover. Parentage: R. sempervirens × 'Mlle Marthe Caron'.

Angela Rippon (Ocarina, Ocaru)   A miniature raised by De Ruiter and introduced in 1978. Medium height. Bushy growth. Parentage: 'Rosy Jewel' × 'Zorina'.

Benson and Hedges Special (Macshana,

Dorola)   A miniature raised by McGredy and introduced in 1982. Parentage: 'Minuetto' × 'Mabella'.

Clarissa (Harprocrustes)   A dwarf Polyantha raised by Harkness and introduced in 1983. Parentage: 'Southampton' × 'Darling Flame'.

Dwarfking (Zwergkönig)   A miniature raised by Kordes and introduced in 1954. Height medium to tall. Parentage: 'World's Fair' × 'Peon'.

Penelope Keith (Freegold, Macfreego)   A miniature raised by McGredy and introduced in 1983. Parentage: not yet available.

Mood Music   A miniature Moss rose raised by Moore and introduced in 1977. Parentage: 'Fairy Moss' × 'Goldmoss'.

Royal Baby (Debrad)   A dwarf Floribunda raised by Bracegirdle and introduced in 1982. Parentage: 'Generosa' × 'Baby Darling'.

Orange Sunblaze (Meijikatar, Sunblaze, Orange Meillandina)   A miniature raised by Meilland and introduced in 1982. Parentage: 'Meichanso' × ('Meidacinu' × 'Duchess of Windsor').

Hula Girl   A miniature raised by Williams and introduced in 1975. Very large, full blooms. Tall. 'Fruity' fragrance. Parentage: 'Miss Hillcrest' × 'Mabel Dot'.

Fashion Flame   A miniature raised by Moore

and introduced in 1977. Medium height. Not reliably hardy. Parentage: 'Little Darling' × 'Fire Princess'.

Baby Faurax   A dwarf Polyantha raised by Lille and introduced in 1924. Parentage: unrecorded.

Petit Four (Interfour)   A miniature raised by Interplant and introduced in 1982. Fragrant. Parentage: 'Marlena' seedling × unnamed seedling.

Mini Metro (Finstar, Rutin)   A miniature raised by De Ruiter and introduced in 1979. Parentage: 'Minuette' × seedling.

Little Flirt   A miniature raised by Moore and introduced in 1961. The colour of the blooms soon fades. Height medium to tall. Parentage: (R. wichuraiana × 'Floradora') × ('Golden Glow' × 'Zee').

Tapis Jaune (Rugul)   A miniature raised by De Ruiter and introduced in 1973. Parentage: 'Rosy Jewel' × 'Allgold'.

Darling Flame   A miniature raised by Meilland and introduced in 1971. Medium to tall. Slightly susceptible to blackspot. Parentage: ('Rimosa' × 'Rosina') × 'Zambra'.

Dreamglo   A miniature raised by E. D. Williams and introduced in 1978. Tall, with upright habit. Parentage: 'Little Darling' × 'Little Chief'.

MINIATURES

Air France

Golden Angel

Lavender Jewel

Little Buckaroo

Dresden Doll

Green Diamond

Pour Toi

Sheri Anne

Swedish Doll

Starina

Yellow Sunblaze

Gypsy Jewel

Josephine

Fairy Ring

Snowdrop

Indian Sunblaze

Royal Occasion

Toy Clown

July 18th, from Wisley

Snowball

July 18th, from Wisley

(Labels in image 2: *Red Ace*, *Blue Peter*, *Anytime*, *Anna Ford*, *Boys' Brigade*, *Bit O' Sunshine*, *Stars 'n' Stripes*, *Little Prince*, *Yorkshire Sunblaze*, *Yesterday*)

Golden Angel A miniature raised by Moore and introduced in 1975. Medium height with fairly large flowers and leaves. Parentage: 'Golden Glow' × ('Little Darling' × seedling).

Lavender Jewel A miniature raised by Moore and introduced in 1978. Large, full blooms. Height medium to tall. Disease resistant. Parentage: 'Little Chief' × 'Angel Face'.

Air France (Meifinaro, American Independence, Rosy Meillandina) A miniature raised by Meilland and introduced in 1982. Parentage: 'Meirotego' × ('Darling Flame' × 'Perla de Montserrat').

Little Buckaroo A miniature raised and introduced by Moore in 1956. Tall, upright growth. Parentage: (*R. wichuraiana* × 'Floradora') × ('Oakington Ruby' × 'Floradora').

Green Diamond A miniature raised by Moore and introduced in 1975. Very small flowers which do not always open completely. Parentage: seedling × 'Sheri Anne'.

Pour Toi (For You, Para Ti, Wendy) A miniature raised by Dot introduced in 1946. Bushy growth. Height medium tall. Parentage: 'Eduardo Toda' × 'Pompon de Paris'.

Dresden Doll A miniature Moss rose raised by Moore and introduced in 1975. Parentage: 'Fairy Moss' × unnamed Hybrid Moss seedling.

Swedish Doll A miniature raised by Moore and introduced in 1976. Parentage: 'Fire King' × 'Little Buckaroo'.

Sheri Anne A miniature raised by Moore and introduced in 1973. Tall, large blooms with good scent. Parentage: 'Little Darling' × 'New Penny'.

Starina A miniature raised by Meilland and introduced in 1965. Large flowers. Parentage: ('Dany Robin' × 'Fire King') × 'Perla de Montserrat'.

Yellow Sunblaze (Yellow Meillandina, Meitrisical) A miniature raised by Meilland and introduced in 1980. Parentage: ['Poppy Flash' × ('Meiridge' × 'Allgold')] × 'Gold Coin'.

Gypsy Jewel A miniature raised by Moore and introduced in 1975. Arching growth. Full, large blooms. Parentage: 'Little Darling' × 'Little Buckaroo'.

Josephine A miniature raised by Moore in 1969. Parentage: (*R. wichuraiana* × 'Carolyn Dean') × 'Jet Trail'.

Fairy Ring (Harnicely) A dwarf Polyantha, raised by Harkness. Short, bushy growth. Free flowering throughout summer and autumn. Parentage: 'The Fairy' × 'Yesterday'.

Snowdrop (Amoru) A miniature raised by De Ruiter and introduced in 1978. Medium to tall height. Parentage: 'Rosy Jewel' × 'Zorina'.

Indian Sunblaze (Carol-Jean) A miniature raised by Moore and introduced in 1977. Parentage: 'Pinocchio' × 'Little Chief'.

Royal Occasion (Montana) A dwarf Floribunda raised by Tantau and introduced in

1974. Parentage: 'Walzertraum' × 'Europeana'.

Toy Clown A miniature raised by Moore and introduced in 1966. Semi-double flowers. Not reliably hardy. Parentage: 'Little Darling' × 'Magic Wand'.

Anna Ford (Harpiccolo) A miniature Floribunda raised by Harkness and introduced in 1980. Parentage: 'Southampton' × 'Darling Flame'.

Red Ace (Amruda) A miniature raised by De Ruiter and introduced in 1982. Parentage: 'Rise 'n' Shine' × 'Sheri Anne'.

Blue Peter (Bluenette, Ruiblun) A miniature raised by De Ruiter and introduced in 1983. Parentage: 'Little Flirt' × seedling.

Anytime A miniature raised by McGredy and introduced in 1973. Very floriferous. Disease resistant. Good in containers. Parentage: 'New Penny' × 'Elizabeth of Glamis'.

Bit O' Sunshine A miniature raised by Moore and introduced in 1956. Height medium to tall. Susceptible to mildew. Parentage: 'Copper Glow' × 'Zee'.

Boys' Brigade (Cocdinkum) A dwarf Floribunda raised by Cocker and introduced in 1983. Parentage: ('Darling Flame' × 'Saint Alban') × ('Little Flirt' × 'Marlena').

Stars 'n' Stripes A miniature raised by Moore and introduced for the US Bicentennial in 1976. Height up to 60 cm. Very large, semi-double flowers. Parentage: ('Little Chief × seedling) × ('Little Darling' × 'Ferdinand Pichard').

Little Prince (Coccord) A dwarf Floribunda raised by Cocker and introduced in 1983. Parentage: 'Darling Flame' × ('National Trust' × 'Wee Man').

Yorkshire Sunblaze (Meiblam, White Meillandina) A miniature raised by Meilland and introduced in 1984. Parentage: not yet available.

Yesterday (Tapis d'Orient) A dwarf Floribunda raised by Harkness and introduced in 1974. Parentage: ('Phyllis Bide' × 'Shepherd's Delight') × 'Ballerina'.

Snowball (Macangeli) A miniature raised by McGredy and introduced in 1984. Unscented. Parentage: unrecorded.

213

R. soulieana

R. majalis

R. fedtschenkoana

R. multibracteata

R. willmottiae 'Wisley var.'

R. farreri 'Persetosa'

R. willmottiae

R. forrestiana

R. nitida

R. × reversa

R. iberica

R. woodsii var. *ultramontana*

R. sericea subsp. omeiensis

R. pimpinellifolia

R. 'Cantabrigiensis'

R. roxburghii

September 2nd, from Valley Gardens, Windsor

Rosa soulieana Crep.   A dainty climber up to 4 m, with lax shoots and numerous curved pale prickles. Leaves pale bluish green or greyish; leaflets 7–9 oval or obovate, rounded at the apex, up to 2.5 cm long, glabrous except for the midrib beneath. Flowers yellow in bud, fading to white on opening. 3.75 cm across, in small corymbs up to 15 cm across. Pedicels and receptacle glandular. Fruit orange red, oval, 1.2 cm long. Native of western China, in western Sichuan, where it grows on rocky hillsides. It was discovered by the French missionary Abbé Soulie and sent back to France in 1895. Distinct in its greyish, rounded, rather small leaflets, and later flowering compared with *R. brunonii*, usually in July.

Rosa glutinosa Sibth. & Sm.   Close to *R. serafinii* (p. 18) but has pedicels and young (and ripe) hips with numerous stalked glands, and leaflets densely glandular and pubescent.

Rosa corymbulosa Rolfe   A shrub up to 2 m high, with few, straight, slender prickles. Leaflets 3–5, ovate oblong, up to 5 cm long, glaucous and pubescent beneath. Flowers in corymbs of 1–12, around 2.5 cm across, deep pink, with notched petals. Pedicels glandular. Hips globose, around 7.5 mm across with persistent sepals. Native of northern China, in Hubei and Shaanxi. Introduced by Wilson in 1907.

Rosa microrugosa Henkel   A hybrid between *R. rugosa* (p. 100) and *R. roxburghii*, with large single pale pink flowers for a long period.

R. nitida (p. 21)

R. glauca (p. 18)

R. 'Wolley-Dod' (p. 29)

R. californica (p. 27)

R. canina (p. 28)

R. rugosa (p. 100)

R. mollis (p. 28)

R. glutinosa see above

R. corymbulosa see above

R. microrugosa see above

R. pendulina

R. moyesii

R. acicularis

R. 'Sealing Wax'

R. 'Geranium'

R. macrophylla
'Master Hugh'

R. bella

R. sweginzowii

R. macrophylla 'Rubricaulis'

R. macrophylla

R. macrophylla
Schilling 2079

September 2nd, from Valley Gardens, Windsor

R. davidii at the Hillier Arboretum, Hampshire

R. moyesii (p. 23)

R. pendulina (p. 23)

R. 'Wintonensis' (*R. moyesii* × *R. setipoda*)

R. setipoda (p. 23)

Rose Suppliers

Australia

Rainbow Roses, 433 Scoresby Road, Ferntree Gully, Victoria 3156.
Ross Roses, St Andrews Tce, P.O. Box 23, Willunga, S.A. 5172.
Swane's Nursery, Swane Bros. Pty Ltd Inc, Galston Road, Dural 2158, New South Wales.
Treloar Roses Pty Ltd, Keillors Road, Portland, Victoria 3305.
Honeysuckle Cottage, lot 35, Bowen Mountain Road, NSW 2753. (Has a garden full of old and rare plants).

Europe

Georges Delbard, 16 Quai de la Megisserie, 75038 Paris Cedex 01, France.
Roseraies Gaujard S.A., 38 Route de Lyon, 69320 Feyzin, Isere, France.
Roseraies Hauser, 2028 Vaumarcus, Neuchatel-Suisse.
Richard Huber AG, Rosenkulturen, 5605 Dottikon AG, Switzerland.
W. Kordes Sohne, Rosenstrasse 54, 2206 Klein Offenseth, Sparrieshoop in Holstein, West Germany.
J. D. Maarse & Zonen B.V., Handels Kwekerijen, Oosteinderweg 489, 1432 B. J. Aalsmeer, Holland.
Meilland Richardier, 50 rue Deperet, 69160 Tassin-la-Demi-Lune, France.
Poulsen Rosen, ApS Hillerodvej 29, 3480 Fredensborg, Denmark.
Rosen Tantau, Tornescher Weg 13, Postfach 1344, 2082 Utersen bei Hamburg, West Germany.

New Zealand

Egmont Roses, Cowling Road, New Plymouth.
Avenue Roses, The Avenue, Levin.
Roselynn Nurseries, McKean Road, Whenuapai, Auckland.
Sam McGredy Roses International, 130b Beach Road, Castor Bay, Auckland.

Canada

Aubin Nurseries Ltd., PO Box 1089, Carman, Manitoba, Canada ROG 090.
Hortico, Inc., 723 Robson Road, RR1, Waterdown, Ontario, Canada LOR 2HO.
Roses by Walter LeMire, Hwy. 3 and Oldcastle Road, North, RR1, Oldcastle, Ontario, Canada NOR 1LO.
Pickering Nurseries, Inc., 670 Kingston Road (Hwy. 2), Pickering, Ontario, Canada L1V 1A6.
Morden Nurseries, PO Box 1270, Morden, Manitoba, Canada ROG 1JO.
Carl Pallek & Son, Box 137, Virgil, Ontario, Canada LOS 1TO.

United States of America

Armstrong Roses, P.O. Box 1020, Somis, Ca. 93066.
Roses by Fred Edmunds Inc, 6235 S.W. Kahle Road, Wilsonville, Or. 97070.
Jackson & Perkins Company, 1 Rose Lane, Medford, Or. 97501.
Roses of Yesterday and Today, 802 Brown's Valley Rd, Watsonville, Ca. 95076.
Stocking Rose Nursery, 785 North Capitol Avenue, San Jose, Ca. 95133.
Thomasville Nurseries Inc., P.O. Box 7, Thomasville, Ga. 31799.
Wayside Gardens, Hodges, SC 29695-0001.
Carroll Gardens Inc, P.O. Box 310, 444 East Main Street, Westminster, Md. 21157.
Sequoia Nursery, Moore Miniature Roses, 2519 East Noble Avenue, Visalia, Ca. 93277.
Nor-East Miniature Roses, 58 Hammond Street, Rowley, Ma. 10969.
Antique Rose Emporium, Rt 5 Box 143, Brenham Tx. 77833.
Gloria Dei Nursery, 36 East Road, High Falls Park, High Falls NY 12440.
Donovan's Roses, PO Box 37, 800, Shreveport LA 71133-7800.
Farmer Seed & Nursery Co., PO Box 129, Fairbault Mn. 55021.
Hastings, 434 Marietta Street N.W., PO Box 4274, Atlanta Ga. 30302-4274.

Heritage Rose Gardens, 40350 Wilderness Road, Branscomb Ca. 95417.
High Country Rosarium, 1717 Downing Street at Park Avenue, Denver Co. 80218.
Historical Roses Inc., 1657 W. Jackson St., Painesville Oh. 44077.
Inter-State Nurseries Inc., PO Box 208, Hamburg Ia. 51640-0208.
Justice Miniature Roses, 5947 S.W. Kahle Road, Wilsonville Or. 97070.
Kelly Brothers Nurseries Inc., Dansville Ky. 14437.
Lamb Nurseries, East 101 Sharp Avenue, Spokane Wa. 99202.
Liggett's Rose Nursery, 1206 Curtiss Avenue, San Jose Ca. 95125.
McDaniel's Miniature Roses, 7523 Zemco Street, Lemon Grove Ca. 92045.
Mellinger's 2310 West South Range Road, North Lima Oh. 44452-9731.
Mini-Roses, PO Box 4255, Station A, Dallas Tx. 75208.
Miller Nurseries, 5060 West Lake Road, Canaduigua NY 14424.
Richard Owen Nursery, 2300 E. Lincoln Street, Bloomington Il. 61701.
Roseway Nurseries Inc., 1567 Guild Road, PO Box 269, Woodland Wa. 98674.
P. O. Tate Nursery, Rt. 20 Box 436, Tyler Tx. 75708.

United Kingdom

David Austin Roses, Bowling Green Lane, Albrighton, Wolverhampton WV7 3HB.
Peter Beales Roses, London Road, Attleborough, Norfolk.
Cants of Colchester Ltd, Agriculture House, Mile End Road, Colchester, Essex CO4 5EB.
James Cocker & Sons, Whitemyres, Lang Stracht, Aberdeen.
Dickson Nurseries Ltd, Milecross Road, Newtownards, Co. Down, N. Ireland.
R. Harkness & Co Ltd, The Rose Gardens, Cambridge, Hitchin, Herts SG4 0JT.
Hilliers Nurseries (Winchester) Ltd, Ampfield House, Romsey, Hants SO5 9PA.
LeGrice Nurseries, Norwich Road, North Walsham, Norfolk NR28 0DR.
John Mattock Ltd, The Rose Nurseries, Nuneham Courtenay, Oxford OX9 9PY.
Notcutts Nurseries Ltd, Woodbridge, Suffolk IP12 4AF.
Wheatcroft Roses Ltd, Edwalton, Nottingham NG12 4DE.
Warley Rose Gardens Ltd, Warley Street, Great Warley, Brentwood, Essex CM13 3JH.

Rose Gardens to Visit

Most rose nurseries welcome visitors to look round their fields when the roses are in flower, and some, in addition to those mentioned below have roses planted in display gardens.

GREAT BRITAIN

Cambridge University Botanic Gardens, Cambridge
Castle Howard, near Malton, Yorkshire
Corsley Mill, Chapmanslade, Wiltshire
Gardens of the Rose, near St Albans, Hertfordshire
Goodnestone Park, near Deal, Kent
Mottisfont Abbey, near Romsey, Hampshire
Queen Mary Rose Garden, Regents Park, London
Royal Botanic Gardens, Kew
Royal Horticultural Society Garden, Wisley, near Woking, Surrey
Sissinghurst Castle Garden, near Cranbrook, Kent
Windsor Great Park: the Valley Gardens Leather Garden, Buckinghamshire; the Savill Garden

FRANCE

Bagatelle, France
Le Roserie de L'Haij-les-Roses, Paris

GERMANY DDR

The Rosarium at Sangar Lausen near Leipzig has probably the most complete collection of roses in the world.

UNITED STATES OF AMERICA
Huntingdon Library, Art Collection & Botanical Garden,
1151 Oxford Road, San Marino, Ca. 91108.
Memphis Botanic Garden, 750 Cherry Road, Audubon Park,
Memphis, Tn. 38117–4699.
Gene C. Reid Park Rose Garden, 900 S. Randolph Way, Tuscon,
Arizona.
Descano Gardens, 1418 Descano Dr., Lacanada, California.
Exposition Park Rose Garden, 701 State Dr., Los Angeles,
California.
Morcom Amphitheater of Roses, Jean St., One Block North of
Grand Ave., Oakland, California.
James P. Kelleher Rose Garden, Park Drive, Boston,
Massachusetts.
Michigan State University Horticulture Gardens, East Lansing,
Michigan.
Lake Harriett Rose Gardens, Roseway Road and Lake Harriett
Parkway, Minneapolis, Minnesota.
Missouri Botanical Gardens, 4434 Shaw, St. Louis, Missouri.
Washington Park Rose Garden, Washington Park, Springfield,
Illinois.
Lakeside Rose Garden, Lakeside Park, 1500 Lake Avenue,
Ft. Wayne, Indiana.
Greenwood Park Rose Garden, Grand Avenue, (45th–49th
Streets.), Des Moines, Iowa.
Reinisch Rose and Test Garden, Gage Park, 4320 W. 10th Street,
Topeka, Kansas.
Deering Oaks Park Rose Circle, 227 Park Avenue, Portland, Maine.
Cranford Memorial Rose Garden, Brooklyn Botanic Garden,
1000 Washington Avenue, Brooklyn, NYC, New York.
Queens Botanical Garden, 43–50 Main Street, Flushing, NYC,
New York.
Biltmore House and Gardens, US 25, Asheville, North Carolina.
Columbus Park of Roses, 3923 N. High Street, Columbus, Ohio.
The Marion F. Rivinus Rose Garden of the Morris Arboretum,
University of Pennysylvania, 9414 Meadowbrook Avenue,
Philadelphia, Pennsylvania.
Samuell-Grand Municipal Rose Garden, 6200 E. Grand Blvd.,
Dallas, Texas.
Ft. Worth Botanic Garden, 3220 Botanic Gardens Dr., Ft. Worth,
Texas.
Norfolk Botanical Gardens, Bicentennial Rose Garden, Airport
Road, Norfolk, Virginia.
Woodland Park Rose Garden, 700 N. 50th Street, Seattle,
Washington.
Boerner Botanical Gardens, Whithall Park, 5879 S. 92nd Street,
Hales Corner, Wisconsin.
Portland, Oregon. Rose test Gardens.
Hershey Rose Gardens, Harrisburg, Pennsylvania
American Rose Society Gardens, Shreveport, Louisiana

Bibliography

General
Gibson, M. *The Book of the Rose* Macdonald 1980
Harkness, Jack *Roses* Dent 1978
Harkness, Jack *The Rose Directory*
Kordes, *Roses*: translated & edited by N. P. Harvey (Studio Vista
1964)
The Rose: The Royal National Rose Society Journal
The Garden: The Royal Horticultural Society Journal
The Journal of the American Rose Society

For Old Roses, Shrub Roses and Climbers
Thomas, G. S. *The Old Shrub Roses* Dent 1955 (revised ed. 1983)
Shrub Roses of Today Phoenix House 1962
Climbing Roses, Old and New Dent (revised ed. 1978)
Beales, Peter *Classic Roses* Collins Harvill 1985
Redoute, P. J. *Les Roses*; text by Thory (Paris 1820)
Willmott, E. asst by J. P. Baker. Drawings by A. Parsons *The
Genus Rosa* 2 vols 1914
Paul, William *The Rose Garden* 1872 (London 1848)

For Hybrid teas, Floribundas and Miniatures
Gibson, M. *Growing Roses* (1984)
Dobson, Bev *Combined Rose List* 1987
Modern Roses 9 American Rose Society, The International
Registration Authority for Roses (McFarland 1987)
Fitch, Charles Marden, *The Complete Book of Miniature Roses*
(Hawthor 1977)

For Rosa species
Bean, W. J. (revised by D. L. Clarke) *Rosa* in *Trees and Shrubs
Hardy in the British Isles* Vol. IV (1980)
Crépin, F. Bull. Soc. Bot. Belg. 8–21 (1869–82)
Fernald, M. L. *Gray's Manual of Botany* ed 8 (1950)
Fisjun, V. V. *Rosa* in *Conspectus Florae Asiae Mediae* (1976)
Hillier's Manual of Trees and Shrubs ed. 4 (1974)
Klastersky, I. *Rosa* in *Flora Europaea* Vol II (1968)
Ku, Tsue-chih *Rosa* in *Flora Reip. Pop. Sin.* t.37 (1985)
Mulligan, B. O. *Rosa* in R.H.S. Dictionary of Gardening
(1951)
Munz, P. A. *A Californian Flora* (1959)
Nilsson, O. *Rosa* in Davis (ed) *Flora of Turkey* 4 (1972)
Ohwi, J. *Flora of Japan* (1965)
Polunin, O. and Stainton, A. *Flowers of the Himalaya* (1984)
Rehder, A. *Manual of Trees and Shrubs Hardy in North America*
(1940)
Zielinski, J. *Rosa* no. 152 in *Flora Iranica* (1982)

Glossary

ACUMINATE: tapering to an elongated point

ALLOPOLYPLOID: hybrid between two species, fertile because
its chromosomes have doubled

ATTENUATE: with a fine point

AURICLE: ear-like lobe at the base of a leaf

BRACT: a visually reduced leaf on an inflorescence

CAUDATE: with a long, tail-like point

CILIATE: with a fringe of hairs on the margin

CLONE: genetically identical individual produced by vegetative
reproduction

CORYMB: broad flat-topped inflorescence with flower stalks of
different lengths

CYME: inflorescence in which terminal flower opens first,
followed by flowers on lower branches

ELLIPTIC: tapering equally at base and apex

EXSERTED: sticking out from its surrounding organs

GLABROUS: without hairs or glands

GLANDULAR HAIRS: hairs with a sticky knob on their apex

GLAUCESCENT: greyish green

GLAUCOUS: greenish or bluish-grey

HISPID: with bristly hairs

INFLORESCENCE: group of flowers

LANCEOLATE: with widest point below the middle

OBLANCEOLATE: with widest point above the middle

OBLONG: with parallel sides and rounded ends

OBOVATE: broadest above the middle

OVATE: egg-shaped; broadest above the middle

PANICLE: branched inflorescence

PEDICEL: stalk of a single flower

PILOSE: with scattered, long hairs

PINNATE: with leaflets on either side of a stalk

PUBESCENT: with fine short hairs

RECURRENT: flowering at intervals through one year

RHACHIS: central stalk of a pinnate leaf

SEPAL: green, usually pointed part of flower behind the petals

STIPULE: small leafy excrescence at the base of the leaf stalk,
often with jagged edge

UMBEL: inflorescence where all the flower stalks are of the same
length and arise from one point

Index

INDEX

INDEX

INDEX